The 100 Show

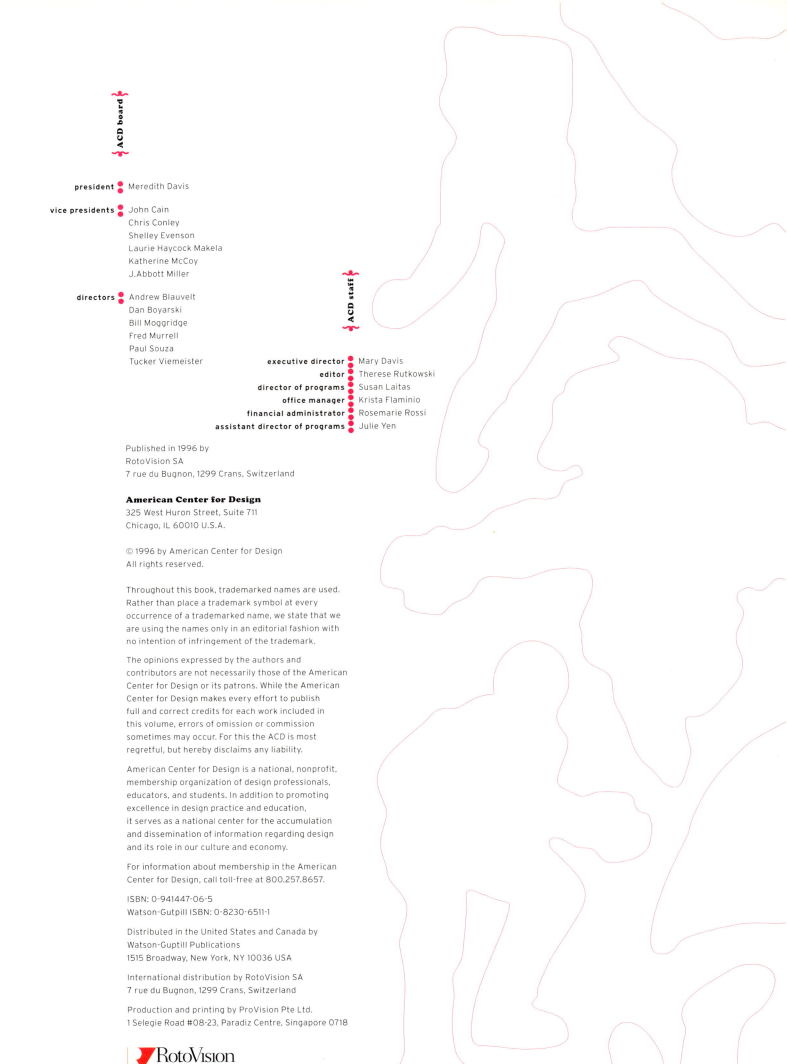

Published in 1996 by
RotoVision SA
7 rue du Bugnon, 1299 Crans, Switzerland

American Center for Design
325 West Huron Street, Suite 711
Chicago, IL 60010 U.S.A.

American Center for Design is a national, nonprofit, membership organization of design professionals, educators, and students. In addition to promoting excellence in design practice and education, it serves as a national center for the accumulation and dissemination of information regarding design and its role in our culture and economy.

For information about membership in the American Center for Design, call toll-free at 800.257.8657.

ISBN: 0-941447-06-5
Watson-Gutpill ISBN: 0-8230-6511-1

Distributed in the United States and Canada by
Watson-Guptill Publications
1515 Broadway, New York, NY 10036 USA

International distribution by RotoVision SA
7 rue du Bugnon, 1299 Crans, Switzerland

Production and printing by ProVision Pte Ltd.
1 Selegie Road #08-23, Paradiz Centre, Singapore 0718

RotoVision

the "100" show

the
eighteenth annual of
the american
center for design

☛ caryn aono's selections

☛ caryn aono's & marlene mccarty's joint selections

☛ marlene mccarty's selections

☛ marlene mccarty's & jan van toorn's joint selections

☛ jan van toorn's selections

☛ jan van toorn's & caryn aono's joint selections

☛ caryn aono's, marlene mccarty's, & jan van toorn's joint selection

reinsur-
ance is
boring
COLORS
LEFT
THE DIAL
Go
Peace on Earth
Summer
of Art
OTIS
College
of Art and Design
in Los Angeles
July 11 - August 5,
THE INFORMATION
MARTIN
AMIS
GAME GENIES
MONEY
Sexual Slang
Attitude
ANGE LECCIA
NO MUSIC
SAY
Have
Seen
MORE PARTNERS
LESS WASTE
interstate
ON

barbara glauber

CHAIR

INTRODUCTION

The tables were set, but the cafeteria's usual diners were not around. In their place stood three judges, one essayist, the American Center for Design staff, me, and 1,700 pieces of graphic design – all ensconced for the weekend in the overly air-conditioned lunchroom of Mies van der Rohe's monolithic IBM skyscraper in downtown Chicago. The mission was simple: to select a total of 100 pieces, no more, no less, "worthy" of inclusion in the Eighteenth Annual 100 Show.

As the chair, however, my choices were limited to the judges themselves. Following the lead of Katherine McCoy, who in 1991 sought to create a more curated competition, I did not select work, but rather picked the judges and determined the specific rules of the competition. By adhering to the McCoy model, each judge was able to select pieces without the need for a consensus vote. As a result, the work chosen reflects the individual vision, experience, and idiosyncratic opinions of judges Caryn Aono, Marlene McCarty, and Jan van Toorn. Each of the trio features prominently in my personal 100 Show. They are extraordinary designers and exceptional typographers whose opinions are not often heard in the graphic design press.

Occupying a unique position at the crossroad of design education and practice, Caryn Aono is a teacher at CalArts as well as the art director of the school's public affairs office, which succeeds in combining design school experimentation with real world publications. Caryn, whose CalArts office has nurtured numerous young designers, keeps abreast of the rapidly evolving design scene, making her particularly well-suited to certify (or debunk) what passes for "cutting edge" design.

Marlene McCarty has followed an atypical career path: starting off with a ruling pen in Switzerland, she has gone on to create graphics for activist groups, run a successful New York design studio, and show typographic paintings in SoHo art galleries. For this show's call for entries, she wrote, "At its best, design is the scout, out in front, making decisions, solving problems, and bravely guiding its audience (and the client, if there is one) to new visions and insights." Along with appreciating this eloquent interpretation, I also happen to share Marlene's fondness for flame type.

In the mid-eighties, my overseas envy shifted from Basel to Holland, where I discovered Jan van Toorn. At the forefront of practice and education, Jan has exhibited a compelling social mission throughout a long and distinguished career. He argues for the inclusion of the designer's viewpoint and recognition of the political context in which the piece functions. From this vantage point, Jan provides a critical reading of American design, a distinctive voice rarely heard in these competitions.

In fact, there aren't many voices at all in most design annuals. In contrast, this competition includes comments from entrants, along with judges, annotating each of their selections. In prior 100 Show annuals, juror comments have ranged from enlightening to confoundingly simplistic. The chronic overuse of clichéd terms such as "it speaks for itself" do not, in fact, speak for anything. They provide the reader with no new information. Alternatively, I have been fascinated to read why Lorraine Wild selected the Time Warner logo in the Fourteenth Annual or why Stephen Doyle cited *Cyclops* in the Seventeenth Annual. Readers and entrants deserve a good explanation.

With this in mind, I asked Caryn, Marlene, and Jan to make selections with an eye toward articulating their take on the work's merit. To further the goal of a more curated approach, I divided the book into separate sections for each of the judges, allowing them to order their discussion, sequence the pieces, and create categories. Pieces chosen by more than one juror appear in both sections (and, in only one instance, all three sections). Since ordering and categorizing are central to designing, the judges responded enthusiastically. I also discouraged frequent overlap, which can function as a seal of approval or to emphasize the judges' common tastes. My suggestion was that judges pick the same piece only if they felt strongly about it and had something important to say about the work.

The day before the judging, I visited the exhibition of the previous year's 100 Show on view at the ACD's old East Ontario Street address. Struck by the physicality and scale of the pieces – difficult to convey in a four-color book format – I wanted to at least recreate a sense of their relative sizes. Hence, the preceding spread serves as a map of all 100 pieces, reproduced at approximately one-tenth scale. This map highlights the difficult task encountered by the judges. Envision the previous spread at ten times its size. Then multiply it by 17. That's what was on the menu that weekend in the IBM cafeteria.

The lengthy process of organizing the 100 Show calls to mind a Mike Kelley artwork entitled "More Love Hours Than Can Ever Be Repaid." Featuring dozens of handmade stuffed animals and crocheted afghans sewn on canvas, the piece addresses the value of these lovingly crafted objects when viewed as commodities – a type of emotional currency that can't be quantified. The 1,700 pieces of design which filled the IBM cafeteria in June of 1995 represented untold years, months, and weeks of work. Of course, with only a tiny percentage of entries being singled out by the 100 Show judges, there remain many more design hours than can ever be rewarded. Competitions like this are but one small attempt to acknowledge those efforts.

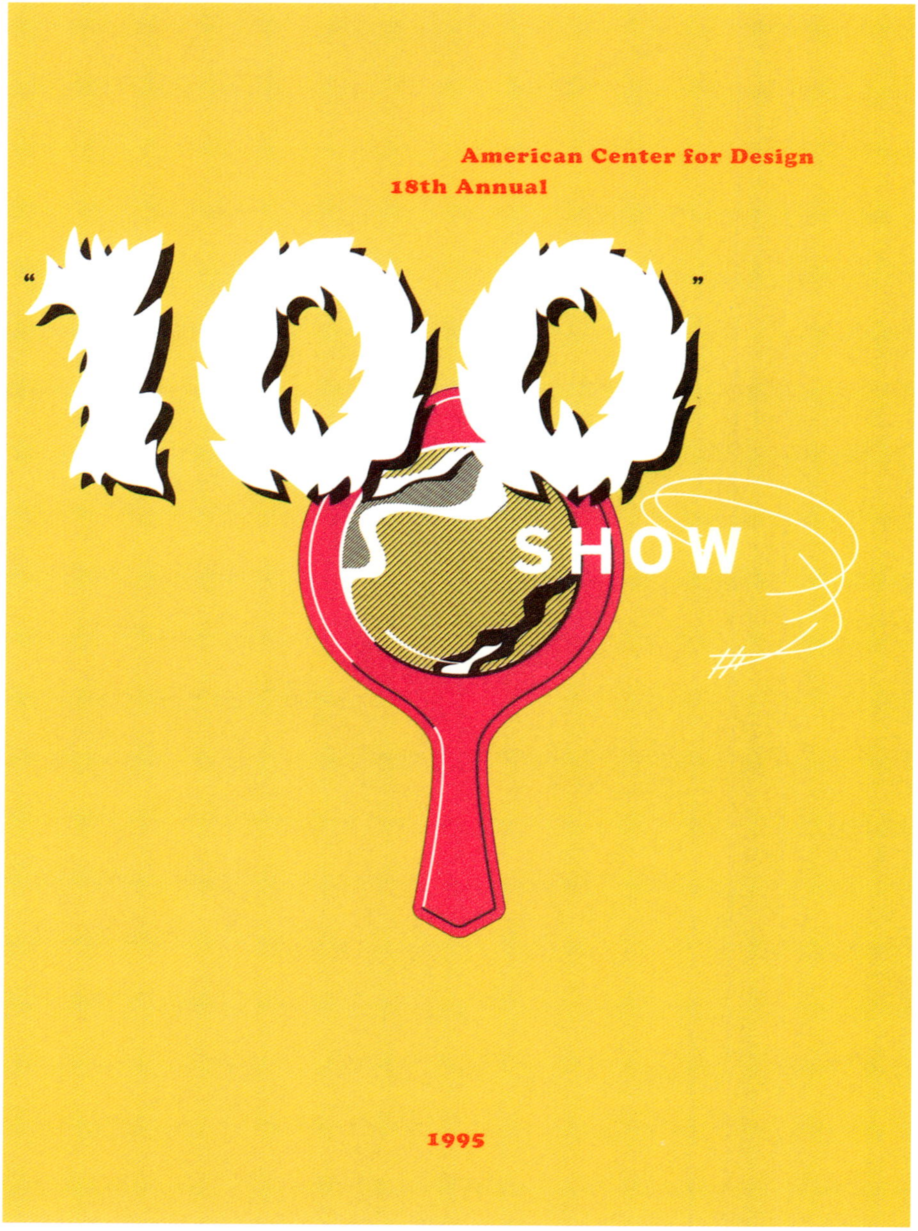

figure 1.

catherine gudis

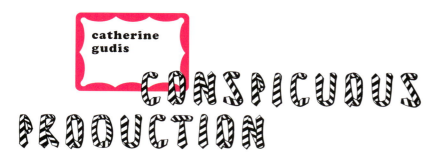

Conspicuous Production

Design competitions are, by their very nature and definition, self-reflexive, self-engendering, and sometimes even self-enclosed enterprises. The American Center for Design's 100 Show is no exception. Designers serve as entrants, chairs, and jurors. An entrant one year might be a juror or a chair in another. In fact, next year's chair just might be the critic of a competition from several years prior. I would guess that most designers who have ever entered, and all of those who have ever been selected, will at least look at the catalog again, if not enter the competition again.

Not that we can expect any professional association run by, for, and with its constituents in mind to offer a nonpartisan opinion. Most design competitions provide the revenue and attention necessary for the maintenance of the organization and helpful to the profession at large. That's their objective. After all, how did the ACD get to be the ACD if not for the cause of professionalism-at-large? With such causes, acronyms come in quite handy. In this case, the genesis is as follows. The ACD was born of the Society of Typographic Arts (STA) in 1988. The STA was formed in 1927, originally as an offshoot of the Chicago chapter of the American Institute of Graphics Arts (AIGA), which was named in 1914 and was a progeny of the National Artists Club, which came into existence not long after a host of other late nineteenth-century associations were formed in law, medicine, the social sciences, and the arts.

But what does the historical lineage of a few examples of white-collar bureaucratization offer? It is a long-winded way of holding up the hot-pink-handled mirror that was the central image for the call for entries to the Eighteenth Annual 100 Show (figure 1). The reflective surface of the mirror is cartooned by distorting waves of white and black, putting us straight in the funhouse – the very hall of mirrors in which the Wizard of professional Oz metaphorically resides. The looking glass invites reflection while it playfully parodies the vanity and narcissism implied by the practice. It is not unlike the flame-spiked sprockets that spell "100" and are enclosed in quotation marks. The quotation marks give us the title and then take its seriousness and authority away with the reminder that this is

figure 2.

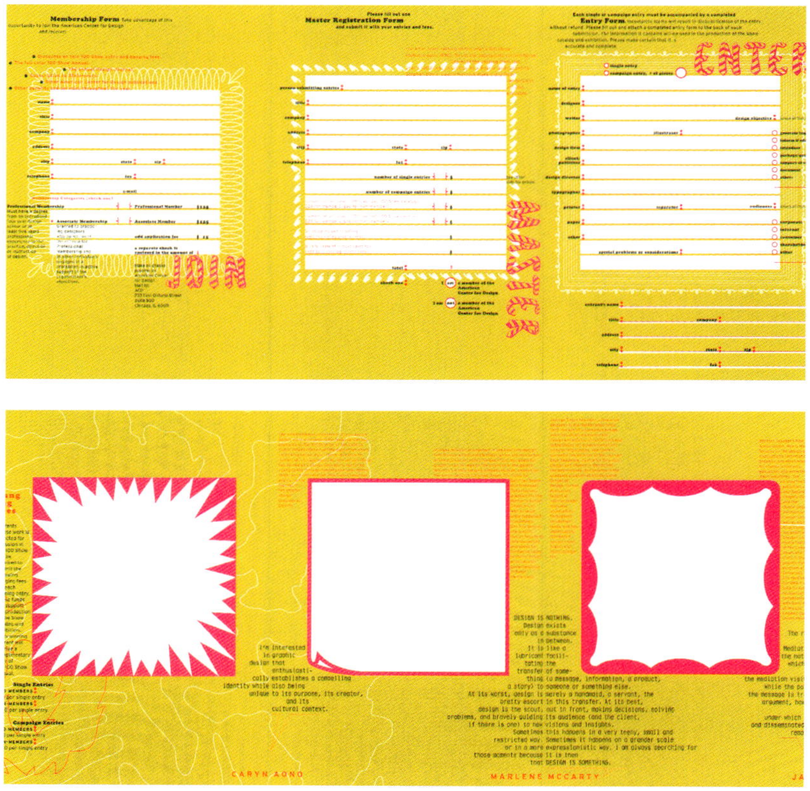

simply what is supposed to be, not what will be or is – that this is a phrase repeated or adduced rather than known firsthand. Those small, smart double-quotes cast doubt, like the mirror, on the givenness of the enterprise, the facticity of what it presents, and the singularity of its authorial intent. They remind us that there is no one Wizard; there is no one grouping of the best 100 designs; there is no summary conclusion to the way we were in 1995.

The quotation marks, the mirror, and the various framing devices employed within the invitation – the spirograph, the pointing fingers, the lifted page – are all part of a good, clean game of self-parody played on a Candyland board gone somewhat psychotically awry (figures 2, 3). By referencing and bracketing the tools of design production, they address the self-consciousness of the artist as producer and they admit to the self-reflexive, self-engendering, and somewhat self-enclosed nature of the design competition. In so doing, the invitation is a call not only for entries, but for another level of reflection upon them.

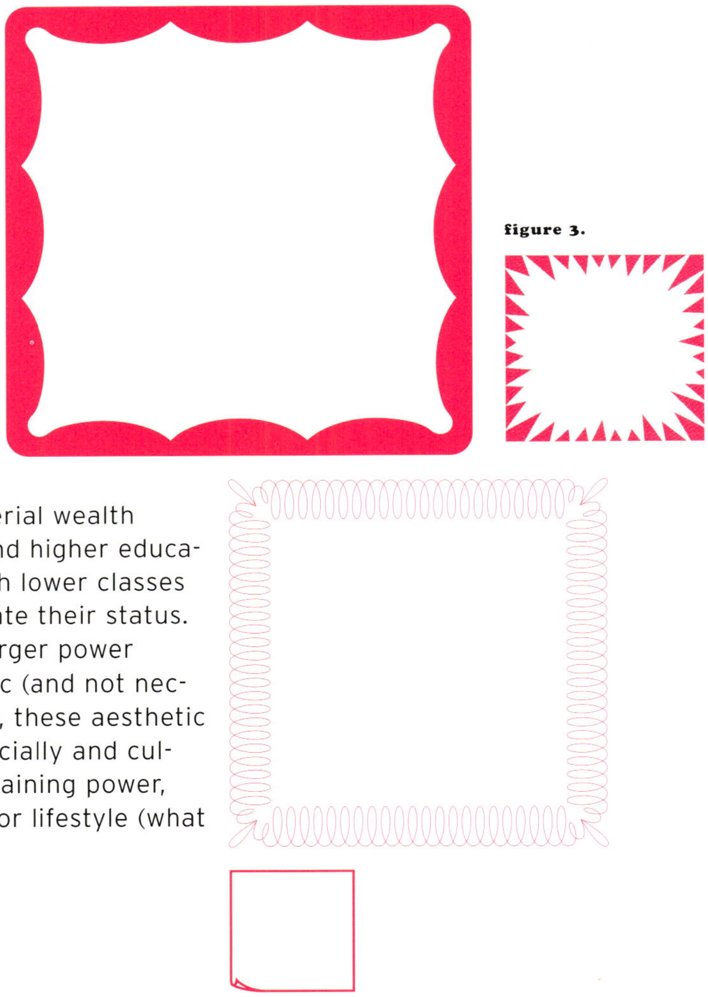

figure 3.

The title of this piece, "Conspicuous Production," is somewhat facetious – a play on Thorstein Veblen's and Pierre Bourdieu's dissections of conspicuous consumption.[1] Veblen directed his critique toward the newly emerging leisure classes of the late nineteenth century (*nouveaux riche*) who strove to assert their status and leisure through exaggerated displays of material wealth indicative of their refinement, cultivation, good taste, and higher education. Bourdieu, in particular, addressed the ways in which lower classes emulated the signs of higher education in order to elevate their status. He also considered the notion of taste to be part of a larger power struggle between not only classes but different aesthetic (and not necessarily vertically hierarchical) subgroups. For Bourdieu, these aesthetic distinctions were not natural or essential. They were socially and culturally constructed according to group interest in maintaining power, and are mediated through one's education, occupation, or lifestyle (what Bourdieu called "habitus").

figure 5. p.47

Switching the focus of Veblen's and Bourdieu's critiques of consumer culture to cultural production (meaning graphic design) brings us to the ways in which different aesthetic subgroups of design are composed and maintained. After all, what is this catalog if not a discussion of the ways in which designers are, among themselves, delivering awards for . . . what? Taste? Refinement? The hackneyed terrain of "good design"? What are the distinctions? How are the aesthetic subgroups of design determined if not by the evidence of education, cultivation, and distance from commercial exchange?

figure 4. p.53

In fact, distinctions between graphic designers are something of an insider's sport. The names of most graphic designers or advertising agencies are unknown to the majority of the general public. The most obvious distinctions between them come from the nature of the work they do, whether it's for nonprofits, schools, or commercial markets. In the case of the 100 Show (at least the past four or five), there is an incredible emphasis on nonprofit and art-related design work, with major corporate clients numbering fewer than most other design annuals I've looked at. Even though many annual reports have been submitted in the last few years, what is striking is that a large number of them are oriented toward the medical profession, design-savvy companies (such as Tupperware), and nonprofits. All of the corporate design that was selected for this year's show has mass-culture clout – sports or entertainment industries, for example.

Nike and Harley-Davidson campaigns express their (sub)cultural cachet so effectively that we hardly recognize them as the monoliths that they are. Accolades in this show have gone to those that targeted marketing to specific audiences, such as Nike's urban youth-oriented NYC Graffiti ads (figure 4) or Coca-Cola's suburban youth-directed OK Cola ads (figure 5) in which there is a ruse of individualism that perhaps is thought to compensate for the usual homogeneity of the corporate image. The niche marketing of the Nike or Coca-Cola campaigns represented here allow us to temporarily forget, or maybe simply feel better for a moment about the power and hegemony of corporate capitalism. It's all wiped clean by a Nike swoosh or an "OK" kind of cola. Nike's logoistic images directed toward specific audiences (its swooshbuckling!) seem to endear it to many designers who would

figure 6. p.84

figure 10. p.81, p.124

otherwise balk at the commercial enterprise (called a town but really an empire). Most of "the 100" mask their connections to corporate commerce or are designs for smaller businesses and nonprofits. This is one area of commonality between them.

Are there other commonalities or ways of evaluating the design submissions without resorting to the mythical essentialism of "good design"? Clearly, this is the problem of recent years, otherwise why this struggle to select 100 works, and why call it a curated show? Why the difficulties of jurors and critics to explain why they chose what they did, and to have it make aesthetic, social, and political sense? There is no denying that there is a paucity of descriptives that can justify why one design is chosen over another. And even though the self-admittedly trite answers to "what is good design?" were published in Michael Bierut's Fifteenth Annual – which included a critique of the institution of the design competition – have we really found better descriptives? Would the problem really be solved if the works *weren't* shorn from their contexts, clients, and audiences?

My choice of the phrase "conspicuous production" is a way of asserting that the primary audience for this work is already in the judging room; that the judges and other entrants are the intended and unintended audience; and that judges, entrants, and clients discern design based on the communication that takes place between themselves inside and out of various judging rooms. In projects such as the 100 Show, design is not judged in terms of its service to commerce or communication, but in terms of the business and distribution of design. And it is a business in which the common understanding between the participants of what constitutes "good design" brings us back to taste, the schools people attended, the professional groups they affiliate with, and the audience of other designers to and for whom they wish to speak. Consequently, there's a predominance of CalArts or Cranbrook references, and the selections of one year seem to spawn more that look the same the next year.

The work an entrant chooses to submit and those selected as "the 100" are discernible in part because they bear the conspicuous signs of their production, because they speak to and of us, or because we recognize the origins of their formal vocabulary. Yes, events such as the

figure 7. p.25, p.93

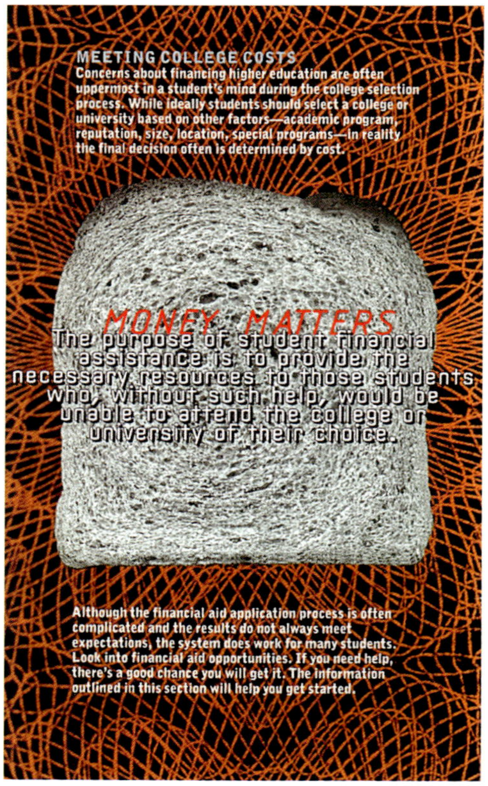

figure 8. p.92

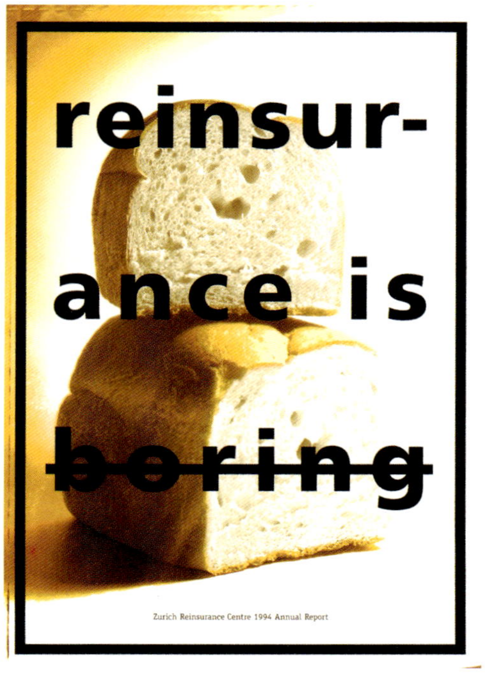

figure 9. p.81, p.124

figure 14. p.139

figure 15. p.104

figure 16. p.66

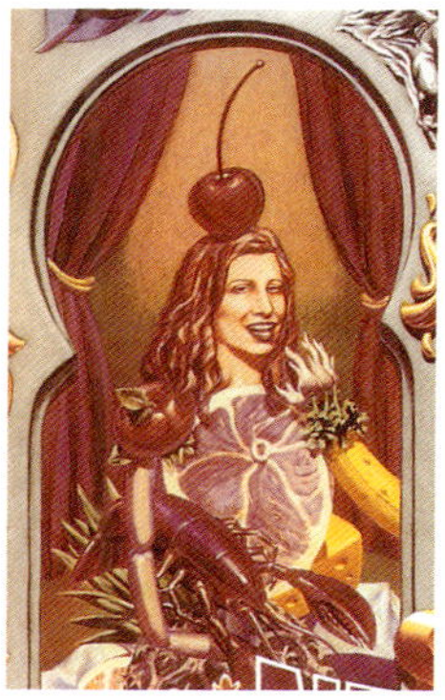

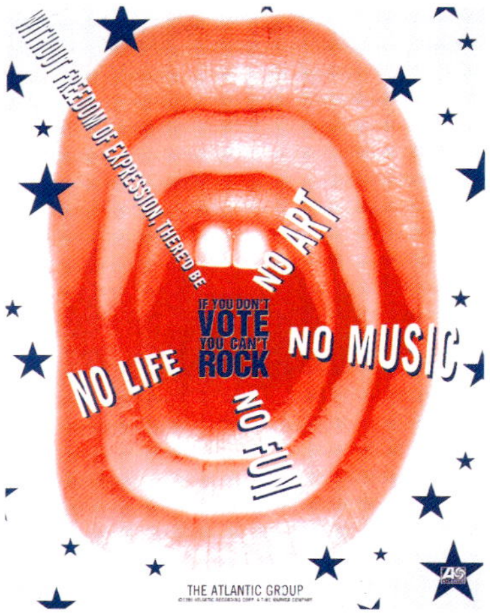

figure 17. p.102

100 Show are conspicuous in their purpose of displaying, emulating, and regenerating an elite distinction from commercial advertising. Yes, they are about professionalism and the maintenance of its hierarchies, whether vertical or not. Nevertheless, what the works say about and to each other makes for some interesting stories.

What are the stories? I've pulled out a few works that make this year's call for entries seem to be a harbinger of motifs to come. Barbara Glauber's choice of notational devices for the entry form – the quotation marks, the frames that serve to bracket information, the somewhat repellent color schemes punched up a few Mad Hatter notches on the color wheel – suggest a history of design and a questioning of its use of the "vernacular," which resonate in the show. The questions come in the form of representational imagery that evokes a glorious age of Americana (figure 6) – the actual historical period of which is fuzzy. It could be the 1920s or the 1950s.[2]

White bread (figures 7, 8, 9), chocolate cake (figures 10, 11), martini olives (figure 12), Red Hots (figure 13). Open mouths (figures 14, 15, 16, 17). Suburbia (figures 18, 19), a Chevrolet (figure 20), a tank of gas (figure 21), and the Interstate (figure 22) to get you there. And Always, perpetually Fresh (figure 32).

figure 18. p.122

figure 11. p.56

figure 13. p.81, p.124

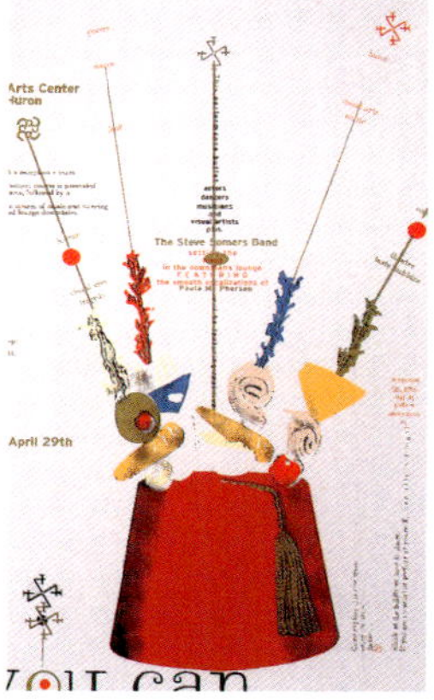

figure 12. p.44

figure 19. p.27

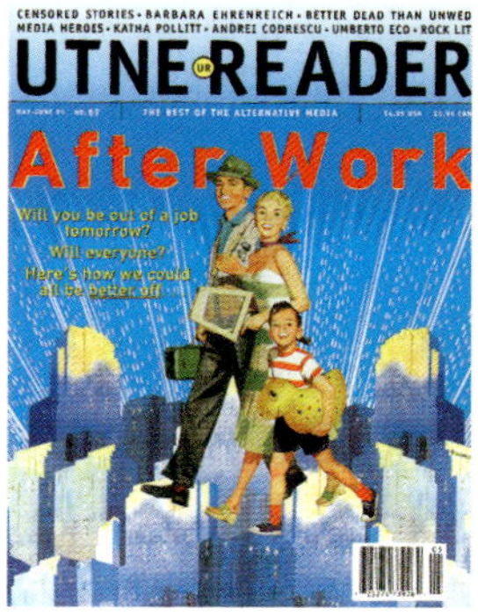

figure 20. p.84

figure 22. p.40

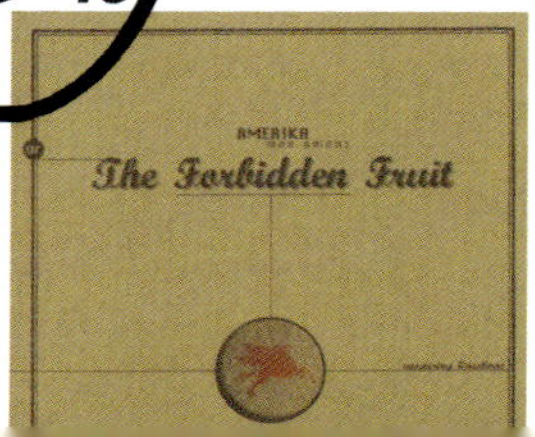

figure 21. p.59

figure 24. p.27

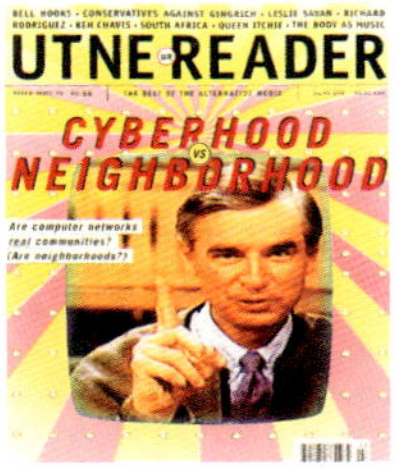

figure 25. p.108

All suggest a hearty American appetite, a consuming desire, a belief in endless resources and prosperity. Why so many references to white, middle-class, American society? Why the stiff mannequins with white smiling faces so happy in their snowboard excursion across the oh-so-blue-sky over which the solid, squat, oval K2-moon beams with industrial clarity (figure 23)? Mr. Rogers is happy in his new cyber-neighborhood (figure 24) as is the robotic Mrs. Realize Change (figure 25). Auras of new-Frigidaire pink and linoleum blue mesmerize. Stock footage and military manuals broadcast messages of Cold War containment. Smash to Face, there is Peace on Earth (figures 26, 27, 28).

Catch-phrases synopsizing these plucked images dominate my attempts to understand this pastiche of the ordinary: "iconic parodic," "Milquetoast for the masses," and "Vance's Trance" (a tribute to the *oeuvre* of Vance Packard).[3] Each phrase gets close to describing the use of images and text that suggest a Technicolor existence we want, yet know we can't have or believe in any longer. (You can substitute Modernist for Technicolor if you want.) By depicting and mimicking those who we believe did believe in white bread and fresh, clean living (or a universal language), somehow we play upon a field of innocence, clarity, and value from a fabled era of abundance gone by.

figure 23. p.24, p.85

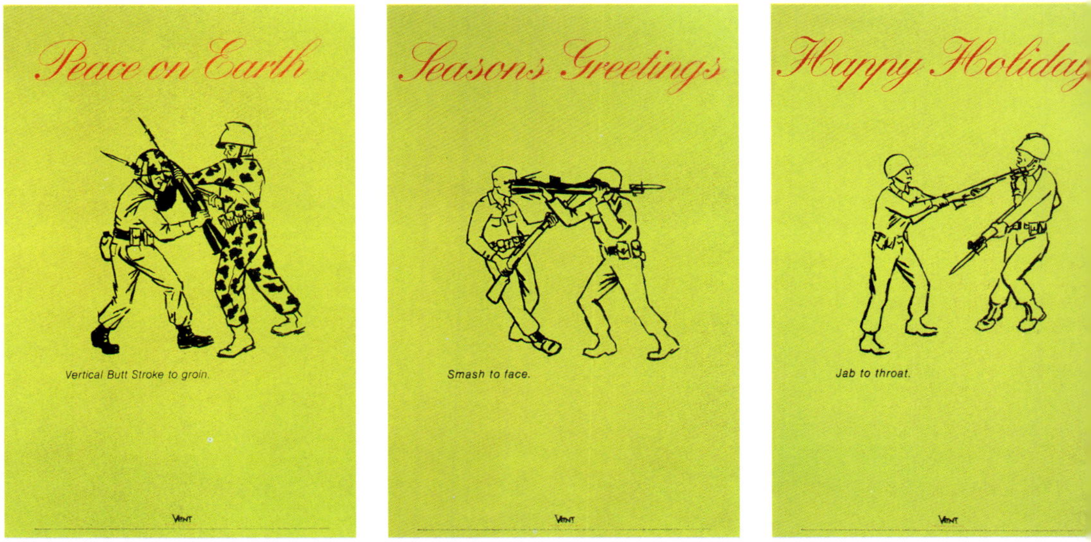

figures 26–28. p.103

figure 29. p.116

figure 30. p.25, p.93

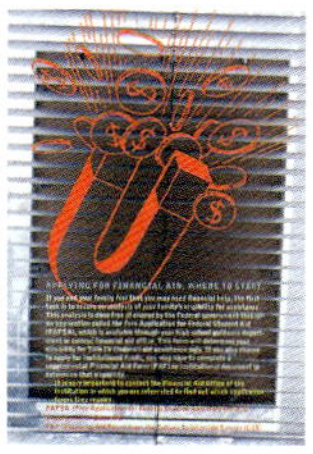

The need to assert the honesty, simplicity, and transparency of meaning offered by an ad has roots in the many "truth in advertising" campaigns of the nineteenth century and first few decades of the twentieth century, when the scientific foundations for what the ad promised and delivered were spelled out as part of the ad itself. Making the truth clearly known was a way of indoctrinating people to the newly emerging professions in advertising and marketing. Some of that history is present in different forms in "the 100." Team TDK claims "the truth" on the outside of its wrapper, which uses a mustard yellow and the straightforward emblem of horseshoe and lightning bolts to suggest there is actually an attainable truth (figure 29). Good luck and magnetism wrapped up in an icon of hopefulness – also found in Toward College in Ohio's promises of financial aid (figure 30) – are stated as true just in case we had any doubts. This is not unlike the San Francisco Art Institute's assertion in three block letters that ART is its business (figure 31). The truths are self-evident in the stylized renderings of the Fresh . . . Always ad (figure 32), AIGA's Basic poster (figure 33), and Vent holiday posters (figures 26, 27, 28), yet not so self-evident that the central message isn't literally spelled out for us anyway.

figures 31. p.92

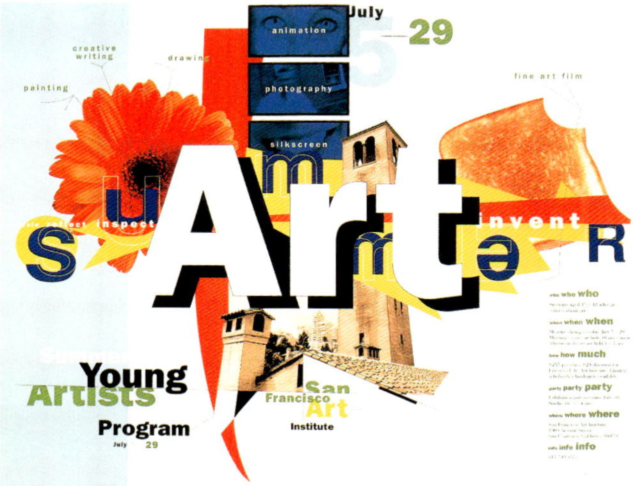

figure 33. p.121

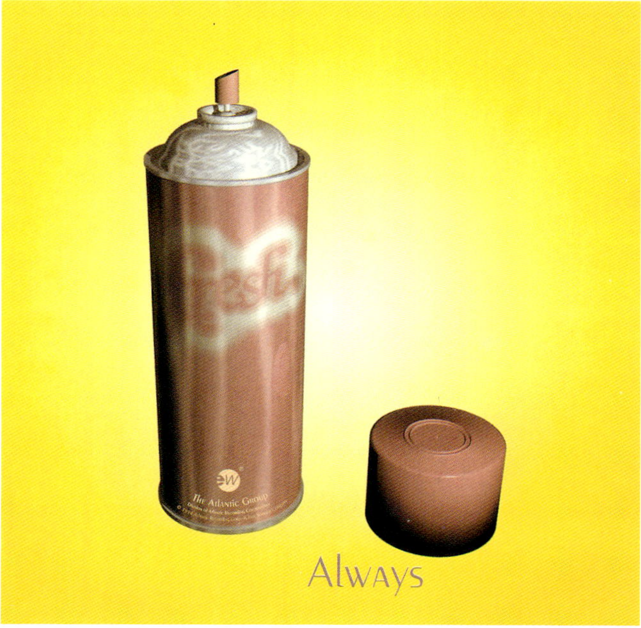

figure 32. p.97

Though there's the risk in many of these pieces of drowning in a soupy haze of nostalgia, most don't go under. They take what have, by now, become the icons of mass culture's excesses and parody their emblematic embrace of consumerism and belief in the attainability of promised satisfaction. By parodying our own familiarity with the vernacular of decades gone by, nostalgia itself is turned into an icon. It works in favor of those pieces that don't joke around too, so that by the time we get to a straight deal, we know it when we see it.[4]

The ultimate parody of mass consumerism comes in the form of that impersonation of a beverage, OK Cola. The packaging features the very automaton that Vance Packard, David Riesman, and William Whyte so feared would be the result of the "bloated excesses" of the post-war consumer economy and the "mass manipulation" of the advertising it spawned.[5] The conformity and homogenization that they foretold is incarnate in the "OK-ness" of OK Cola. "OK" is less than generic: the bar codes of early 1980s packaging are replaced by an "OK" perspective drawing of a can, a floor plan of the 12-pack, and a bird's eye view of the supermarket display, which maps the way just in case you get lost.

The entrant's comments say that they "took to calling it the self-evident campaign." But whose "self" are they talking about? One possibility is that they were speaking to and of themselves, and to and of the other designers who would read, understand, and appreciate the campaign. Printed on the inside of the carton (does the intended teen audience really look there?) is a nonsensical board game, a scramble of letters, and an "OK Decoder." Beneath that we find "Instructions: Assemble and play as instructed" (figure 34). Though circular, the instructions really are "OK," and could just as easily be stamped on the back of the Candyland board gone awry – a game whose assembly and play is instructed by its participants, and whose production is as conspicuous as its consumption.

figure 34. p.46

1 Thorstein Veblen, *Theory of the Leisure Class* (1899; London: Unwin and Allen, 1970) and Pierre Bourdieu, *Distinction: A Social Critique of the Judgment of Taste*, trans., Richard Nice (1979; Cambridge: Harvard University Press, 1984).

2 Landmark periods in advertising, historically, are the years from the end of World War I until the Crash of 1929 and from the years after World War II (late 1940s) through the recessionary early 1970s. They mark heydays in new strategies of advertising, marketing, and distribution to foster a rate of consumption to match increased production.

3 Caspar Milquetoast was a character from a 1950s comic strip. He is the prototype of timidity, born of soft living, seemingly emasculated by the women around him. Vance Packard was a popular critic of advertising from the same post-war period whose searing diatribes against consumer culture ended up being taken by the public as a how-to manual for consumption. Both were responses to anxieties about loss of identity that were supposed to come with mass production and consumption and the rise of the middle-class bureaucrat, or "organization man," who shuffled the paper or managed the ads that made the system work.

4 The clearly fake bodies and snow of the K2 Snowboard catalog end up being as direct an expression as those book covers made up solely of type (see *The Information*, p.77 and p.138; and *Who Will Run the Frog Hospital?*, p.30 p.72), or the UNIFEM annual report that uses straight color photographs that show exactly how the money from the year past was spent (see p.78 and p.128). In its contrast to the quotation – the impersonation – of the vernacular, design such as UNIFEM's perhaps become even more clear and "universally true" than they would be outside of this context.

5 David Riesman and William Whyte, similar to Packard but with different conclusions than his, expressed anxieties about the environmental impact and social conformity that would result from mass production and consumption.

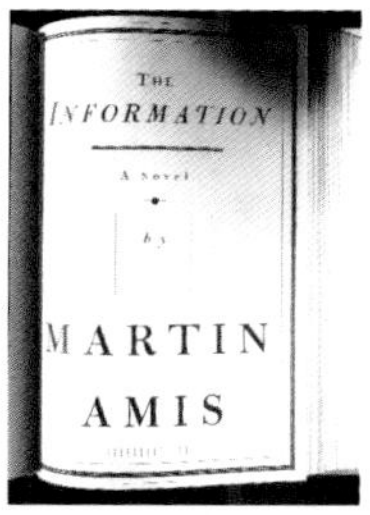

Who Will Run the Frog Hospital?
a novel by
Lorrie Moore

selections by

caryn aono

3SIXTY
GILLY
Alegria
Who Will
Run the Frog
Hospital?
a novel by
Lorrie Moore
Cinema
Our Fall
1994 Season
of 25 events
includes:
Errant Bodies
time
you
REVOLUTION RADIO
NEVILLE
MORE SO-
BRODY
PUNCH
EXTRAORDINARY
THUR. P.M.
A113
Toward
College
in
Ohio
Attitude
High Five
UTNE READER
CYBERHOOD
NEIGHBORHOOD
TAGS
YOU'RE IT
OK
AMERICAN TYPE CORP
all you can
ART.
OK
I can't
read
this

caryn aono

Previous 100 Show chairs and judges have laid the groundwork for what is perhaps the most rigorous competition and certainly the most intelligently constructed. Each year the rules of the curatorial approach, initiated in 1991 by Katherine McCoy, are amended by each chair in an effort to improve "the 100" competition. This curated show says as much about the work selected as it does about the jurors' concerns at the time. Only time will tell, and maybe shed some light on, why certain forms of a period look the way they do, were singled out and selected, were considered important and of value.

Most graphic design competitions are perplexing, primarily because the subjective criteria by which a work is judged often do not and cannot consider the objective criteria by which the work is made. Not knowing the specifics or briefs of the work was frustrating and resulted in a continuous reevaluation in the two-day judging period. In the end, I picked work that spoke in the languages and formal dialects with which I am most familiar.

From my perch, designing and teaching at California Institute of the Arts, I am constantly looking forward. An academic environment is always considering the future. The unbridled experimental activity swirling around in the studios and classrooms downstairs will eventually emerge as the "new guard" of tomorrow. The next generation of designers, musicians, actors, and dancers is not patiently waiting on the sidelines; rather, their fingertips are on the torch.

I came to the judging full of optimism. At CalArts, the design program had just graduated a fresh new crop of students, and promise was high for their launch into the great unknown. Like the work of young people everywhere, theirs is enthusiastic, intelligent, inquisitive, fresh – all descriptions of "new" and "next" – all descriptions of what I thought would be on view in Chicago.

This expectation was quickly dashed upon viewing the plethora (tables and tables and more tables!) of corporate annual reports in the IBM cafeteria. I was reminded that Chicago (and the Midwest) relies on the corporate industrial sector to make it "the city that works," and it, in turn, relies on the design community to polish "the city of broad shoulders" image. The vehicle that best showcases this image is the annual report.

The number of entries submitted was overwhelming, as were the sight of tables dripping with inks, the smells of varnish and blanket wash, and the sounds of spines cracking as we made our rounds. At one time, corporate annuals were the vehicles that showcased significant new trends in graphic design. Perhaps this is not the case now. Most of this work did not push formal and/or conceptual boundaries or necessarily point to new directions. The look of these annuals is best described as "dutiful." Being "good" in the sense of effectively satisfying client desires *is* deserving of recognition, yet because of limited information and judging criteria, this was nearly impossible to evaluate.

If the design of these annuals was not progressive, their use of the latest and best technology was. The high level of production techniques and materials was amazing. What may look like "excess" is perhaps just what the client requested. The design takes a back seat to the applied "veneer." I thought of the vendors and production industries that back this work and realized that design competitions such as this probably would not exist without them, since so many entries are from this market.

Currently, it seems that progressive design emerges out of work for the youth market rather than the corporate sector. Styles aimed at youth culture were plentiful and were applied to materials for colleges, soda pop, car audio, sneakers, and, of course, the omnipresent design competition standard – the snowboard catalog. This year's version appeals to Generation X's affinity for 1970s American vernacular (see the K2 Snowboard catalog by Modern Dog on p.24 and p.85). The "more is more" approach (sometimes bordering on schizophrenia) is used to recruit the college bound (see Toward College in Ohio by Schmeltz + Warren on p.25 and p.93 and Attitude by Lee Allen Kreindel on p.26, p.87, and p.125). The idea of "more" aids in "reflecting attitude" for a radio station's identity. It can't be confined to just one logo mark, so six are developed to do the job (see REV 105 logos by Thorburn Design on p.40).

Technology's latest influence on graphic design is undoubtedly in multimedia. Curiously, we saw some examples of interactive work, but at this time the designer's struggle with this medium (or is it the struggle with the design?) seems to be at an intermediate level. Interest in interactivity as applied to print-based work is starting to emerge as a visible trend. *Wired* magazine by Plunkett + Kuhr (see p.23, p.109, p.119, and p.120) is probably the most widely seen work of this genre. This style is highly complex and exciting since it tries to simulate in two dimensions what takes place in four. Traditional design criteria, such as composition and hierarchy, are modified in reading (and designing) these pieces to imply a nonlinear narrative and motion.

Designer-initiated work and design for designers – what is academically referred to as "visual research" – is not taboo in my milieu. The best experimental work is produced for familiar audiences, such as design for designers. This kind of work is the core of examination, implementation, and movement that drives our field forward. However, visual research can also be seen as a subtle and sophisticated form of self-promotion. Authoring new ideas, or at least being credited with them, has always been a subject for discussion and debate. This may also explain part of the current motivation for designers to write.

Over the past few years, noticeable work has been coming out of Indianapolis, no doubt a stone's throw from the university design program at Herron School of Art. Antenna on p.43 (Many Can Argue bookmark) and p.54 (Tag! You're It Christmas tags) and Mirelez/Ross on p.49 (American Type Corp. promotion) and p.61 (Who Makes the Cut? booklet) have created absolute design gems which are distinctly odd yet fresh. Their works cleverly dare and provoke audiences to join in the communication and challenge designers to join in the *fun*!

Another trend this year was a return to austerity. This preference for nonembellishment seems to cycle around every few years, with designers exercising various degrees of restraint. To me, these pieces resonate in their functional beauty. See Barbara deWilde's book cover design for Knopf on p.30 and p.72 (*Who Will Run the Frog Hospital?*), Laurie Haycock Makela's book cover design for the Getty Center on p.29, (*Empathy, Form, and Space: Problems in German Aesthetics, 1873-1893*) and Adams/Morioka's identity for the Pacific Design Center on p.38.

More than a year has passed since we took stock of our profession in the Chicago IBM building, and I wonder about the work that did not answer the call for entries. I wonder about the pieces I admire that I know were not on the cafeteria tables in June of 1995. I am curious about the work that I see exhibited in the recent storm of new books on typography and graphic design (*Typography Now, Typographics 1, Cutting Edge Typography*, etc.) – each one proclaiming to be the newest of the new. These books feature some of the freshest work, much of it not repeated in the annuals and competitions. Are the entry and presentation fees truly prohibiting entries of the work these annuals seek to document? Are consensus juries canceling out "forward-looking" work? And are these new books their adjunct platforms? Are there too many forums or not enough?

Given the expansion in areas that graphic designers now practice, the venues to showcase this work should grow. Growth may also accommodate specificity. Maybe this will level the playing field and enable judges to consider the specific criteria that went into conceptualizing a piece, rather than simply considering its looks.

Gauging by the quantity of submissions received for the Eighteenth Annual 100 Show, designers will continue to seek recognition of their work by people in the field. I actually see this increasing as the numbers in our ranks grow. Established competitions and annuals will continue to attract the numbers, as they always have, and their companions, which showcase more specialized kinds of work, will grow in popularity too.

Having had this opportunity to see what is going on in our field, or at least view 1,700 pieces of evidence, I am left asking more questions than before. During the judging, one piece appeared as an epiphany.

Jim Ross of Mirelez/Ross cut the top off the textbook *Typographic Design: Form and Communication* by Rob Carter, Ben Day, and Philip Meggs. He submitted the remaining 1-1/2-inch book under the title "Who Makes the Cut?" (p.61). What one sees in this booklet is a contents page *sans* listings. *Sliced* halftones of seminal works follow chapter titles with no text. Blank pages *intermittently* appear between slashed specimens of type families. A timeline lists only *selected* historical events. And toward the end, an *edited* index references a folio-less book. It gets points for making points about design competitions.

caryn aono

In the spirit of "more is more," this two-dimensional design embraces the dimensions of multimedia work. Although the information hierarchy seems a bit erratic, it ebbs and flows like a moving sound piece. Perhaps an interactive-savvy audience is more patient snaking through all this stuff. Sidebar-information-as-chat-room is added fun. –ca

entrant's comments

By perusing these catalogs, you get the feeling that you are inside a CD-ROM program. Our goal was to replicate the sense of discovery that comes through the use of CD-ROMs. The pages are chock-a-block with information – at first glance seemingly dense and layered. The curious and careful reader realizes that the information on the pages is, in fact, arranged in a logical, useful, and informative manner. These differ from traditional software catalogs in several ways. Our objective was to treat them as magazines, featuring a curated selection of CDs published by Voyager and others. No one paid to be included. There is an emphasis on writing, with the belief that the informed consumer would demand information and opinion rather than facile hard-sell blurbs.

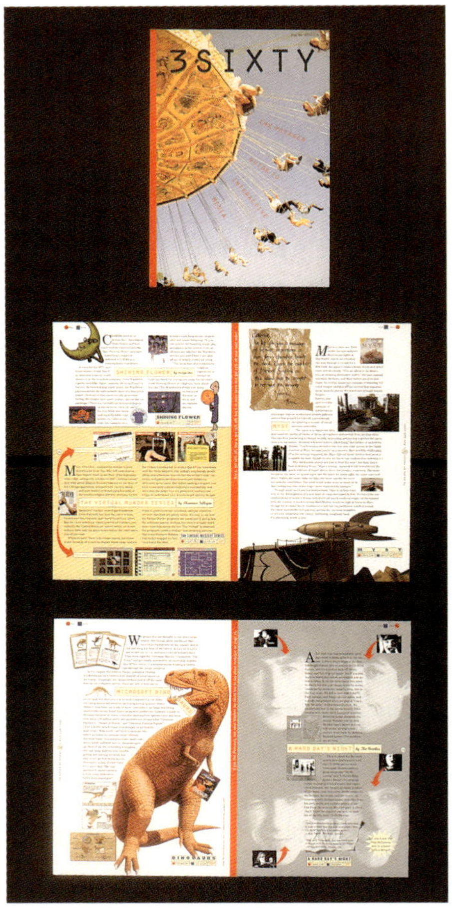

3Sixty

CATALOGS

Designer : Paul Donald
Art Director : Alexander Isley
Writer : Ashton Applewhite
Design Firm : Alexander Isley Design
Client/Publisher : The Voyager Company
Other : mail-order catalog

caryn aono

also selected by Jan van Toorn, see p.120

Wired submitted several magazine spreads, but I chose these from the "Electric Word" front section of the magazine because it's chock-a-block with stuff. This section is designed with maximum impact and is quite accessible. It reminds me of Richard Saul Wurman's "Access" books and it has some of the same qualities of Voyager's 3Sixty catalogs. The design is hyper-urgent, like the hyper-content. It offers the reader the option to read now or surf later. –ca

entrant's comments

"Electric Word" is a monthly department of late-breaking news and gossip. (We call it "bulletins from the frontlines of the digital revolution.") We use this section to try to reflect in print the feeling of navigating through the Net by experimenting with a less-linear-than-normal presentation of information. Text is not anchored to a grid and headlines are not necessarily where one expects to find them. In addition, the gossip column slices horizontally through the pages and stories, so that, in the end, we have a collection of seemingly random bits floating across a series of pages.

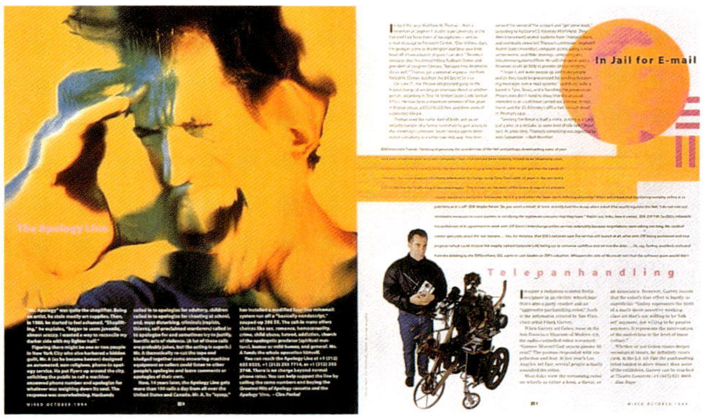

Wired 2.10 Electric Word

MAGAZINE SPREADS

Designer : John Plunkett
Design Directors : John Plunkett, Thomas Schneider
Design Firm : Plunkett + Kuhr/*Wired* Magazine
Client/Publisher : *Wired* Magazine
Printer : Danbury Printing & Litho

caryn aono

also selected by Marlene McCarty, see p.85

Another year and another snowboard company catalog. There were a lot of submissions in this style for snowboards, car audio, sneakers, even colleges. For the past several years, snowboard catalogs have borrowed from some genre of American vernacular. Happily, this one resurrects the now-defunct Sears catalog. Even though this lifts some direct elements from the "Wish Book," it has an updated, clunky-tech feel to it. The fun and excitement are hard to resist. –ca

entrant's comments

Since snowboarding is such a trend-driven industry, the catalogs can't be even one second behind what's hip at the moment. And something that's cool one week is a joke the next. What's difficult is that you need to be able to forecast the cool stuff one year or more in advance. We kept a close eye on snowboard trends and attitudes, and decided to follow the muse of Sears, summer of '72. But we didn't want it to look too kitschy or tongue-in-cheek. Just fun, yet taking itself somewhat seriously.

K2 Snowboard

CATALOG

Designers : Michael Strassburger, Vittorio Costarella, George Estrada
Design Director : Michael Strassburger
Writers : Michael Strassburger, Vittorio Costarella, George Estrada
Illustrators : Michael Strassburger, Vittorio Costarella, George Estrada
Photographers : Eric Berger, Jeff Curtes, Jimmy Clarke, Aarron Sedway, others
Design Firm : Modern Dog
Client/Publisher : K2 Snowboards
Typographers : Michael Strassburger, Vittorio Costarella, George Estrada
Printer : Valco
Separator : WY'east
Paper : Simpson Evergreen

caryn aono

also selected by Marlene McCarty, see p.93

There is an odd sense of schizophrenia flipping through this booklet. Particular styles currently in vogue are scattered throughout. Some spreads present serious graph information and look like they're from AAA guidebooks; others are more ambiguous with Scott Makela-esque type/photo collages; while others are overtly obvious. A headline reads "Be aggressive" over an image of Godzilla. This is aggressive communication – like watching ten minutes of MTV. –ca

entrant's comments

Each year, the same necessary, but dry and basic, information about colleges and universities in Ohio is presented to high school juniors and seniors. We try to wake it up. A quote from our client, "Realizing that TCIO (Toward College in Ohio) must also be user-friendly to parents and counselors, we may have felt that some of the graphics and text designs were a bit 'far out.' We are willing to forego personal likes and dislikes because the evidence indicated that the design is working."

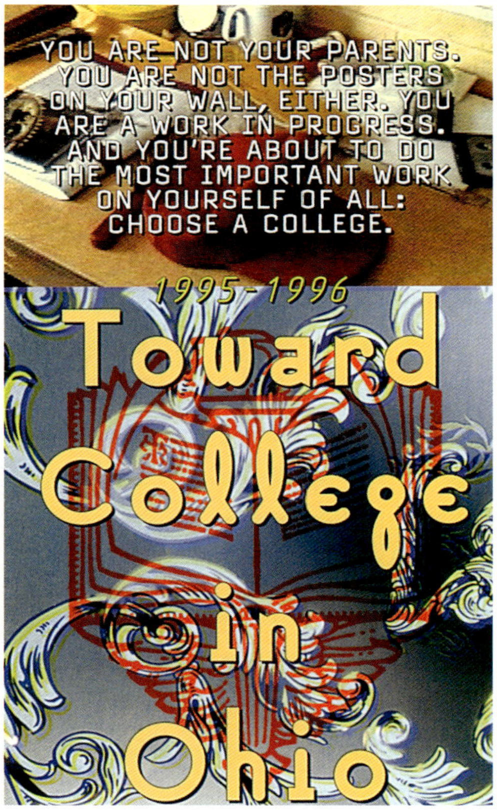

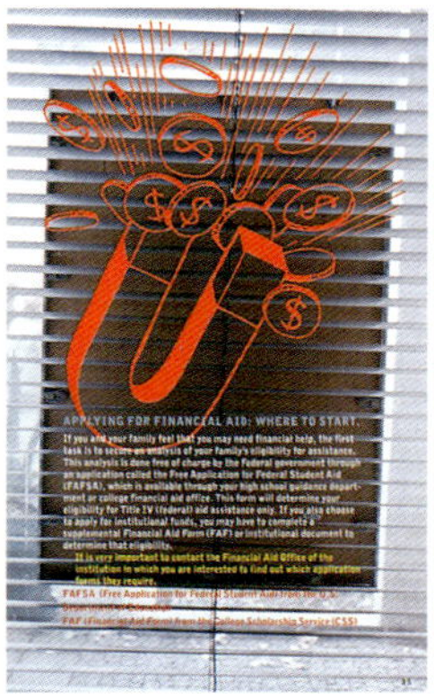

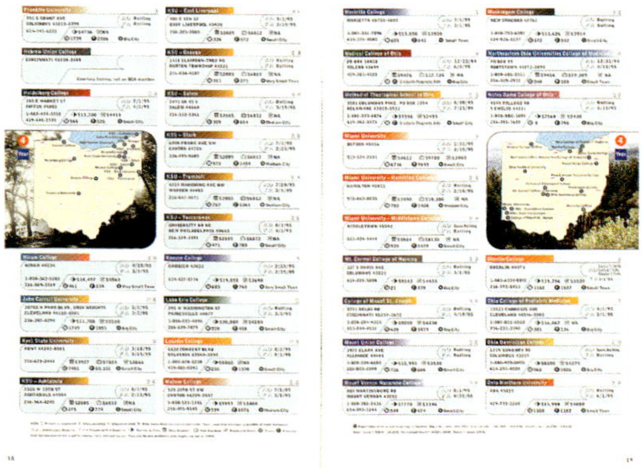

Toward College in Ohio 1995–1996

BROCHURE

Designer : Crit Warren
Design Director : Crit Warren
Writer : George Felton & Others
Photographer : Crit Warren
Design Firm : Schmeltz + Warren
Client/Publisher : The Ohio College Association
Typographer : Schmeltz + Warren, Macintosh
Printer : West-Camp Press
Separator : West-Camp Press
Paper : Futura Matte 70 lb. Text

caryn aono

also selected by
Marlene McCarty, see p.87; and Jan van Toorn, see p.125

It is interesting to note that the one piece we all chose is designed in a style aimed at MTV audiences. Attitude, as this piece is called, is its purpose and attraction. This is sassy, like the magazine, and spars with its hip and knowing audience. This language, which can sell $100 sneakers, is also convincing in selling education. This catalog is a very strong synthesis of editorial and design objectives.
–ca

entrant's comments

In response to a gradual drop-off in enrollment, Pine Manor College was looking to make a radical departure in how its viewbook read and looked. The viewbook was reeingineered to appeal to the prospective student rather than the parent. It takes into consideration the profile of the typical PMC student, both academically and socially. The viewbook uses the layout and writing style of teen magazines, such as *Sassy* and *Seventeen* as its model.

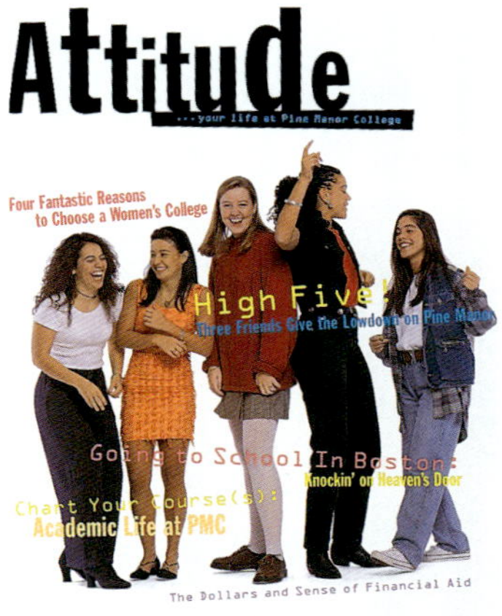

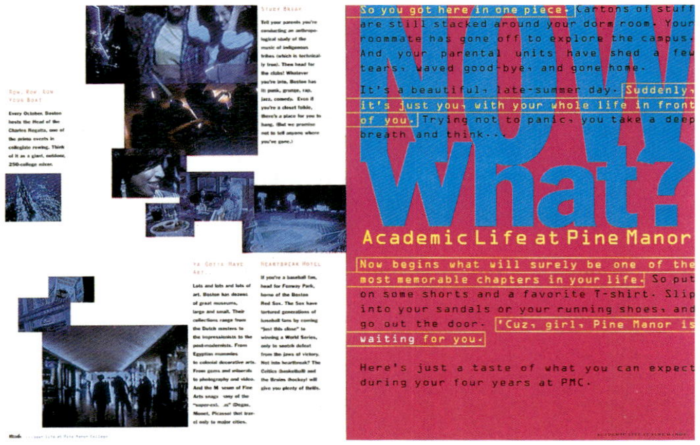

Attitude – Pine Manor College

VIEWBOOK

Designer : Lee Allen Kreindel
Design Director : Lee Allen Kreindel
Writer : Christine Kane
Photographers : Molly Lynch, Charles Barclay Reeves
Illustrators : Diane Bigda, James Kraus, Jeff Tate
Design Firm : Lee Allen Kreindel Graphic Design
Client/Publisher : Pine Manor College
Typographer : Lee Allen Kreindel
Printer : Dyngraf, Inc.
Separator : Dyngraf, Inc.
Paper : Repap Multieffect Gloss Text and Cover

caryn aono

These pages have a peculiar balance of beauty and beast. Brutish heads contrast with photos and strict, delicate subheads and section titles. Article openers are visually arresting with carefully cropped photos and sure, bold headlines. Some details look Dutch-influenced in their practical, yet elegant orderliness. Overall, a beautiful redesign that lassos the magazine's strange eclecticism. –ca

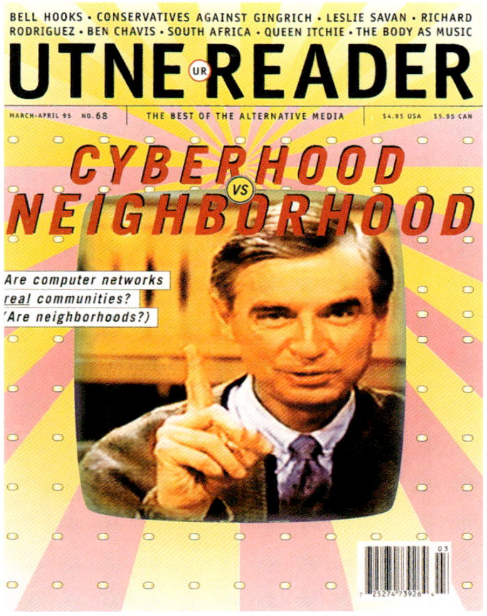

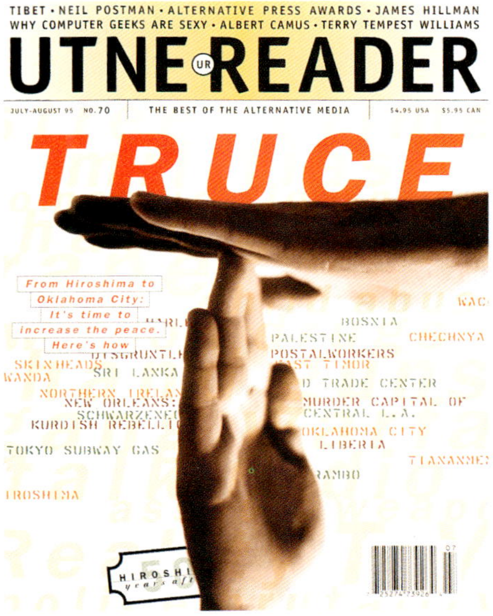

Utne Reader

MAGAZINE

Designers : Jan Jancourt, Andrew Henderson
Art Director : Andrew Henderson
Client/Publisher : *Utne Reader*
Printer : Quad Graphics
Separator : Superior Graphics, Smartset
Paper : Penagra Suede Recycled

entrant's comments

Question 14 – responses: It's cool + It's fine + It's like I'm picking it up for the first time + It's too digital + It's ugly and drab + It's great design and I'm a designer! + It's very user-friendly + It's got too many eye-crossing fonts + Its new format is easier to read + It's too cluttered + It's an interesting '90s concept, I'm game + It's like any other magazine + It's a slick design, but I like slick + It's OK + It's fine + Its new design is great + It's too much like *Wired* + It's not a computer, you are a magazine + It's a nice look + It's design 101.

caryn aono

Earlier books from this ongoing architectural history series have been selected in prior ACD 100 Shows. I chose them again this year. They are quite wonderful. This is an example of book design at its best: an interesting and substantial project; a progressive client; and two intelligent designers working in tandem producing very smart designs. These books are executed with a keen, daring, edginess to them. It would be great to view the series in its entirety, since good collaborations are rarely noted. –ca

entrant's comments

The cover uses one of Friedrich Gilly's perspective study drawings to call attention to the theoretical aspect of his work. The combination of typefaces on the cover – Poster Bodoni, Walbaum, and Weiss – is a reference to Gilly's historical position on the cusp between Classicism and Romanticism. The use of the title block/book label format to hold the title information is part of the graphic identity for the separate titles in the "Texts & Documents" series. Gilly's drawing is allowed to break into the space of the title block/book label as a contemporary graphic gesture – to emphasize the contemporariness of the publication.

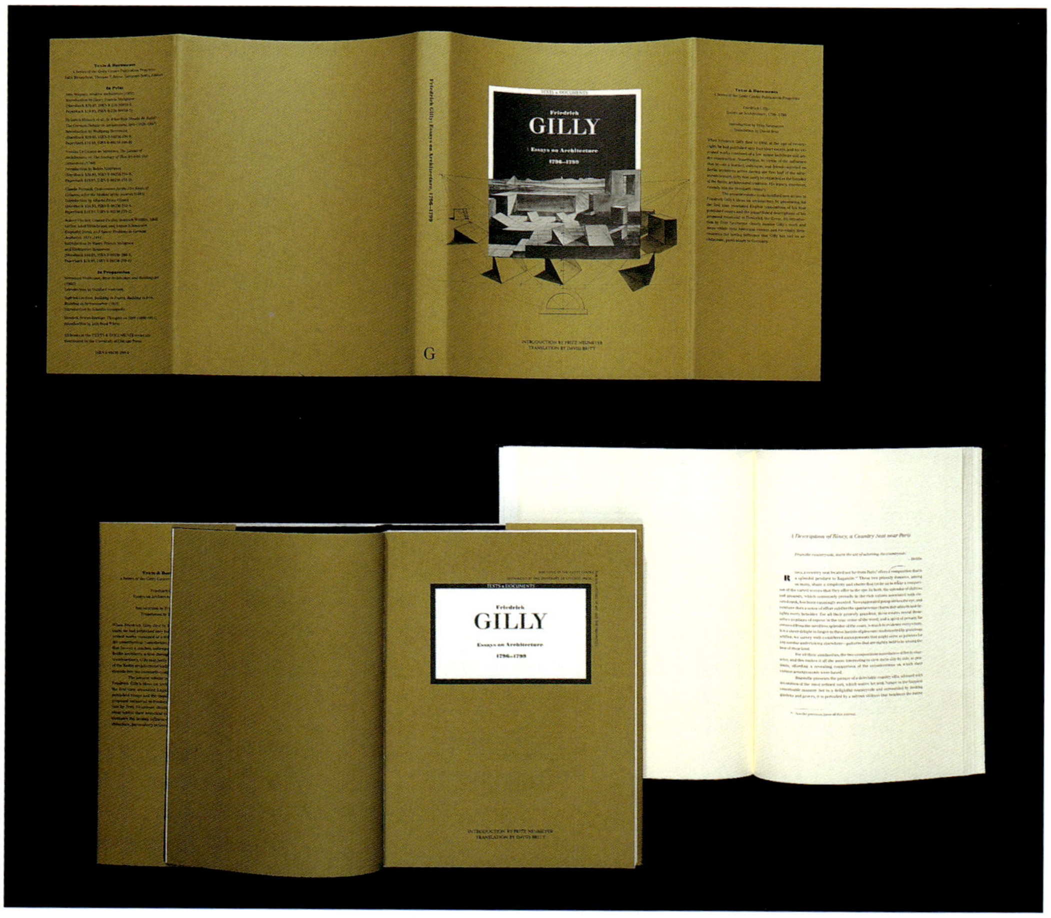

Friedrich Gilly: Essays On Architecture, 1796–1799

BOOK

Designer : Lorraine Wild

Design Firm : ReVerb

Client/Publisher : The Getty Center for the History of Art and the Humanities

Typographer : Wilsted & Taylor

Printer : Gardner Lithograph

Paper : Text: Mohawk Superfine, White and Softwhite, Smooth Finish, 80 lb. Text
Jacket: Mohawk Superfine, Softwhite, Smooth Finish, 100 lb. Text

caryn aono

entrant's comments

The title of this book is so beautiful and evocative that the cover really needed very little else in the way of imagery. I wanted the words "empathy, form, and space" to feel lyrical and light, so I used Zuzana Licko's new font, Quartet. The type falling outside of the label on the cover and the combination of white and cream is meant to refer to the idea of form and space in an elegant, restrained way. Inside, the white pages indicate new writing, and the cream pages carry the actual translations of historical material. The real challenge for the "Texts & Documents" series has always been to convey historical and conceptual content within a postmodern context using the highest editorial, typographic, and printing standards. Working with a profoundly dedicated editorial staff gave me the opportunity to locate the details that make typography enhance readability.

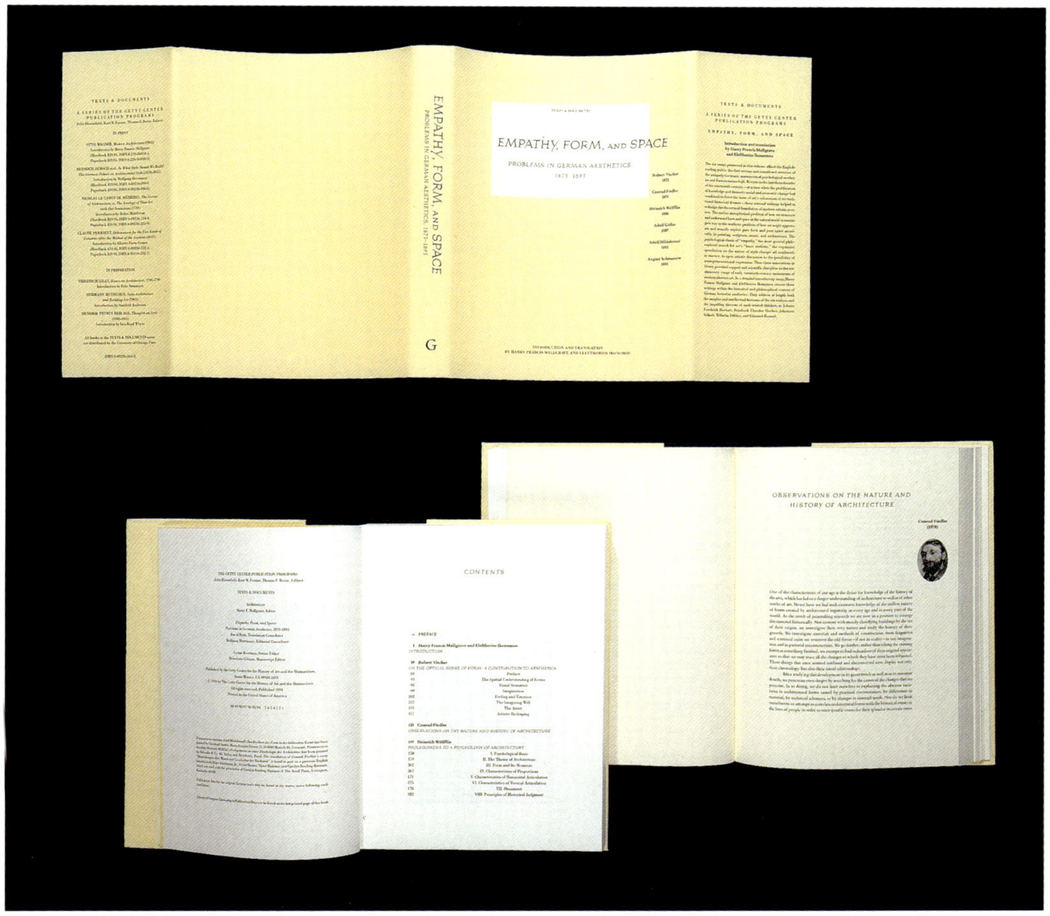

Empathy, Form, and Space: Problems in German Aesthetics, 1873–1893

BOOK

Designer : Laurie Haycock Makela
Client/Publisher : The Getty Center for the History of Art and the Humanities
Typographer : Archetype
Printer : Gardner Lithograph
Paper : Text: Mohawk Superfine, White and Softwhite, Smooth Finish, 80 lb. Text
Jacket: Mohawk Superfine, White, Smooth Finish, 100 lb. Text

caryn aono

also selected by
Marlene McCarty, see p.72

The influence of Knopf in-house design on book design and marketing is unprecedented. I enjoy the cover designs most after having read them since they so cleverly and intelligently interpret the narrative. Quite a few were submitted, but I chose this one specifically since I read it, and I read about the cover in a book review. It is rare that the mention of the book design or designer is associated with a book's popularity. In the review, the designer thoughtfully explained the design process and her concerns with misrepresentation, appropriateness, and reasons for the final cover look. Since the book title is a bit strange, the designer chose to emphasize these words and exercise a bit of restraint in setting it clearly in Bell Gothic. To me, the cover design and review acknowledge the graphic designer's role in popular culture. –ca

Who Will
Run the Frog
Hospital?
a novel by
Lorrie Moore

entrant's comments

With such an evocative title, any embellishment of the jacket seemed to border on the perverse. This novel is a first-person reminiscence of a woman named Berie, who is gifted with the author's deadpan wit and brilliantly ironic observations. As *The New York Times* noted, "Berie realizes, as she recounts the story of her youth, that she is romanticizing events, allowing memory to colorize all the blacks and whites and grays." I agree. Such coloring is often best left to the memory and the imagination.

Who Will Run the Frog Hospital?

BOOK COVER

Designer : Barbara deWilde
Design Director : Carol Carson
Design Firm : Barbara deWilde
Client/Publisher : Alfred A. Knopf
Typographer : Barbara deWilde
Printer : Coral Graphics
Paper : white coated stock

caryn aono

also selected by Jan van Toorn, see p.137

The designers have intelligently used typographic metaphors to interpret the theme of cross-cultural representation throughout this catalog. The visually striking front cover title is especially compelling and syncs thoughtfully with the artist's photograph. This idea is also applied in the headlines, which cross a few fonts to create a distinct new one. Interior sections carefully sequence essays and color plates on complex grids. Overall, a respectful design that eloquently interprets the voices represented in the artwork. –ca

entrant's comments

The artists included in this exhibition show in their work the negotiations that they have undertaken in their respective journeys across a constantly shifting bicultural landscape. Because there are no clear divisions or boundaries, but, rather, multiple perspectives across cultural, historical, and artistic issues, we set up a page grid with a central horizon line defined by certain typographic details, while other elements hug either the top or the bottom of the page. The typefaces used are all sans serifs, playing into the idea of visual difference with a superficial similarity at first glance, which is loosely analogous to the use of one geographic term to describe so many widely varying cultures. Each of the three essays is treated differently, with the typography of the opening spreads referring to border crossings and the multiple voices that shape one's identity. In the cover typography, we tried to refer to non-Western alphabet forms without using stereotypical "thematic" typefaces that mostly derive from Chinese or Japanese characters. A shift occurs in the title treatment in the front matter, reiterating the impossibility of representing the relationship between Asia and America as a fixed form.

IDENTITIES IN CONTEMPORARY ASIAN AMERICAN ART
ASIA
AMERICA

Asia/America

BOOK

Designers : Somi Kim, Lorraine Wild, Andrea Fella
Publication Director : Joseph Newland
Writers : M. Machida, V. Desai, J. Tchen
Photographer : assorted
Design Firm : ReVerb
Client/Publisher : The Asia Society Galleries, New York
Typographers : Somi Kim, Lisa Nugent, Andrea Fella
Printer : Typecraft
Separator : Typecraft

caryn aono

These pages have a lyrical quality to them, down to the smallest details. The typography is highly manipulated, especially on the bilingual pages which are quite poetic. A beautiful, intimate piece. –ca

entrant's comments

This was the perfect project. The client and printer were amazing. They said "yes" to everything (only in Holland). The essays in the front of the book were written by separate people and addressed different aspects of the career of Joe Cillen, the artist. It seemed appropriate that the typography support that difference. The essay by Leslie Jaye Kavanaugh was interesting to design. As the translator grew increasingly angry due to the untranslatable language, I suggested that we run the essay in Dutch as a literal translation and only print the sentences that made sense. The entire Dutch translation took away from the piece, and by eliminating the unnecessary, the essay had meaning and the page took on a rhythm of its own. In contrast to some of the typographic play in the essay section, I wanted a simple and clean treatment of the type for the second section of the catalog so that the focus was undoubtedly on Joe's work.

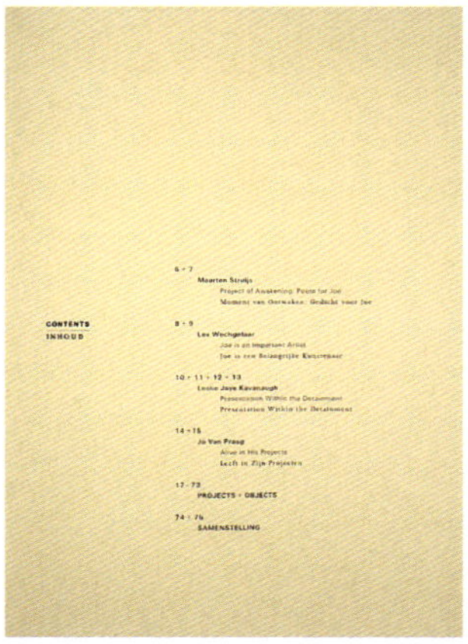

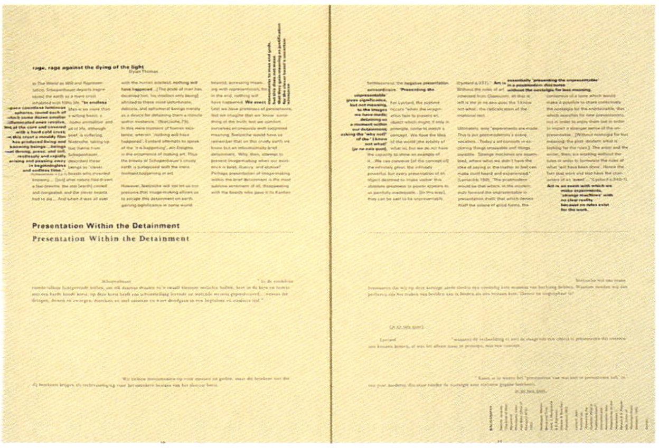

Projects + Objects

CATALOG

Designer : Kali Nikitas
Writers : various
Photographer : Rob Kamminga
Design Firm : graphic design for love (+ $)
Client/Publisher : Joe Cillen
Printer : Studio Pascal Frans Boon, Utrecht

caryn aono

This is more active than typical investment materials. It has to be, in order to reach its intended, though reluctant, audience. The exaggerated hierarchy with soft photo vignettes clearly illustrates growth over time. –ca

entrant's comments

Aid Association for Lutherans is one of the nation's largest fraternal benefit societies. Its market has traditionally been people over the age of 50. Downey Weeks & Toomey was asked to find a way to reach an under-40 market to sell the concept of retirement saving. Although this generation faces greater economic challenges than the previous one, the one advantage it has for retirement is time. We chose to emphasize this through the use of graphics and words that continually reinforce the advantages of beginning a savings plan early, and benefiting from the compounding of interest. Our goal was to break through the boredom of traditional financial messages and target this specific market segment with graphics that appeal to them, not to their parents. There was some initial hesitation by our client, until some informal testing was done with members of this age group. This approach won over a more traditional execution unanimously.

Make Time Work For You

BROCHURE AND POSTER

Designers : Michael Glueckert, M. Perez
Design Directors : Lynda Decker, Byron Weeks
Writer : Bill Trembath
Design Firm : Downey Weeks & Toomey
Client/Publisher : Richard Redman, Nancy McMillan, Aid Association for Lutherans
Typographer : DWT
Separator : Pasani Graphics
Paper : Simpson Kashmir

caryn aono

I like pieces that have dual formats. The exteriors of these pieces work as handheld pamphlets. When unfolded, the interiors work as posters. The designers have done a good job of shoe-horning the copy (of which there is too much) on the page. These could use some editing since the copy is almost to the brink of forcing a new page size or format. On the calendar side, the imagery is a nice ethereal contrast to the straightforward typography. –ca

entrant's comments

This series of calendars, created three times annually for the experimental film organization San Francisco Cinematheque, functions as the organization's only printed piece of public communication. For this reason, each piece had to function as a calendar of upcoming film-screening events, as well as a newsletter to reach new and current members. To achieve this, we developed a flexible system in which the typography and grid structure could shift between calendars, while still creating a unified identity. The imagery for each calendar was selected from the featured films, which allowed us to highlight the work of many film makers and use the images to create a collage with the text.

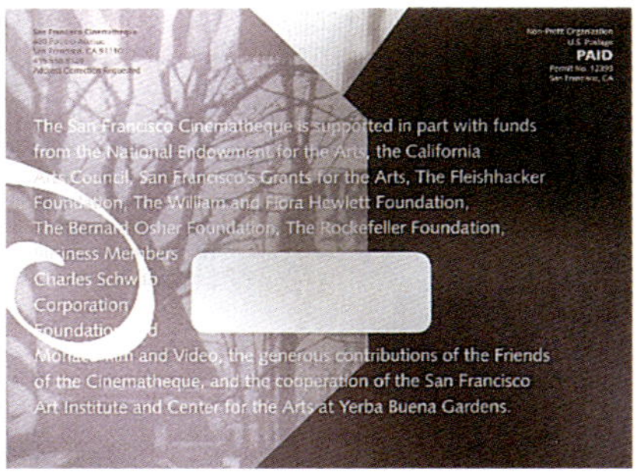

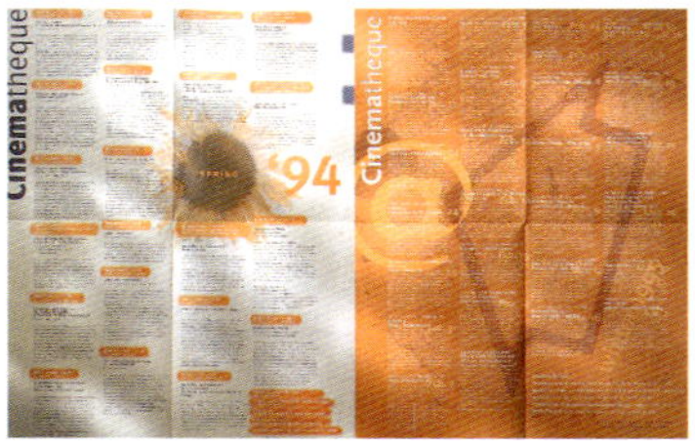

San Francisco Cinematheque

CALENDARS

Designers : Jeff Zwerner, Deborah Whitney
Writer : San Francisco Cinematheque
Client/Publisher : San Francisco Cinematheque
Printer : Alonzo Printing
Separator : Omnicomp
Paper : Husky 80 lb. Cover

caryn aono

A fun, functional piece that helps streamline the drudgery of prepress. A really beautiful example of information design. –ca

entrant's comments

This project deals with two very real issues: an industry coping with rapidly changing technology, and discovering the role of design and communication in maintaining or competing for market share. The Dynagraf Prepress Envelope provides a customer-friendly vehicle designed to perform a variety of functions: to collect disks, proofs, and project information; document basic information from the customer (input); and provide in-house technical specifications and job tracking information (output). In addition, this project was designed to address this commercial printer's marketing need to appear fully capable, completely up-to-date with digital prepress technology.

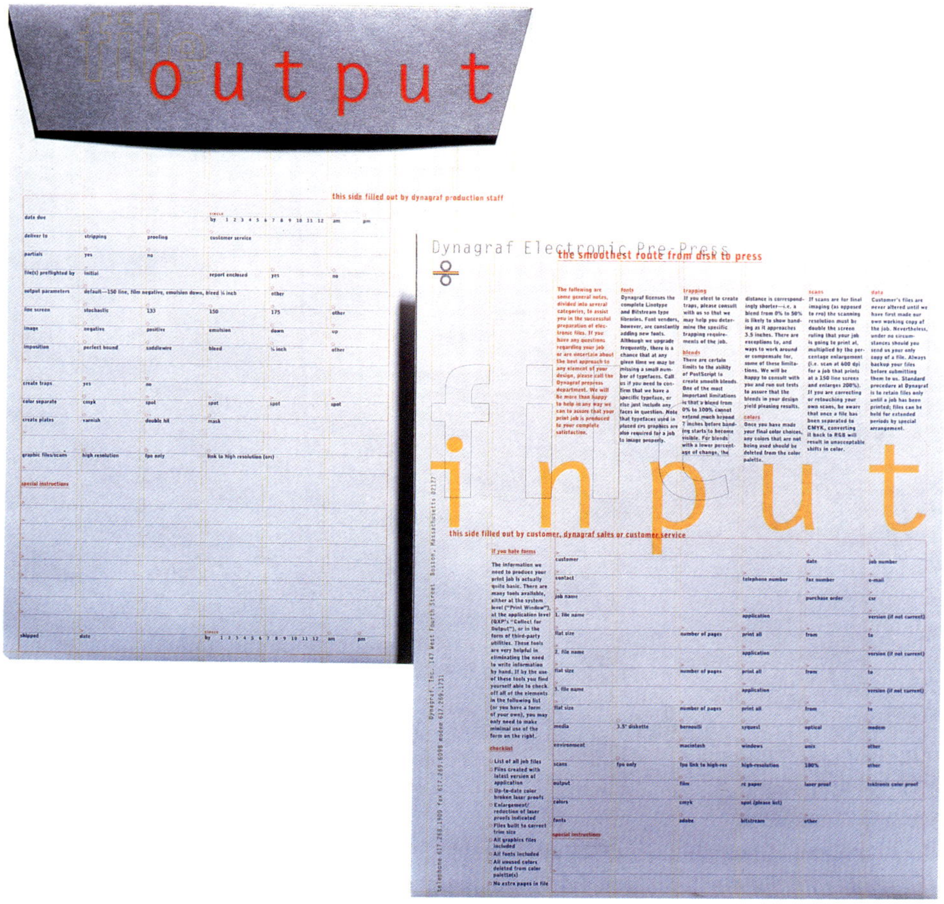

Dynagraf Prepress

ENVELOPE

Designer : Lee Allen Kreindel
Design Director : Lee Allen Kreindel
Writer : Roy Fischer
Design Firm : Lee Allen Kreindel Graphic Design
Client/Publisher : Dynagraf, Inc.
Typographer : Lee Allen Kreindel
Printer : Dynagraf, Inc.
Separator : Dynagraf, Inc.
Paper : Simpson Starwhite Vicksburg Tiara Cover

caryn aono

entrant's comments

The Unity Temple Restoration Foundation looks after one of architect Frank Lloyd Wright's most well-known structures. This report refers to the architect's use of blueprints to communicate intention and accomplishment – the efforts that keep the building alive. The blueprint process allowed us to work within a budget that diminishes each year.

This annual report is one of the most thoughtful pieces I came across in the judging. Copy is carefully set to notate architectural details, such as the renowned columns. This actual blueprint functions as a unique and inexpensive memento for the donors who support the foundation. –ca

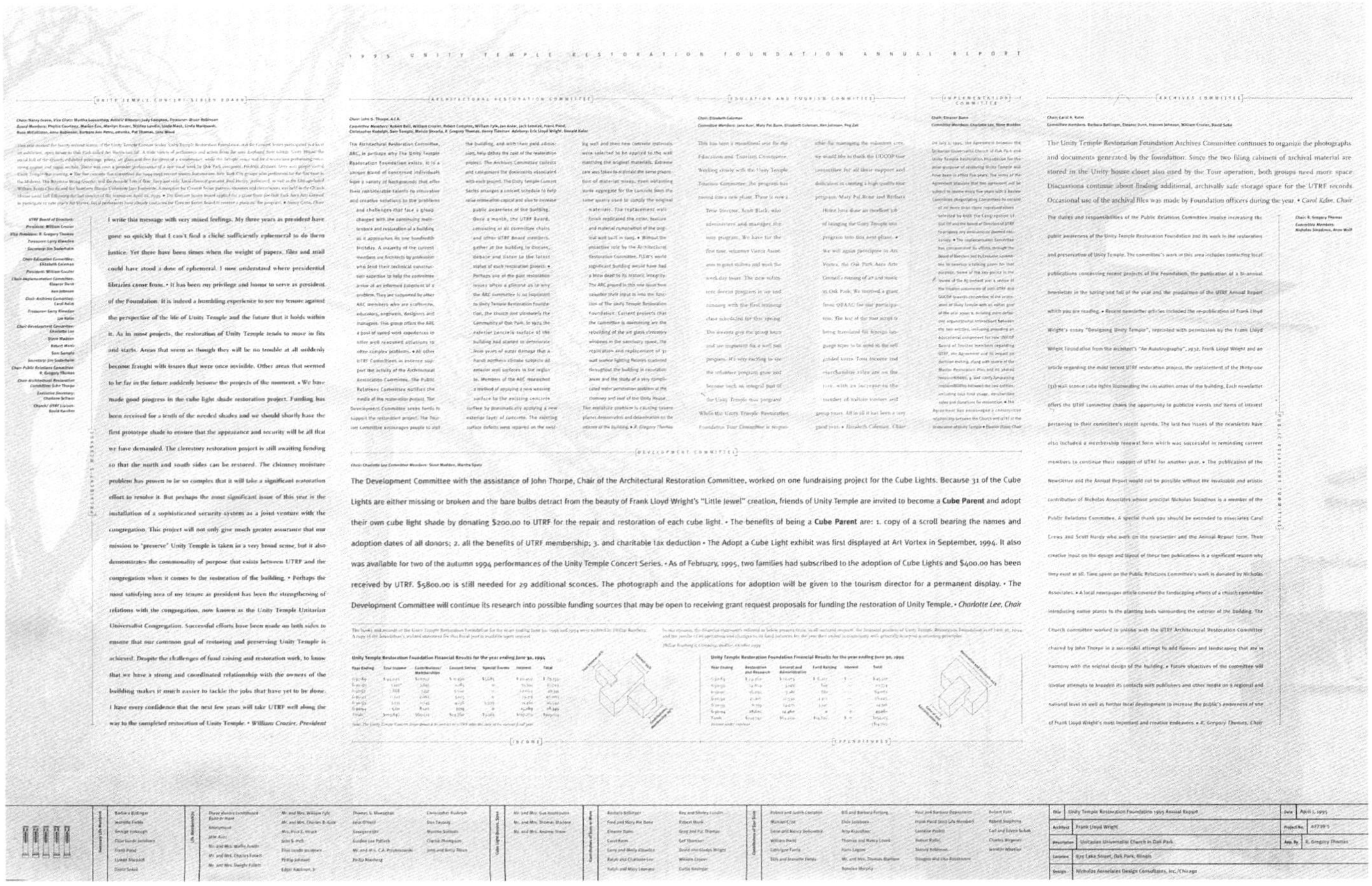

The Development Committee with the assistance of John Thorpe, Chair of the Architectural Restoration Committee, worked on one fundraising project for the Cube Lights. Because 31 of the Cube Lights are either missing or broken and the bare bulbs detract from the beauty of Frank Lloyd Wright's "Little Jewel" creation, friends of Unity Temple are invited to become a **Cube Parent** and adopt their own cube light shade by donating $200.00 to UTRF for the repair and restoration of each cube light. • The benefits of being a **Cube Parent** are: 1. copy of a scroll bearing the names and adoption dates of all donors; 2. all the benefits of UTRF membership; 3. and charitable tax deduction • The Adopt a Cube Light exhibit was first displayed at Art Vortex in September, 1994. It also was available for two of the autumn 1994 performances of the Unity Temple Concert Series. • As of February, 1995, two families had subscribed to the adoption of Cube Lights and $400.00 has been received by UTRF. $5800.00 is still needed for 29 additional sconces. The photograph and the applications for adoption will be given to the tourism director for a permanent display. • The Development Committee will continue its research into possible funding sources that may be open to receiving grant request proposals for funding the restoration of Unity Temple. • *Charlotte Lee, Chair*

Unity Temple

ANNUAL REPORT

Designers : Nicholas Sinadinos, Scott Hardy

Design Director : Nicholas Sinadinos

Writers : Elizabeth Coleman, William Crozier, Eleanor Dunn, Nancy Greco, Carol Kelm, Charlotte Lee, R. Gregory Thomas

Design Firm : Nicholas Associates/Chicago

Client/Publisher : Unity Temple Restoration Foundation

Typographer : Strong Silent Type

Printer : Photographic & Reprographic Group

Papers : Dietzgen Dri Print, Diazo Media 20 lb. White

caryn aono

This is quite an elegant book. A highly articulated grid structures generous white space throughout the layout. Wide letterspacing and leading, wispy, fine, three-point type, and hairline rules make for pages that someone observed, "a slight breeze could blow away the design." This design firm submitted several entries with this similar style. I picked this one specifically because designers are the audience and they could most appreciate (tolerate?) three-point type.
–ca

entrant's comments

This running narrative and photo essay, which divides *AR 100* into categories, spotlights not only those reports that were produced in celebration of banner years, but those in which the results were nothing to brag about as well. The series of black and red photos are intended as humorous interpretations of business terms that are commonly used to relate earnings news – both good and not so good: merger and acquisition, downsizing, strategic alliance, start-up, take over, belly up.

AR 100

BOOK

Designers : Steven Tolleson, Jennifer Sterling
Design Directors : Steven Tolleson, Jennifer Sterling
Writer : Lindsay Beaman
Photographer : John Casado
Design Firm : Tolleson Design
Client/Publisher : Black Book Marketing Group
Typographer : Tolleson Design
Printer : D.L. Terwilliger
Separator : D.L. Terwillger
Paper : Celesta Litho Dull by Westvaco

caryn aono

This identity looks a bit deceiving to me. It is very stark and simple, yet consciously considered. The multilingual copy and placement of the elements suggest more than what appears. Perhaps it is designed for multiple formats and uses. Crowning touches are the buildings on the envelope flap which cut the horizontal space like the buildings rising on the L.A. horizon.

–ca

entrant's comments

The Pacific Design Center (PDC) identity needed a clear message interfacing and inclusive of the Pacific Rim. It needed the landmark building as a very unmistakable part of the program. It needed to function within a range of media – from print, signage, digital formats, and video to the Internet. It needed to give more control to the user. The PDC identity did not need another layer of graphic design on top of the incredible richness within the building itself. It did not need a big logo à la IBM. It did not need hip, groovy design. It did not need 14 colors, 2 varnishes, and 37 typographic elements. This was accomplished with a kit of parts: Pacific Design Center in four languages, a corporate alphabet, "Pacific," open boxes, and the image (photographic) of the building. Although there are five most-used configurations of these elements, theoretically, anyone could create their own and it would always remain clearly Pacific Design Center.

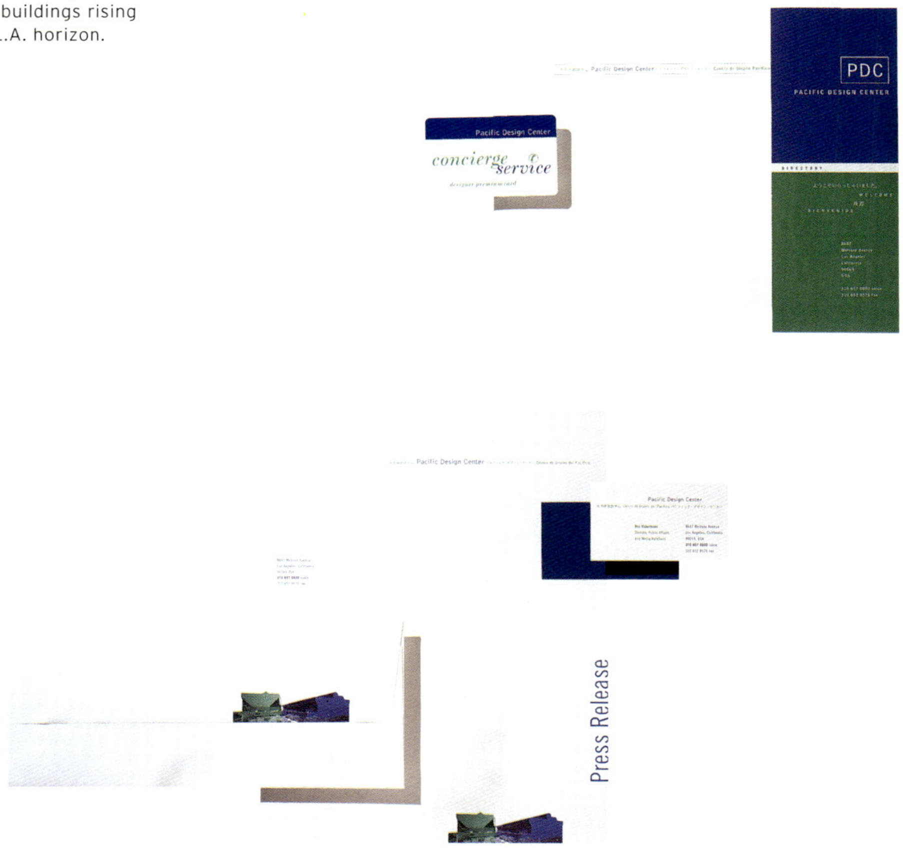

Pacific Design Center

IDENTITY

Designers : Sean Adams, Noreen Morioka
Design Director : Sean Adams
Design Firm : Adams/Morioka
Client/Publisher : Andrew Wolf/Pacific Design Center
Typographer : Icon West
Printer : Coast Litho
Paper : Strathmore Writing

caryn aono

The fusing of the letter forms and the diminuendo in the type size makes wonderfully odd shapes in this very simple, yet elegant, logotype. –ca

entrant's comments

The International Design Network Foundation (IDNF) is a nonprofit organization devoted to strengthening and enriching the field of design by linking different design groups in various countries and helping to expose design to a broader public. The logo is meant to symbolize the mission of IDNF by the connected letters, which represent the contact that different areas of the design community will have with one another as a result of IDNF's efforts.

International Design Network Foundation

LOGO

Designer : Takaaki Matsumoto
Design Director : Takaaki Matsumoto
Design Firm : Matsumoto Incorporated
Client/Publisher : International Design Network Foundation
Typographer : Matsumoto Incorporated

caryn aono

With the variety of the logos presented, I wondered if REV 105 was one of those radio stations that changes format every six months to remain progressive in the eyes (ears) of its audience. I'm uncertain if these logos were used simultaneously or if only one (or none) was chosen. If all six were used, kudos to the client for presenting themselves as this multifaceted. –ca

entrant's comments

REV 105 is a critically acclaimed alternative radio station. The station has a devoted following due to its large playlist rotation and loose format. We felt it would be the perfect opportunity to create a similar approach for the identity. Thus, we came up with a series of logomarks, which, while not always consistent in vernacular, are always high on the curiosity scale. Large companies need a corporate identity, but a local progressive radio station like REV can reflect an attitude as its identity.

REV 105

REVOLUTION RADIO

REV 105 .1 .3

REVOLUTION RADIO

ReV radio revolution 105

rev R 105

REV 105 .1 .3

revolution radio

REV 105

LOGOS

Designer : Chad Hagen
Design Director : Bill Thorburn
Design Firm : Thorburn Design
Client/Publisher : REV 105

caryn aono

This is a design for an independent label anthology. It has a nostalgic feel for place-as-memory and is very carefully executed. The embossed maps are tactile impressions of the studio's old neighborhood and the photo collages piece together vignettes as if they were spaces remembered. The color palette is unexpected and doesn't make the nostalgia idea too sentimental. –ca

entrant's comments

This is Fort Apache is a recording studio in Boston specializing in alternative rock music. In 1994, they entered into an agreement with MCA Records and became a record label. This package was created to introduce the Fort Apache label and explain its past. As the first sentence of the text states, "born out of the original punk, do-it-yourself spirit," we decided to create a new package as opposed to conforming to an already existing one. The idea was simple: take people on a trip to Fort Apache starting with an aerial view of Cambridge and the Boston area, through the neighborhood, carry them over the fort-like fence at the entrance, and then into the studio. The materials we chose were recycled and raw – a little like the bands, and in line with the politics of the principles.

This Is Fort Apache

CD PACKAGING

Designers: Robin Cottle, Tim Stedman, Todd Gallopo, Pia Koskela
Design Director: Tim Stedman
Writer: Karen Schoemer
Photographer: Michael Wilson
Client/Publisher: Fort Apache/MCA
Typographers: Tim Stedman, Robin Cottle
Printer: AGI Inc.
Separator: L.A. Filmco
Paper: Exterior: 18.0 Recycled Newback
Interior: Mead 100 lb. Offset Enamel

caryn aono

The photos in these pieces are quite engaging. These images are highly manipulated and reveal some software tricks, but they don't distract from their richness. I am curious if the music resonates as these images suggest.
–ca

entrant's comments

Each of the six CDs was designed to fit together to form an elaborate composite. Initially, I designed an overall format for each title to adhere to and built in certain links that would graphically join them. The hexagon became the series' identity, with each of the CDs represented by a color-coded triangle. The images were a mixture of X-ray plates, location shots, and elaborate still-life setups, all of which were scanned into the computer and put together in Photoshop.

The Hafler Trio – The Golden Hammer

KUT 1–6

CD INSERTS

Designer: Giles Dunn
Design Director: Giles Dunn
Writers: Jon Wozencroft, Andrew McKenzie
Design Firm: Giles Dunn
Photographer: Giles Dunn
Client/Publisher: Touch/The Gray Area of Mute Records
Typographer: Giles Dunn
Printer: Mute Records
Separator: Mute Records
Paper: 140 Matte Color-Dex

caryn aono

Another piece produced with minimum means – two colors on chipboard. I like that they put this message on a bookmark as a periodic reminder about the act of conversing. The deliberate cropping of the two-handed saw is quite clever. –ca

entrant's comments

This bookmark was used in support of the Campaign for Civility by the Indiana Civil Liberties Union (ICLU). The mission of the ICLU is to defend and protect the Bill of Rights of the United States Constitution. We used the Alcott quote "many can argue, not many converse" to make a point about civility and listening. We used the image of the double-handled saw to suggest that if two people work in harmony, they can accomplish their goal; but if communication is severed, nothing is gained.

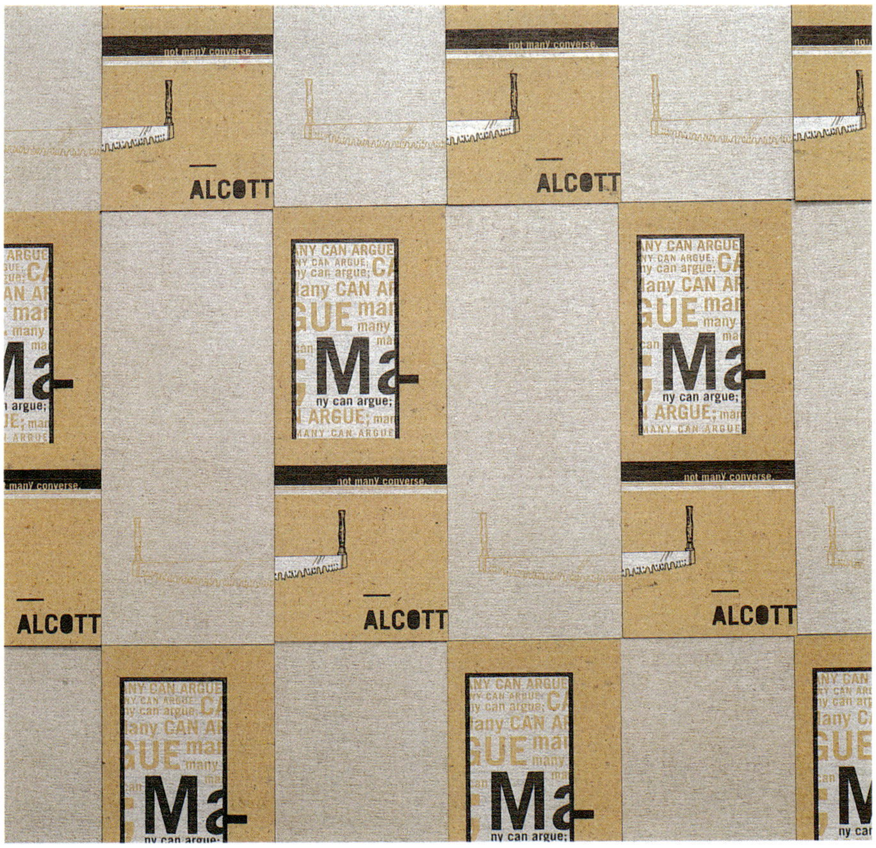

Many Can Argue
Indiana Civil Liberties Union

BOOKMARK

Designers : James Sholly, Laura Lacy-Sholly
Writer : Louisa May Alcott
Design Firm : Antenna
Client/Publisher : Indiana Civil Liberties Union
Printer : Faulkenberg Printing
Paper : chipboard

caryn aono

This poster is quite funny and sarcastic. The imagery and zippy type swing like the life of the party. -ca

entrant's comments

This poster announced an evening of visual and performance arts in a former Masonic temple. The intent of the event was to create a sampler of the types of events that community members could attend or become a part of in the new art center. Performances and demonstrations were offered buffet style, and the audience was free to roam and participate at will. The poster juxtaposes the fez, symbolizing club membership, with hors d'oeuvres, representing the works of art to be produced and consumed. The ironic visual approach is further heightened by the use of flocking and metallic embellishment to create a more theoretical representation of a big-ass party.

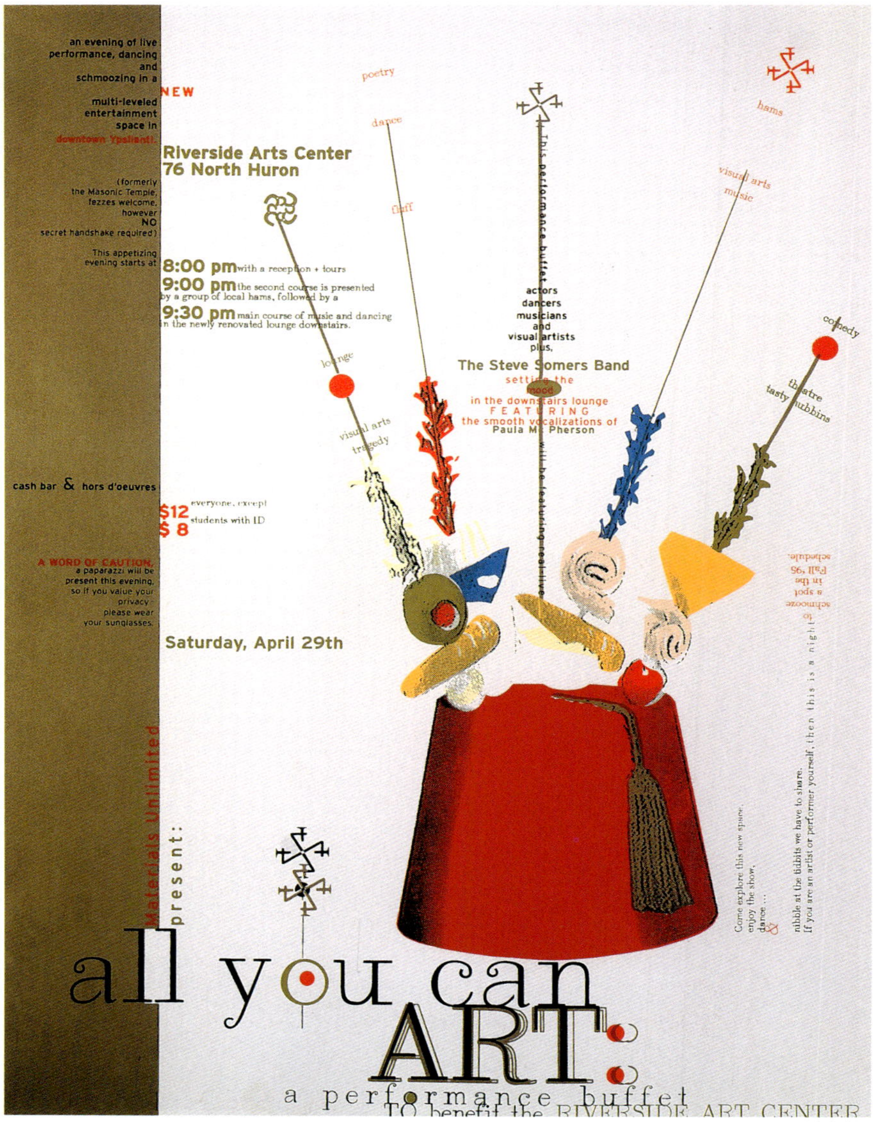

All You Can Art

POSTER

Designers : Sue LaPorte, George La Rou
Writers : Christine Marshall, Sue LaPorte, George La Rou
Illustrators : Sue LaPorte, George La Rou
Photographers : Sue LaPorte, George La Rou
Design Firm : Exquisite Corps
Client/Publisher : Petey The Dog Productions
Typographers : Sue LaPorte, George La Rou, Dingbats by Kindra Murphy
Printer : David Morris
Separator : George La Rou
Paper : floor stock

caryn aono

This is a striking poster for an art exhibition. Map imagery, photography, and a quirky code font subtly suggest places of origin. A smaller repeat of the headline in the right corner is a nice touch. The combination of elements create an odd, ominous feel that I don't necessarily associate with Indiana, but then, I don't know the dark side of that state.
–ca

entrant's comments

Direction is the first exhibition including all of the fine-arts faculty in the entire Indiana University system. The faculty, the schools' locations, the styles, and media are quite diverse. The landscape, maps, compass, rose, and type are all motifs meant to represent the vast logistics involved in its organization rather than any single artist. This press sheet can be cut in different ways to make the following: the dust jacket of a hardbound exhibition catalog (the top half, cut approximately in the middle) with a list of artists on the flaps; a poster announcing the exhibition's tour (cut minus the left side) with the list included at the insistence of the sponsor; a poster announcing the inaugural exhibition of one gallery on the tour (cut minus left and bottom one quarter); and a tiny all-purpose announcement.

Direction Exhibition

POSTER

Designers : Edwin Utermohlen, Christa Skinner
Design Director : Edwin Utermohlen
Design Firm : dcubledagger
Client/Publisher : Indiana University
Typographers : Edwin Utermohlen, Christa Skinner
Printer : Benham Press
Separator : Benham Press
Paper : Vintage Velvet

caryn aono

It is rare that soft drink packaging is so hip and clever. Its plainness, and self-effacing humor – to the point of almost being dumb – implies something more than the obvious. This challenges the consumer to put a 12-pack in the grocery cart, while also gauging their hipness quotient. -ca

entrant's comments

OK soda is a brand for teenagers. Therefore, it contains many contradictions. It is obvious and obscure, stupid and smart, sullen and exuberant. Graphically, it sustains many variations on a few simple themes. So far, we've produced seven cans, two 12-packs, and four 12-pack interiors. The exterior depicts a teenager in a supermarket and the cans contained inside the 12-pack. On each interior, there's a pretense of interactivity: a board game you can't win; absurd objects to cut out of the cardboard (ice cube trays, scissors); and, shown here, a "secret decoder" with the message already decoded. Teen life is hell, but fun. Fun hell.

OK 12-Pack

BOX

Designer: Todd Waterbury
Design Director: Todd Waterbury
Writer: Peter Wegner
Illustrators: Daniel Clowes, Todd Waterbury
Design Firm: Wieden & Kennedy
Client/Publisher: The Coca-Cola Company
Typographer: Todd Waterbury
Printer: Ivy Hill
Paper: Mead Duplex, Recycled

caryn aono

Like the packaging, this video continues the "it's OK" theme and maybe is the most successful in conveying OK-ness as a motion graphic with sound. It's interesting how this video design pulled up the flat, two-dimensional package design by scanning over the can and activating those mundane graphic elements, which are givens in the design brief. "Burns Boy," in particular, speaks an inside message to designers, such as when the zebra stripes of the UPC label, upon closer inspection, reveal a typographic OK-ness. Other activated elements add a zippiness not seen in the two-dimensional work and also cut the cool (almost chilly) austerity of some of the images.

–ca

entrant's comments

Two small perceptions gave rise to this brand. First, the core values of OK could be built into the package designs. Second, those designs could then be extended indefinitely and would always support the brand. Packaging = advertising = packaging = advertising. In this campaign, the camera treats the flat art with appropriate respect, which is to say, none. We tilt, lock, spin, push in, pull back, skid, and careen across the shallow landscape of each design. All in the service of a deeply conventional strategy: launch a new product by showing the pack. We took to calling it the "self-evident" campaign.

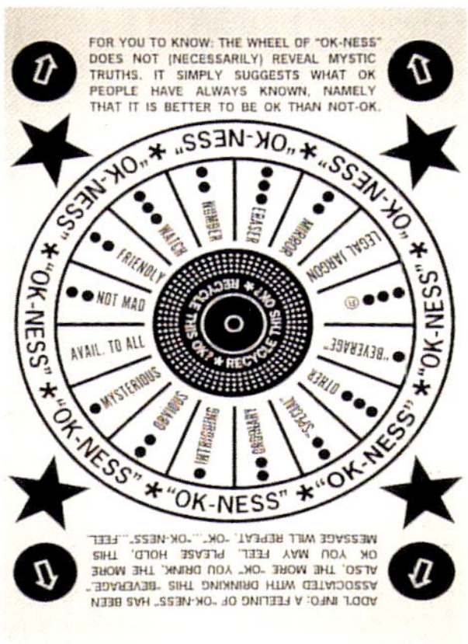

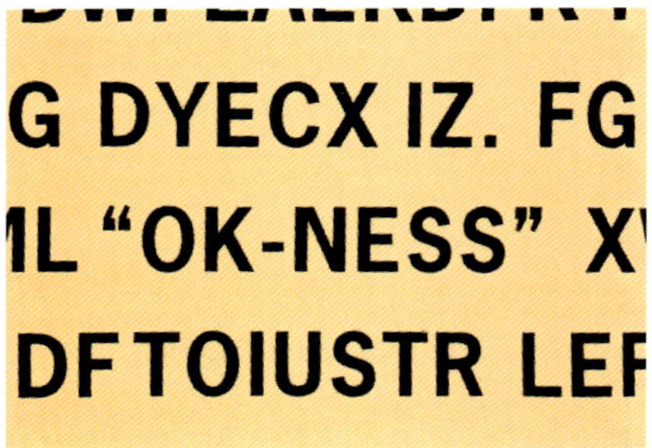

OK Animation

TELEVISION ADVERTISING SERIES

Designer : Todd Waterbury
Design Director : Todd Waterbury
Writer : Peter Wegner
Illustrators : Daniel Clowes, Charles Burns, David Cowles
Design Firm : Wieden & Kennedy
Client/Publisher : The Coca-Cola Company
Typographer : Todd Waterbury
Directors : Donna Pittman, Mark Hensley, Pittman Hensley
Producer : Amy Davenport

caryn aono

For starters, this is a pretty silly icon font. It is perfectly suited for animation, which shows it at its most charming.
–ca

entrant's comments

When designing Zeit Guys, we were interested in making images that had implied, rather than overt, levels of meaning. Our intent was to have the images acquire meaning over time, independent of us. Certainly, we have thoughts about what some of the images might mean, but we have tried as much as possible to create images that must be completed by the viewer. The interactive presentation was purposefully kept small enough to fit onto one high-density floppy disk. The small size allows for easy distribution of the project and also ensures that it can be quickly downloaded from Emigre's bulletin board (now serving). We see this project as the beginning of the contextualization of Zeit Guys. We also think it's a lot of fun.

Zeit

INTERACTIVE COMPUTER ANIMATION

Designer: Bob Aufuldish
Writer: Mark Bartlett
Illustrators: Zeit Guys designed by Eric Donelan and Bob Aufuldish
Design Firm: Aufuldish & Warinner
Client/Publisher: Emigre
Typographer: Bob Aufuldish
Sound: Scott Pickering, Bob Aufuldish

caryn aono

These are smart (and a bit smarmy) promotions for a garage font company. I like how the catalog shows alternative fonts by treating the promos as clever trinkets. These are nice keepers. –ca

entrant's comments

This catalog, business card, and postcard were produced to introduce the new digital type foundry known as The American Type Corp. The company was born out of the desire to share and make available these great typeface designs. To keep production costs low, common staples of office supply stores were used as the materials to fabricate the pieces. All pieces were designed using Adobe PageMaker 5.0 and printed on a laser printer. Type designers include Edwin Utermohlen, Brian Horner, and Christa Skinner.

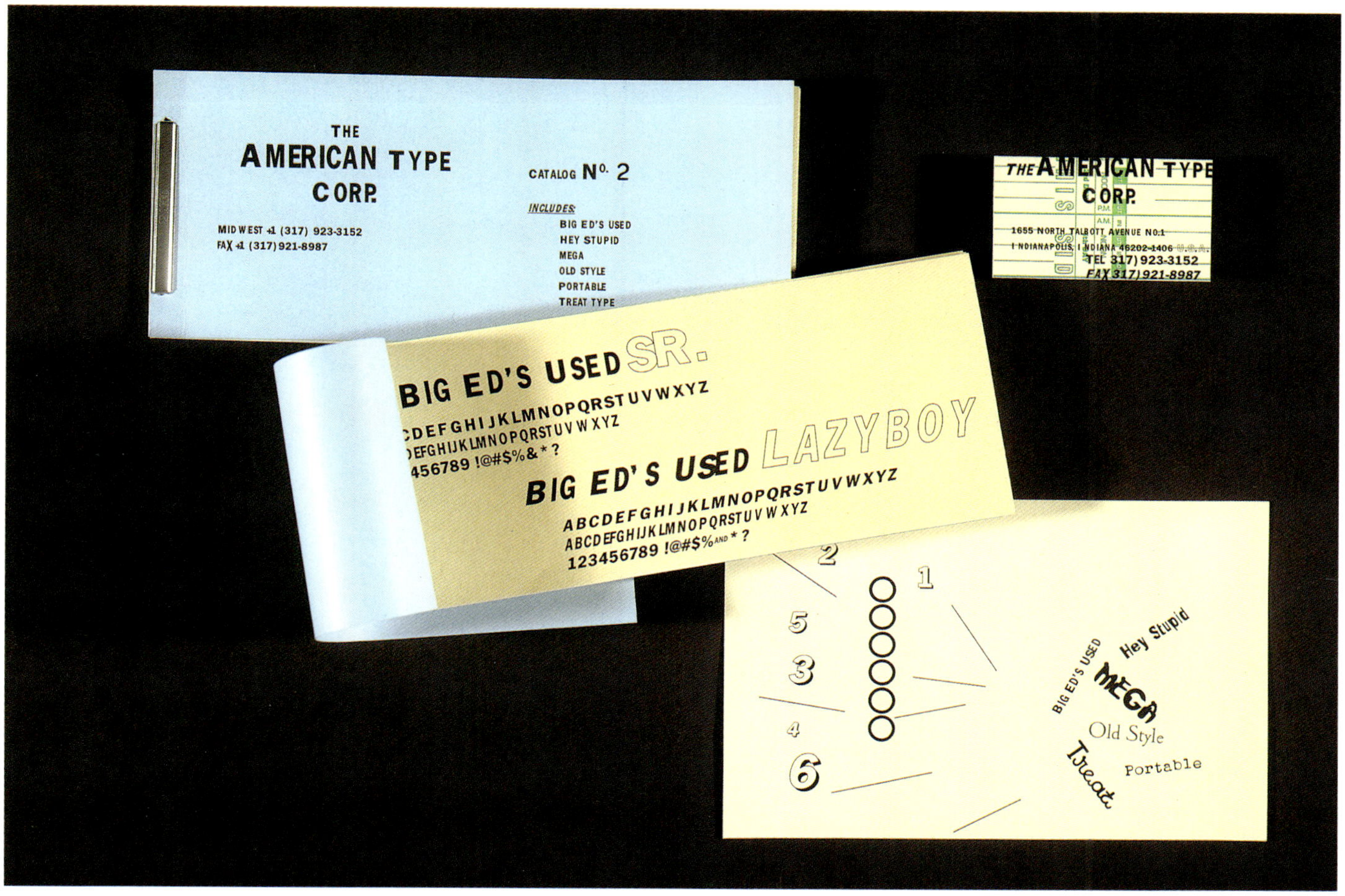

American Type Corp.

PROMOTION

Designer: Jim Ross, Mario A. Mirelez
Design Firm: Mirelez/Ross, Inc.
Client/Publisher: American Type Corp.
Paper: Bristol, Manila, Kraft

caryn aono

These books showcase an incredible amount of work and are invaluable type resources. I appreciate the variety of type treatments and the way the book is structured to reveal all the font's characteristics. It still has the traditional typeface presentation look – reminiscent of metal type catalogs, showing the type in use on a jar label or store ad. –ca

entrant's comments

The Nueva typeface evokes a sense of things new, poised to unfold. The design of the Nueva specimen book reflects this. Text, artwork, and sequencing showcase this typeface, demonstrating the breadth of expression for which Nueva was designed.

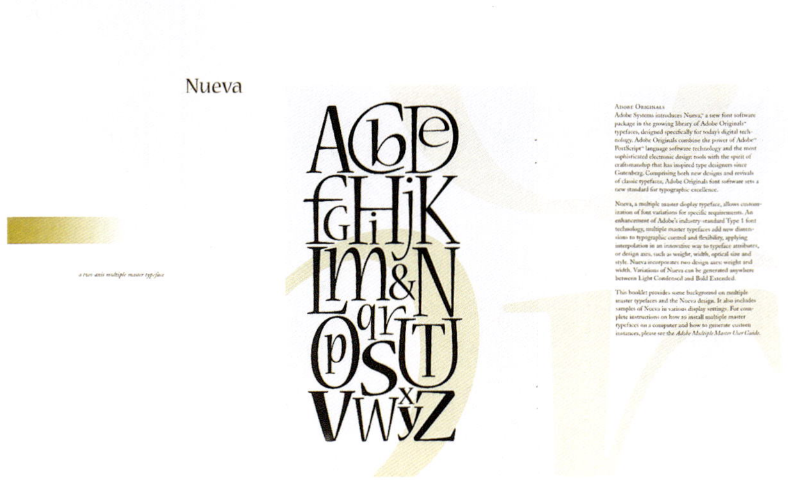

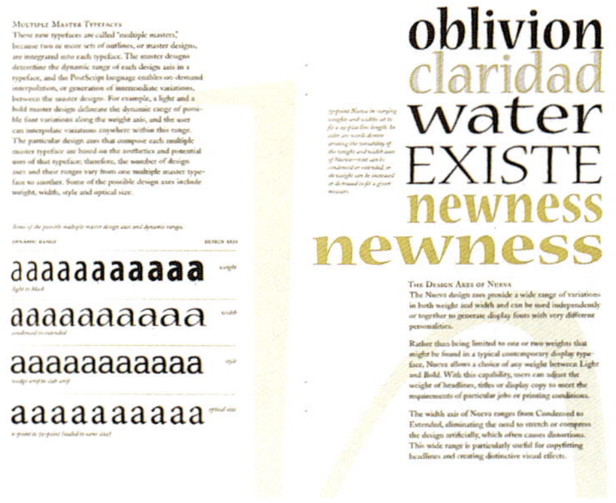

Nueva

SPECIMEN BOOK

Designer : James Young
Art Director : Gail Blumberg
Writer : Adobe Originals Group
Design Firm : Adobe Systems Creative Services
Client/Publisher : Adobe Systems
Typographer : James Young
Printer : West Coast Litho
Separator : in-house
Paper : Mohawk Superfine

caryn aono

This is a beautiful script font rendered less beautiful and – perhaps now – more contemporary in its connotations. This is one of those typefaces that demands your full attention and patience. It looks blurred, yet it is focused and committed to the words it represents. –ca

entrant's comments

Indelible Victorian gives a historical perspective to those who cry that the new typography is illegible. It views the scripts of the past as artifacts; that is, with the ancient roots and connotations still dangling from them. When the reader trusts a strange memory of letter shape inside them, the text is surprisingly present.

The poem excerpt, which was written independently of the typeface, addresses this same cultural shadow: how vocabulary and meaning changes within the same code-set (language) throughout time and space. –daniel x. o'neill

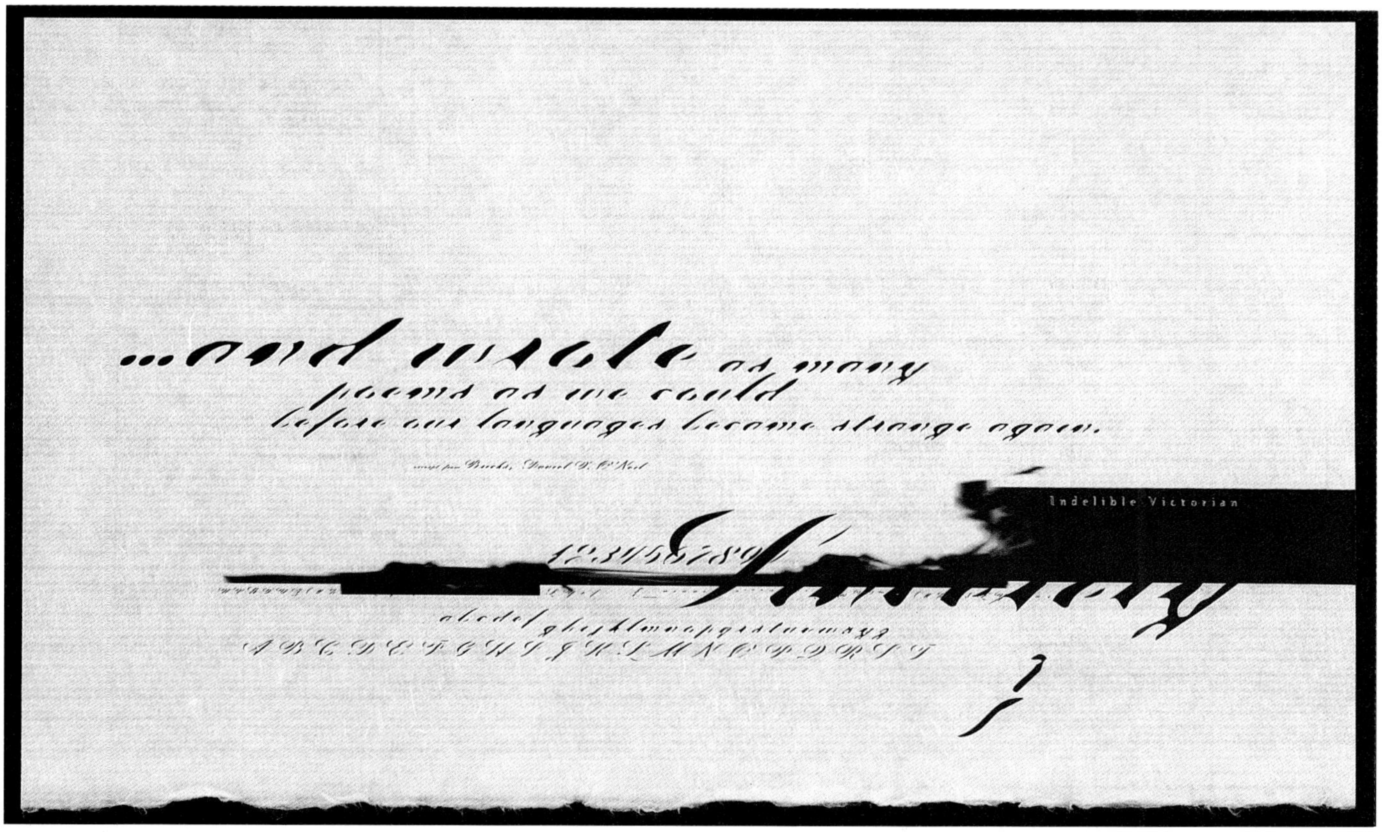

Indelible Victorian Typeface

FONT SPECIMEN SHEET

Designer : Stephen Farrell
Writer : Daniel X. O'Neil, specimen sheet text
Design Firm : Stephen Farrell Design
Typographer : Stephen Farrell
Printer : Laserwriter
Paper : Kayasuki

caryn aono

This is one in a series of posters that Ed Fella has been working on for several years. It is inexpensively produced (11-inch by 17-inch format, one ink, on bond paper), but its impact on design is worth noting. This designer works in his own vernacular, speaking in a highly personal yet approachable language. These are very rich, formally and poetically. Different messages and forms reveal themselves on subsequent readings. What I also find intriguing is the designer's obvious amusement in creating intentional misreadings like "Brody Bunch" for "Brady Bunch." Groovy.
–ca

entrant's comments

This is one of a series of after-the-fact announcements for visiting designers' lectures at California Institute of the Arts. The piece conveys all of the information of the actual event, but in a style (or aesthetic) and content opposite to (or different from) the subject's work. For example, the punning of "The Brody Bunch" with reference to the Brady Bunch television sitcom of the 1970s, and the all hand-lettered "typography" is done in American supermarket/circus vernacular, while the source for the fuse project is "electrical."

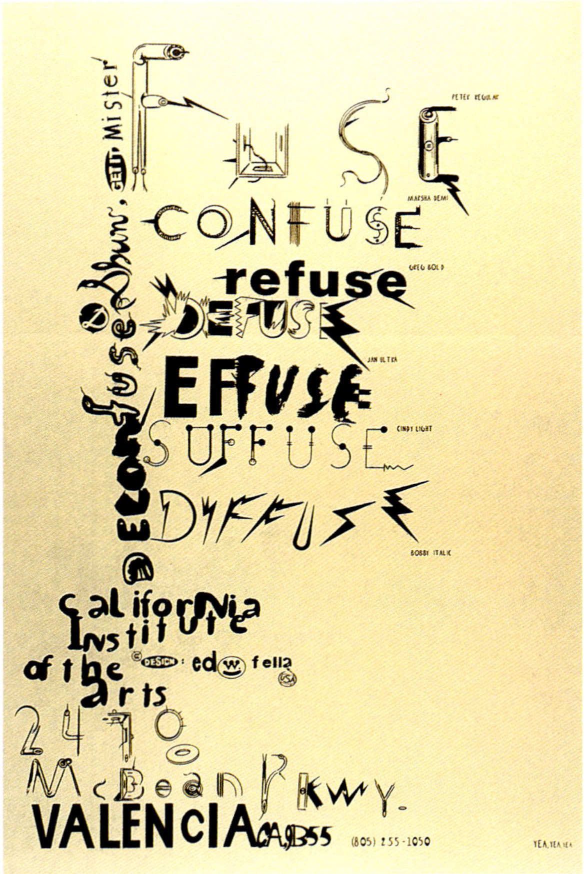

Neville Brody Visiting Designer

POSTER

Designer : Edward Fella
Writer : Edward Fella
Illustrator : Edward Fella
Client/Publisher : California Institute of the Arts, Graphic Design Program
Typographer : all hand lettering/Edward Fella
Printer : Printmasters #115, Valencia, California
Paper : text bond, ivory

entrant's comments

Nowhere does basketball reach such mythical status as in New York City. Here, the sport transforms into a religion, where a single act of superb skill can live for decades beyond the actual moment. Reputations developed on its fabled playgrounds become neighborhood folklore, and, through word-of-mouth, real legends are made. The Nike "NYC" campaign is a celebration of that special spirit – that love of the sport that transcends today's definition of success. It's a celebration of a unique style of play as well – a style that has power as well as elegance. Like the city itself, it expresses a knack for one-upmanship, a unique verbal skill of storytelling, and a dramatic sense of contrasts.

caryn aono

It's always interesting to see how this company presents itself each season. Lately, its ads seem to be paring down to the bare minimum – like the "swish" logo appearing sans "Nike." These billboards dazzle with very few elements. I like the impact of the graffiti-style illustrations and how the name brand "tags" the whole billboard. I would be curious, though, to see what these look like after being reappropriated by actual tagging.

–ca

Nike NYC Graffiti

BILLBOARDS

Designer : Imin Pao
Art Director : John Jay
Creative Directors : Dan Wieden, Susan Hoffman
Illustrator : Javier Michaelski
Design Firm : Wieden & Kennedy
Client/Publisher : Nike

caryn aono

entrant's comments

We developed these gift tags because we felt that tags were the most neglected member of the holiday gift-wrap family. It was only fair.

These humorous witticisms speak more about the gift-giver than the receiver. I appreciate the designers' fondness for communication folly. The odd word breaks, strange croppings, and bold borders deliver small, wry presents.

–ca

Tag! You're It

CHRISTMAS TAGS

Designers : James Sholly, Laura Lacy-Sholly
Design Firm : Antenna
Client/Publisher : Antenna
Printer : PIP
Papers : tagboard and chipboard

caryn aono

This is a witty look at the ongoing legible/illegible debate among designers. Although I enjoy reading the quotes and seeing skillful parodies of textbook design samples, the punchlines are always the same — the typography is legible.

—ca

entrant's comments

I Can't Read This and I Designed It using 22 quotations from renowned graphic designers and avant-garde typographic styling as paradox and parody — attempts to graphically portray the seemingly never-ending quarrel over the use of illegible and unconventional typography. Produced in a limited edition and sold commercially, *I Can't Read This* is the second in a series of chapbooks documenting designers' quotations.

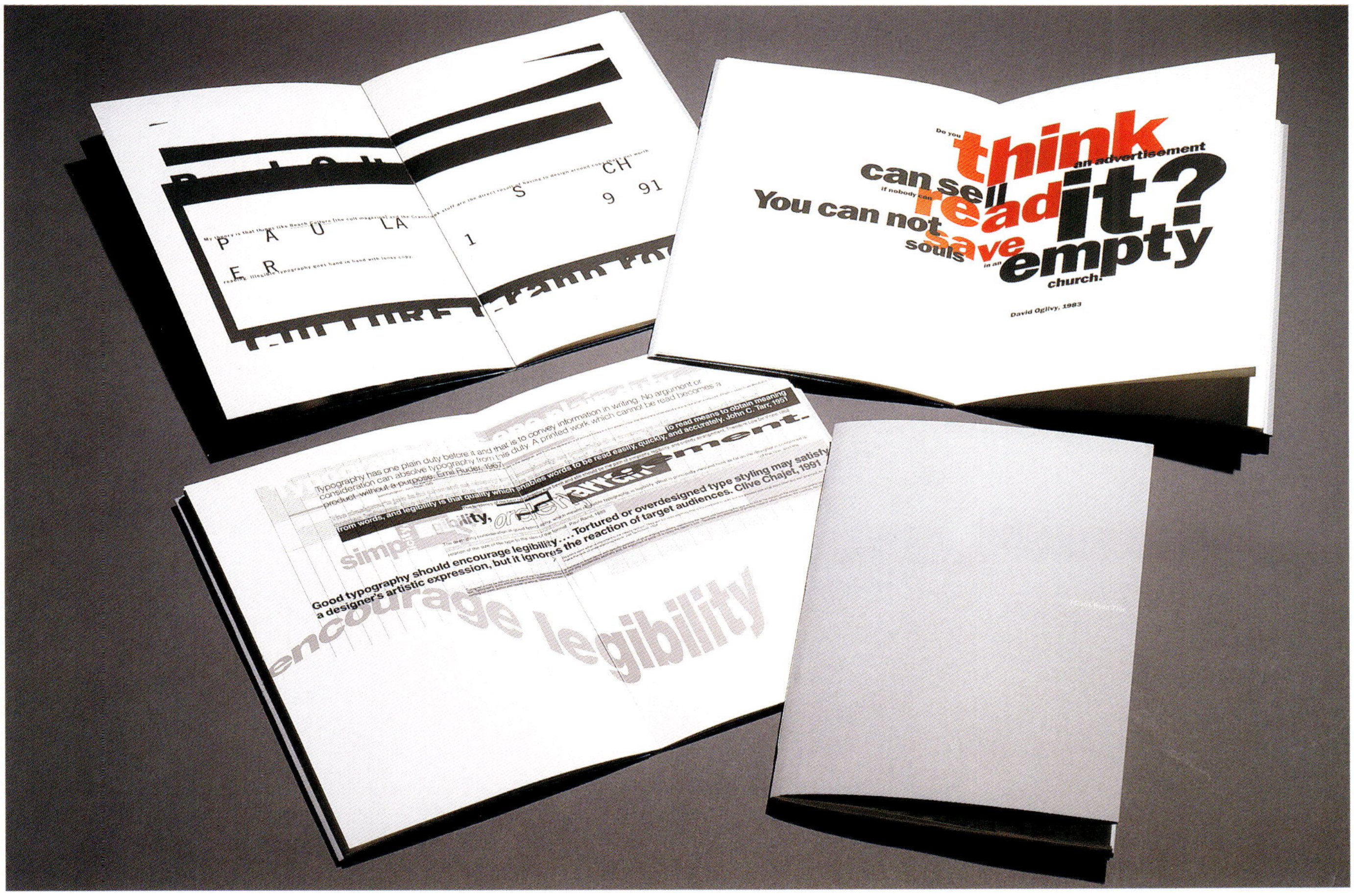

I Can't Read This

CHAPBOOK

Designer : Michael Skjei
Design Director : Michael Skjei
Writers : various
Design Firm : M. Skjei Design Co.
Client/Publisher : Shay, Shea, Hsieh, and Skjei Publishers
Typographer : ASAP, Minneapolis
Printer : Custom Color, Lakeville
Paper : Mohawk 50/10, Curtis Gradations

caryn aono

There is a plucky spirit to this book with a genuine sense of enthusiasm for the subject matter. This book reminds me of a cookbook, especially since a thought-as-food metaphor is overtly suggested. Pages are designed and consumed as eye/mind candy.

–ca

entrant's comments

In the second issue of *Errant Bodies*, the design, as well as an editorial introduction, is used to explore: ways of knowing; the means by which knowledge is acquired; and the value systems that different forms of knowledge represent. Chocolate cake recipes are juxtaposed against dense theoretical texts; page numbers are simultaneously food and information; images waver between things you look at, things you eat, and representations.

Errant Bodies

JOURNAL

Designer: Louise Sandhaus
Design Director: Louise Sandhaus
Writers: various
Photographers: various
Client/Publisher: Errant Bodies/Brandon LaBelle
Printer: Nations Printing
Paper: Simpson Springhill Tag, Offset Opaque, French Dur-o-tone Butcher

caryn aono

This is a student-designed publication. These are difficult to pull off, with students collaborating (probably for the first time), showcasing their own artwork, and limited by time constraints and budgets. Pages are designed with intelligence and restraint. This is quite a handsome piece. I particularly like how advertisements are carefully relegated to the thumb margins – so as not to interfere with editorial, yet visible to showcase its supporters. –ca

entrant's comments

Iowa State University's College of Design comprises undergraduate and graduate students with majors in architecture, art and design, biological pre-medical illustration, community and regional planning, craft design, drawing/painting/printmaking, graphic design, interior design, landscape architecture, and visual studies. Desire, inspiration, passion, obsession, compulsion, drive. From an interdisciplinary perspective, internal motivation is ubiquitous. All disciplines use basically the same tools: problem solving, line, color, value, the universal truths of composition – all used so specifically depending upon our discipline. Regardless of media, the innate need to create something of ourselves unites us. Personal drive must be discovered by each individual in order to mature creatively. Classes and professors are merely catalysts in the manifestation of individual ideas and goals. Real development comes when there aren't assignments and deadlines, but when creation itself is its own justification.

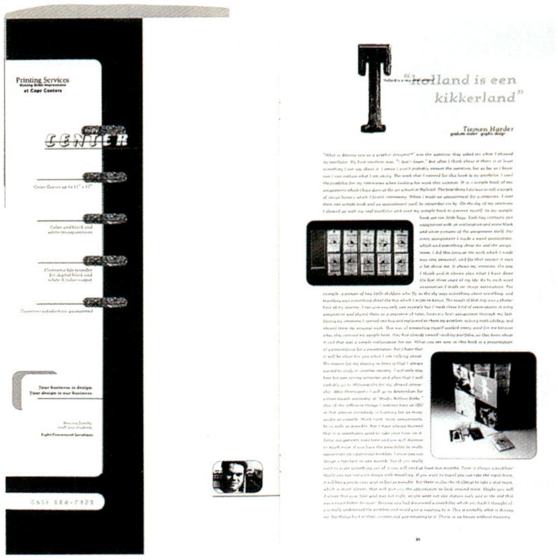

Drive – Iowa State University College of Design

MAGAZINE

Designers: Angie Burr, Jason Endres, Brad Johnson, Kelly Konwinski, Sally Slavens
Writers: Steven Lee Schmiers, Sally Slavens
Photographers: Jason Endres, Pete Kumhardt, René Larson
Design Firm: I.S.U. College of Design Magazine
Typographers: Angie Burr, Jason Endres, Brad Johnson, Kelly Konwinski, Sally Slavens
Printer: I.S.U. Printing Services
Separator: I.S.U. Printing Services
Paper: Cross Pointe Genesis Tortoise, Hammermill Cream White
Faculty Advisor: Lisa Fontaine

caryn aono

Another student-generated publication, although with a very different attitude. Eclectic pages are sequenced together, probably designed by different designers. Typography is enthusiastically approached, some more successfully than others. Overall, it flows quite beautifully.

–ca

entrant's comments

To what extent does the design of literary works affect their content? *Cellar Roots* is a literary magazine in which student work has a chance to be published. Our design revolves around the idea of organizing the book and structuring the pages using the conventions of a classic grid that English department papers are based on. Our idea was to use this structuring system to start to push the boundaries of how art and literary materials are presented, and to begin questioning the extent to which the designer shares the role of author.

Cellar Roots

MAGAZINE

Designers : Andy Slopsema, Kindra Murphy, Kevin Sams, Ann Bourselethe, Lori Young
Design Director : George La Rou
Writers : various
Photographers : various
Design Firm : Eastern Michigan University Visual Communications Area
Client/Publisher : Eastern Michigan University Student Media
Typographers : Andy Slopsema, Kindra Murphy
Printer : Frye
Paper : 85 lb. uncoated floor stock

caryn aono

There is an obvious joy (probably mixed with tears) in the research, exploration, and execution of these books. The designer-generated messages, both verbal and visual, are quite intriguing. Pages are thought-laden, yet accessible. Like most graduate theses, this is personal research, yet it has the very real potential of being a stronger and pertinent voice in the future.

–ca

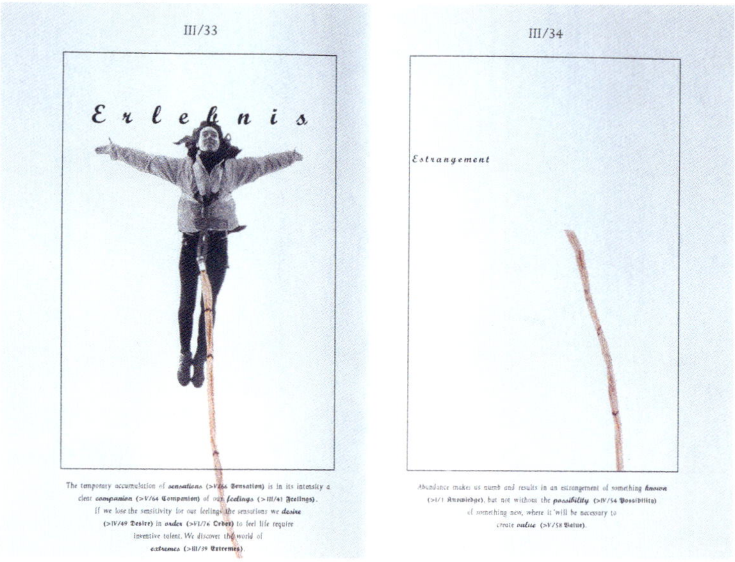

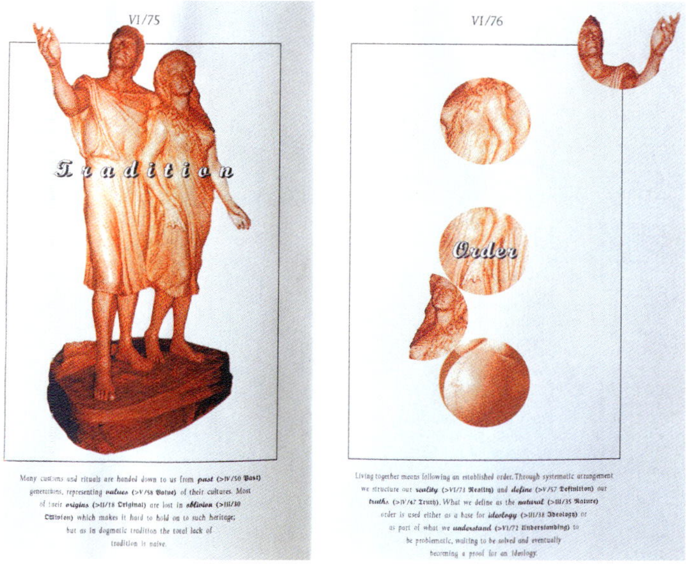

entrant's comments

(Frau Steinbeck's Platitudes, inspired by Luther's 95 Theses) An everyday dictionary of steadily asked and never really answered questions...keep asking. First statement: At the end of the second millennium wo/men looked at a rich past. They saw the mistakes of their ancestors and thought that all problems came from dogmatic claims for Truth. They came up with the idea that there is no Truth, and created the ideology of "I'm OK, you're OK," "Whatever," and "A Place for Everybody's Voice." There was no place for disagreement in their new Truth. The idea left them in an undefined space where no one was wrong or right, nothing was bad or good, nothing ugly or beautiful. Then they began to reform, recreate, and reconstruct lost Truths. The only other world they could have escaped to was the virtual world – a world that seemed to remain foreign because of its untouchability. Second statement: The cover page of my sketchbook says, "How to write a dictionary, or What to do if your sketchbooks never look as pretty as those of other people, or What to do if no one wants to answer your questions, or How to teach yourself a foreign language, or How Cranbrook affects one's mind, or How deals a somewhat young European woman with the experience of two years in America," or,...I did not know it either. I was going through my notebooks and through the stacks of photographs I took since I arrived in this country. I tried to put everything together in order to make sense out of all these fragments that I collected and saved throughout two years.

AMERIKA
mon amour or
The Forbidden Fruit

THESIS PROJECT

Designer : Frau Steinbeck
Writer : Frau Steinbeck
Illustrator : Frau Steinbeck
Photographer : Frau Steinbeck
Design Firm : Cranbrook Academy of Art
Typographer : Frau Steinbeck
Printer : self-published on HP DeskWriter 550C
Paper : Archiva

caryn aono

also selected by
Jan van Toorn, see p.142

This is a friendly computer-interface design proposal. The intended audience for this is highly visual (designers?), and the subject matter – a future TV movie service – is a great forum for experiments in interactive communication. The design is fun and accessible like late-night rerun television or Nickelodeon. Some of this is a bit clunky, but there are moments that are really terrific, such as the weird speech bubbles. This kind of visual experimentation works best as a moving piece (as it was intended). But I like how that working method influenced the two-dimensional design in the digital essay too.

–ca

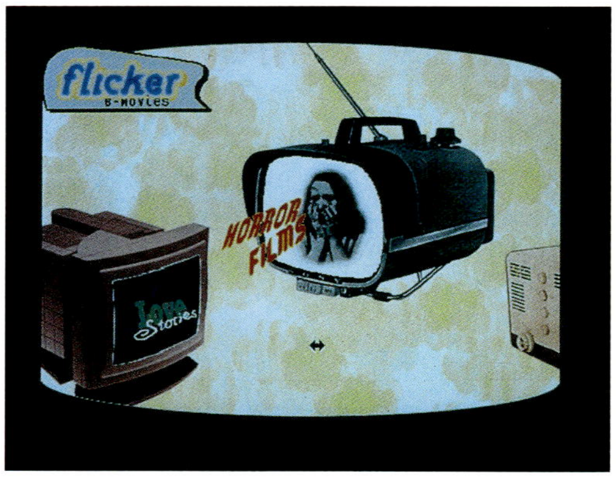

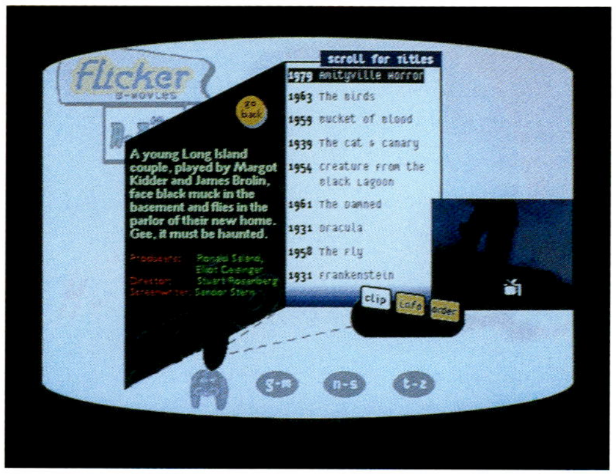

entrant's comments

This is a California Institute of the Arts MFA thesis consisting of two complementary parts. First, I wrote and designed the book *Print is Dead* as a way to organize the research I amassed about interface design. Through it, I raise issues such as, What makes a fluid, intuitive interface design? What constructs exist in multimedia interfaces today that can be built upon or should be dropped? And what new constructs should be developed to make navigation through digital spaces more customizable and expressive? The digital companion "Flicker" implements many of these issues. It is a proposal interface for an on-line B-movie service. Using Flicker, customers would be able to access menus listing available cult-classic movies, view a clip of the movie, receive information about the film on screen or by fax, and then instantly download the film to their televisions to view. The interface I've designed explores different levels of navigability from simple point-and-click buttons to hot type and scrolling lists. Interface design will need to become more expressive and intuitive to reflect the many different voices that interactive television will introduce.

Print is Dead – Or So It Seems

THESIS PROJECT

Designer : Richard Sienkiewicz Shanks

entrant's comments

We had our copy of *Typographic Design: Form and Communication* cut to make a body comp for our own book cover design commission. The leftover material conjured up several ideas relating to graphic design. We now choose to let the viewers discover these ideas for themselves.

caryn aono

The top one-and-a-half inches of *Typographic Design: Form and Communication* is left intact, bound, collated, and "selected." I thought this was an appropriate metaphor for the whole judging process. –ca

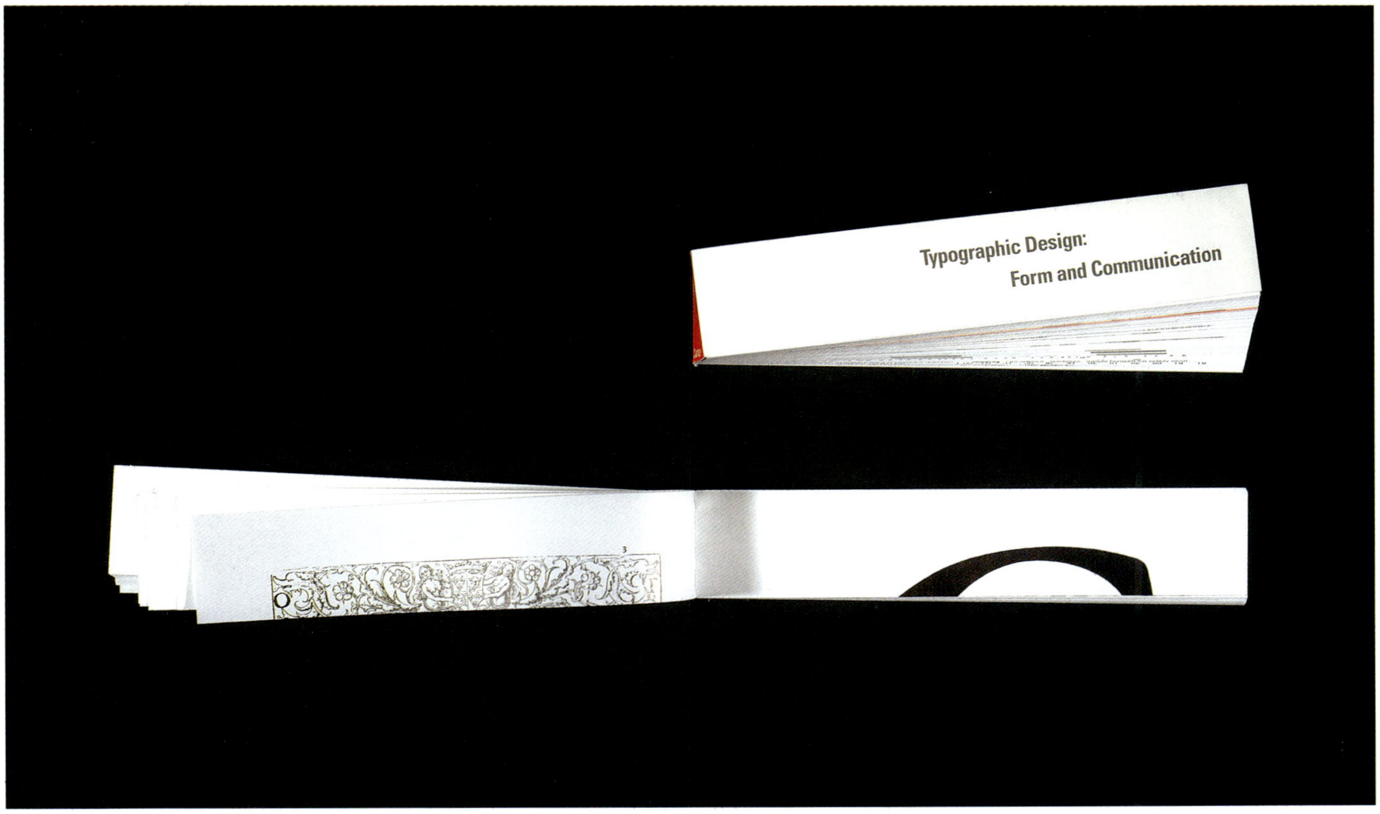

Who Makes the Cut?

BOOKLET

Designers : Jim Ross, Mario A. Mirelez
Design Firm : Mirelez/Ross, Inc.

selections by

marlene mccarty

GAME GENIES
Video Game Champions
Part of a complete video game arsenal!
Graduate exhibition
poster children!
blur
HOT WHEELS
MATTEL
Always
NO LIFE
NO ART
VOTE ROCK
NO MUSIC
NO FUN
Toward College in Ohio
reinsur-
ance is
boring
NEMESISTERS
ON
Attitude
High Five
ANGE LECCIA
SAN FRANCISCO
if I were a Carpenter
Sexual Slang
AMERICAN MUSIC CLU
THE BEST OF SHOUKICHI
now available at all fine record
earing for the first time in the US with RY COODER
CENTRAL PARK SUMMERSTAGE
JULY 17, 1994 · 3 PM
At CalArts, we place strong emphasis on
95-96
Peace on Earth
interstate
pell mell
MAKELA
Vertical Butt Stroke to groin.
VENT
Have You Seen Me?
Seattle Center
THE JIMI HENDRIX MUSEUM ROCK ARENA
at Bumbershoot
SEPT 2-5, 1994
HARLEY-DAVIDSON INC
1994 ANNUAL REPORT

marlene mccarty

Design SURE is something. Walking into the "redone-more-warmly" IBM cafeteria in Chicago to face table after table, row after row, of "things that have been graphically designed" is like walking into a place that might be called "The Design Barn." A wave of over-saturated consumer oblivion swept through me. It was a pretty quick read: the attempt to engage or articulate the actual pieces through any "deep thoughts" would be virtually impossible. The potential essence of any individual piece was smothered by the sheer numbers. To simply move somewhat thoughtfully through all the submissions became a bit of an endurance test. Sadly, a traditional discussion of form became the way out.

In retrospect, I harbor a bit of frustration. I spend a great quantity of my time trying to figure out how to make graphic design more than a styling profession. Yet, there I was, faced with piles of design, and the only way to move efficiently through the work was by recognizing stylistic or form-oriented relationships. I guess the inverse is that most of the work was primarily form-based. Content-driven work (especially visually interesting content-driven work) was a clear minority. The difficulty of choosing 100 pieces was evident.

Good, better, and best judgments seemed to be ridiculous in such a situation. However, curating – rather than reaching a consensus – promised to be a constructive manner of survey. It would let the work reveal the momentary tendencies of the designers who chose – and could afford – to enter this competition. In this way, I've allowed for a dialog among the pieces.

One piece in particular provided the keystone for this strategy. The Babes in Toyland Nemesisters poster by Tom Recchion for Reprise Records (p.66) was probably the most raucous piece in the whole show. Jarred by its rowdy implications, the air cleared. Inclinations shared by numerous pieces of work then were revealed.

The most vital body of work in the show seemed to be the "Throbbing Type" category (category 1, pp.66–73). There is a trend of work driven by expressive but relatively flat typography – perhaps a reaction to the layers of pictorially based Photoshop work that has recently prevailed. Typography ("I'm not dead yet") is doing its own thing, whether it's down-and-dirty for the Woman Made Gallery cards (p.71), or ultimately trendy like a *blur* magazine cover (p.69), or classically restrained for the cover of *Who Will Run the Frog Hospital?* (p.30 and p.72).

A more traditional subcategory of type-driven work is that which relies on "The Organization of Type as Guide to the Inner Sanctum" (category 2, pp.74–79). This work ranges from the meat-and-potatoes type usage found in the Internet Guides (p.74) and the UNIFEM 1993 annual report (p.78) to the sublime of the Asyst Technologies lab book (p.75).

In another category of work, we see less expressive typography juxtaposed with symbolically loaded images. I call this the "It Has Something To Do with Semiotics" category (category 3, pp.80–83). This is a smarty-pants category. Chip Kidd's *Sexual Slang* book cover (p.80) is a charming example. Within this category, the pieces could be arranged in a rather even progression from the ones in which the *interplay of type and image* is the concept to the ones in which the *lack of type (or image only)* is the concept. Check out Sunja Park's If I Were a Carpenter 7-inch record set (p.82) and Irma Boom's *Arrangement* book (p.83).

Following through with the implications of "concept," a grouping of pieces based on "Even Bigger Concept" (category 4, pp.84–87) coalesces. This work moves beyond the one-liners of category 3 into a realm in which the concept is the prime motivator. These pieces were among the most intriguing and challenging in the competition. Each piece is constructed with layers of meaning and multiple references. This is the category upon which theory projects could be based. Don't miss Modern Dog's K2 Snowboard catalog (p.24 and p.85) or Lee Allen Kreindel's Attitude – Pine Manor College viewbook (p. 26, p.87, and p.125). At first glance, you think Attitude is *Sassy* magazine. But it's a school catalog. It crosses into an entirely different interest group.

"If It Ain't Broke, Don't Fix It: The School Industry" (category 4a, pp.87–94) is the next category. For a number of years, we have seen the education industry paving the way for new design, especially in the realm of computer-based design. California Institute of the Arts and Cranbrook Academy of Art, in particular, have been very progressive. These schools were among the first institutions to provide access to computers, and to encourage the then-considered progressive design development into the electronic realm. Definitely to be applauded. Much of this work was truly groundbreaking. However, the rest of the world has caught up. Schools seem very attached to layered computer styling. They seem reluctant to move on. I must make the assumption that this is working for them. If it ain't broke don't fix it. Perhaps this style is successful for academic institutions because it is similar to the style of "Music Industry" products (category 4b, pp.95–105) and kids like it.

Though similar in tenor to the school work, the music industry sports a much broader and looser spectrum of aesthetics. Over the years, the music industry has provided an important "safe house" for graphic design(ers). It has traditionally condoned a more licentious attitude toward irony (meaning) and materials (form). Graphic designers – often drained within an inch of their lives by the constraints of their clients – have found vital breathing room in the music industry. It was June of 1995 when the judging took place, and Rose Marshak's Poster Children "Junior Citizen" interactive press kit (p.105) for Sire/Reprise was the only good interactive piece in the competition. Graphic design is no longer just print on paper. Graphic design is morphing into many shapes and guises, but little or none of this was evident. The lack of significant new media did cause me to wonder: are we living in the past?

Answer: not all of us are. Three very different projects "Touch the Future" . . . (category 5, pp.106–109). In advertising, we see the strategies of Nike (p.106). Instead of doing market research to appeal to the masses, Nike is deliberately focusing their ads on smaller markets and varying them from market region to market region. This can develop into an amazing consumer strategy – market diversity as opposed to market homogeneity.

More forward movement is sensed in Rick Valicenti's ads for Gilbert paper (p.107 and p.108). His development is more form-oriented and less strategically based. Bye bye, computer-layered look. Hello, amazingness.

And then there's *Wired*. *Wired* is waiting for us. Some will go willingly, some with mild trepidation, others kicking and screaming. But we're all gonna be there.

Keep the lights on, but don't wait up.

marlene mccarty

entrant's comments

We wanted the stuff to look like an old circus poster for a freak side-show. Through a series of meetings with the band members, Dan Kalal pinned down each of their secret desires. What kind of freak of nature did they want to be? Sketches were delivered and we talked. He can draw and paint very well. The final painting is truly magnificent.

THROBBING TYPE

If I had a grand prize to give in this jury, I would give it to this poster. The thing that I have been most discouraged about in this competition has been the lack of "looking forward," the lack of breaking prescribed methods of design, the adherence to academics and computer design. This poster blows all of that out of the water in such an enormous way that it is awe-inspiring. The imagery is just so bad, it's good. –mm

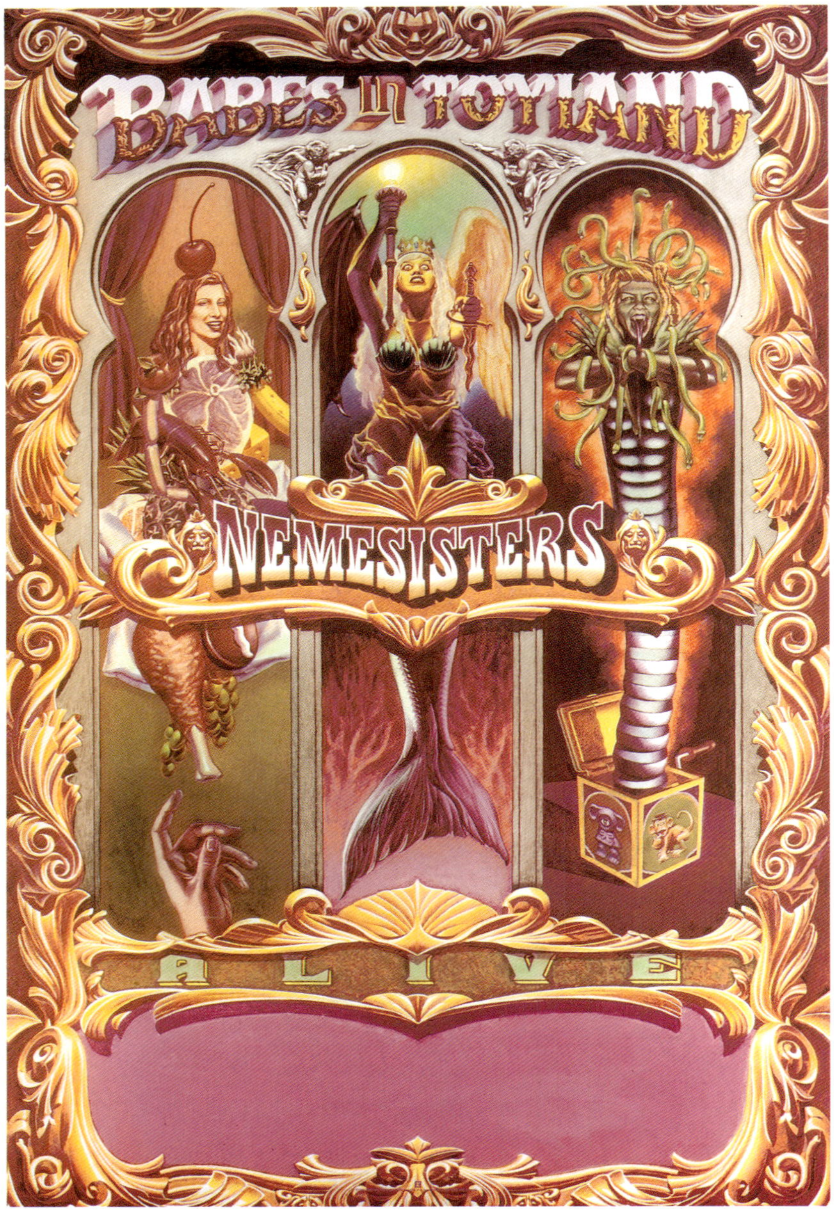

Babes In Toyland Nemesisters

POSTER

Designer : Tom Recchion
Art Director : Tom Recchion
Illustrator : Dan Kalal
Photographer : Bill Phelps
Client/Publisher : Reprise Records

entrant's comments

A wonderful painting done by Jean Lowe through discussions with the various band members. This was used as a front cover. It made sense to use this art for the poster. When the artwork was stretched to fit the format, the center needed something to counteract the elongation of the image. It needed another element. Dennis Keeley had taken some beautiful photographs of the band. I created a vignette oval around the group and stripped it in Photoshop. This seemed to solve the problem that I was facing. To enhance the nostalgic, mysterious, and delicate nature of the finished piece, I chose an uncoated stock.

THROBBING TYPE

This poster and Babes in Toyland go together. The Babes in Toyland poster is stronger, but the American Music Club poster is also groundbreaking. When I first uncurled it, I thought, "Oh my God, it's one of those weird movie posters." You know how they always have those heads of people airbrushed into landscapes. But, as I unrolled it, it became completely obvious to me that it was not a movie poster and that it had to be in my selection. Both of these posters are amazing. They are both so strong that their use of recognized styles steps beyond the limits of affectation and becomes something else. –mm

American Music Club San Francisco

POSTER

Designer : Tom Recchion
Art Director : Tom Recchion
Photographer : Dennis Keeley
Illustrator : Jean Lowe
Client/Publisher : Reprise Records

marlene mccarty

THROBBING TYPE

To be quite frank, I chose this campaign because of the snowboards. (I have a hard time resisting anything with flames on it.) It was all or nothing. The snowboards embodied such a moment – such a sort of Zeitgeist – that I wanted to have them in. So I had to take the rest of the campaign, which I'm not so crazy about, with the snowboards. I do love the poster with the pictures of all the snowboards. –mm

entrant's comments

In a category in which it's very difficult to possess a point of difference, our task to create memorable and intrusive boards was a challenge. Most of the board designs have a concept, and, while some are more tangible than others, the combination of design and ideas gives birth to a new style. Some concept examples are: the "Crown" gives the feeling of being in control, you're king, conquering that downhill slide; "Spike," with its saw blades, cuts through anything, nothing can stop it; "Hot Rod" (flame) – this one really moves; "Heart" signifies the internal need to express yourself, with the barbed wire as the element of danger; "No Wonder" (a spoof on Wonder Bread, no white bread around here); "DeChute" borrows from the classic '60s surfboards; "Spike Face" equals attitude.

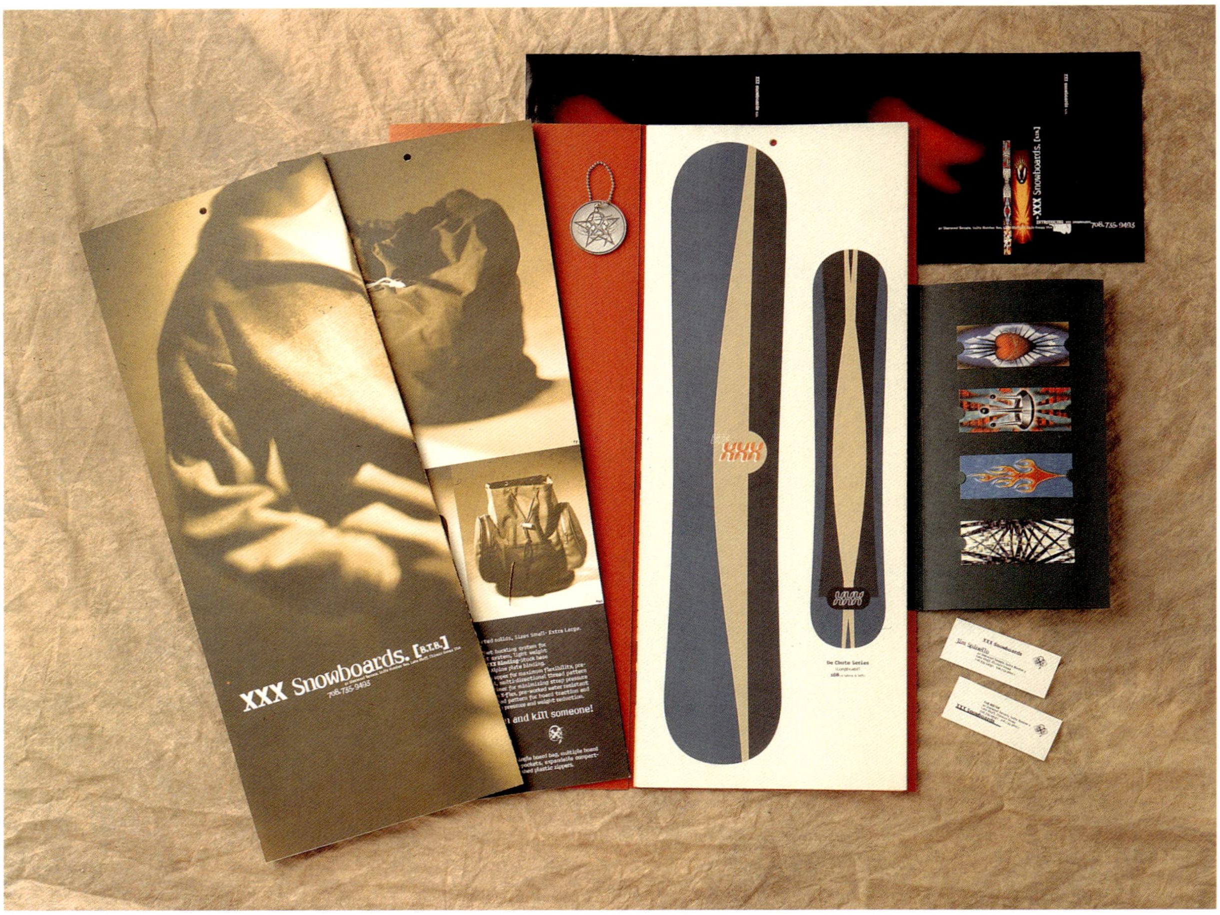

XXX Snowboards

SNOWBOARDS AND CATALOG

Design Firm : Segura Inc.
Creative Director : Carlos Segura
Art Director : Carlos Segura
Designer : Carlos Segura
Additional Designers : Jennifer Weiss, Marilyn Devedjiev
Photographer : Jeff Sciortino (brochure only)
Illustrators : Tony Klassen, Carlos Segura
Fonts : Amplifier
Printer : Bradley
Client/Publisher : XXX Snowboards B.T.B.
Medium : snowboards

marlene mccarty

THROBBING TYPE

See the Lewis Galoob Toy, Inc. 1995 Toy Fair Catalogs (p.86). Parody just keeps looping back in upon itself to such an extent I don't even know what to say, except that, as I've already said (see XXX Snowboards on previous page), I have trouble resisting anything with flames. –mm

entrant's comments

blur has been described as an overlap of art, music, and comics. It's a current of energy that comes from these areas and is guided in form by design. The Hot Wheels cover came from our appreciation of this subdivision of aesthetic. There has always been an energy from the design of the Hot Wheels packaging. It's exciting to look at because it's about the speed and movement. These are great elements of design, and this is what we like to capture in *blur*. It's about taking the extra steps to see something new.

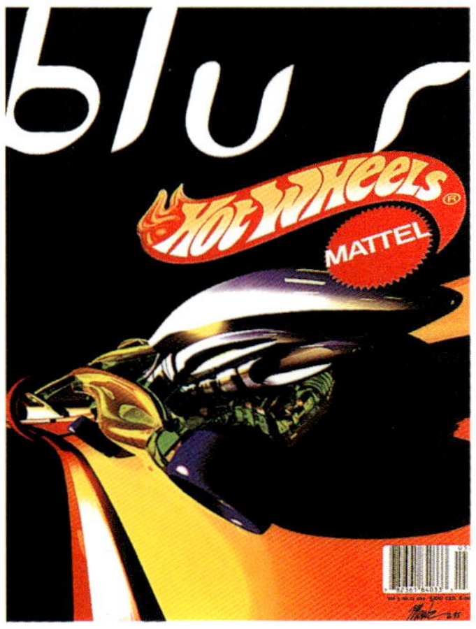

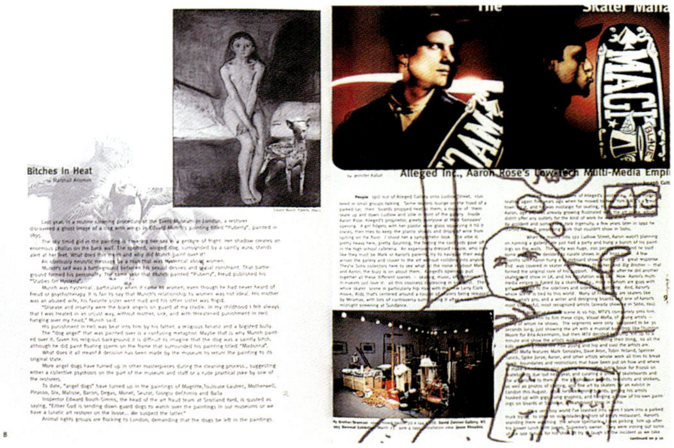

blur Cov 11

MAGAZINE COVER AND SPREADS

Designer : Scott Clum
Design Director : Scott Clum
Illustrator : Mark Jones
Design Firm : Ride Dsgn
Client/Publisher : *blur* Magazine
Typographers : Cyberotica typeface by Barry Deck

THROBBING TYPE

Through the cyber-breakdown of typographical boundaries, there has been a rebirth of typography as expression. This spawning has included a burst of typographic flowering that is not computer-based. Whether it's a reaction to the computer or not, I don't know. This poster is a perfect example of such. –mm

entrant's comments

The psychedelic posters of the '60s really inspired me. I thought of this poster as the expression of an illustrator who is totally into the music and the bands and really living that whole trip. So I spent a lot of time spacing out on the artwork with a pen, thinking about the music and the bands, and looking forward to the shows.

Jimi Hendrix Museum Rock Arena at Bumbershoot

POSTER

Designer : Michael Strassburger
Design Director : Susan Pierson
Illustrator : Michael Strassburger
Design Firm : Modern Dog
Client/Publisher : Experience Music Project
Typographer : Michael Strassburger
Printer : George Rice & Sons
Separator : Modern Dog
Paper : Simpson Evergreen

marlene mccarty

THROBBING TYPE

Speaking of expressionist typography, these three invitations are wonderful little jewels. Printed in one color on really cheap stock, they are bursting with energy. They say so much with so little (no gigabytes needed here!)

–mm

entrant's comments

Woman Made Gallery is a small gallery in a Chicago neighborhood. Since there are many galleries in the city, it is important that its cards stand out from a heap of mail when they are delivered, or catch one's eye if they are posted on a billboard. Due to its small budget and time limitations, I set up guidelines for myself. The cards are always one color (canned colors, only a PMS color when I beg the printer); they are consistent in size for the purpose of recognition; and I work off of the computer with found type/press type along with computer-generated material. There are 11 shows a year, which are unlike one another, and I try to reflect that in my design of the cards. It seemed appropriate that the "Gayly Forward" cards (for a show of work by lesbian artists) be printed on some of the colors from the rainbow — a symbol of freedom and diversity in the gay community.

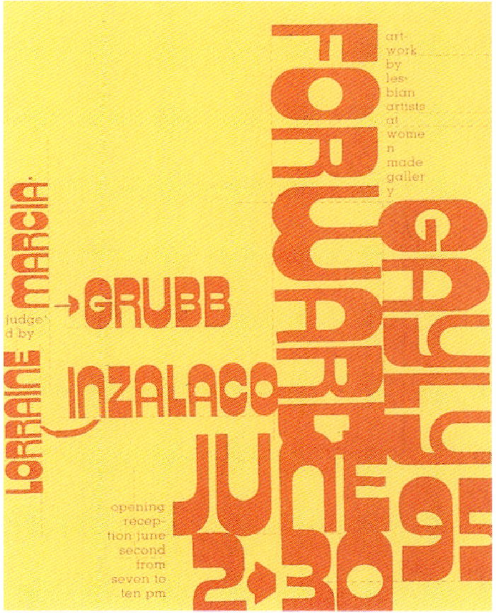

Woman Made Gallery

CARDS

Designer : Kali Nikitas
Design Firm : graphic design for love (+ $)
Client/Publisher : Woman Made Gallery
Printer : Alpha Graphics, Skokie

also selected by Caryn Aono, see p.30

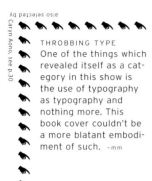

THROBBING TYPE
One of the things which revealed itself as a category in this show is the use of typography as typography and nothing more. This book cover couldn't be a more blatant embodiment of such. –mm

entrant's comments
With such an evocative title, any embellishment of the jacket seemed to border on the perverse. This novel is a first-person reminiscence of a woman named Berie, who is gifted with the author's deadpan wit and brilliantly ironic observations. As *The New York Times* noted, "Berie realizes, as she recounts the story of her youth, that she is romanticizing events, allowing memory to colorize all the blacks and whites and grays." I agree. Such coloring is often best left to the memory and the imagination.

Who Will
Run the Frog
Hospital?
a novel by
Lorrie Moore

Who Will Run the Frog Hospital?

BOOK COVER

Designer: Barbara deWilde
Design Director: Carol Carson
Design Firm: Barbara deWilde
Client/Publisher: Alfred A. Knopf
Typographer: Barbara deWilde
Printer: Coral Graphics
Paper: white coated stock

marlene mccarty

THROBBING TYPE

I almost see a complete category within the 100 Show of typography – typography as a means of expression. Of course, we all know this has been brought on by the computer. The one thing I loved about this Xerox logo is that it is graphic design in the most traditional and classic sense. It infers movement into the computer age, but it's articulated in the exquisite manner of old-fashioned design. It's so smart. –mm

entrant's comments

The Xerox Corporation had been synonymous with leading-edge technology since the release of its first photocopier in 1959. By 1992, Xerox had worldwide revenues of $14.6 billion and more than 99,000 employees. Although Xerox had grown to offer many scanning, printing, imaging and faxing products, and consulting services, the company was still primarily known for its copiers. In an effort to move beyond this image, Xerox developed the tagline "The Document Company" to reflect its expanded role in the creation, use, and transmission of business documents and databases. The existing Xerox identity system reflected the company's early copier positioning. The identity was rigid and corporate, and the black bar underscoring the Xerox name did not allow for maximum impact in packaging or advertising. Landor's challenge was to communicate a new, re-energized Xerox, while broadening "The Document Company" positioning. The new identity system needed to incorporate youthful appeal, creativity, and flexibility while reflecting Xerox's wide range of high-performance products. After extensive research, Landor recommended emphasizing "The Document Company" phrase by permanently placing it above the Xerox signature. The new name, "The Document Company Xerox," now clearly communicates the company's ability to handle all document-related products and services. Landor also created a bold, partially digitized red "X" to increase Xerox's visibility on all advertising, packaging, and print promotion materials.

Xerox Digital "X"

PROMOTIONAL SYMBOL

Designer : Margo Zucker
Design Director : Margaret Youngblood
Design Firm : Landor Associates
Creative Director : Courtney Reeser
Client/Publisher : The Document Company Xerox

entrant's comments

The design is about connections.

marlene mccarty

THE ORGANIZATION OF TYPE AS GUIDE TO THE INNER SANCTUM

These are very simple, straightforward guides through the not-so-simple, entangled, and opaque world of the Internet. Anything that can do that deserves a little design recognition. –mm

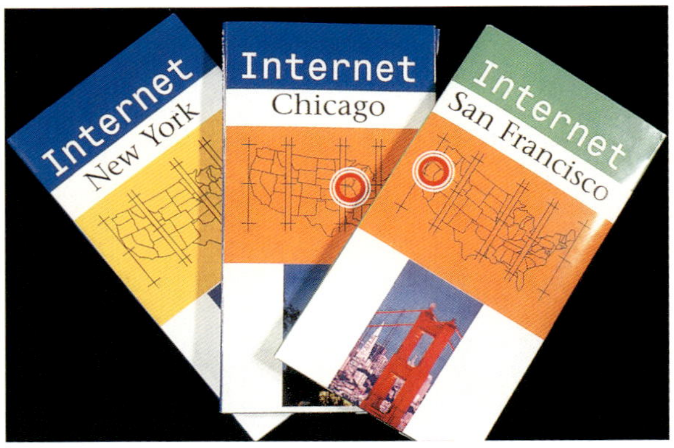

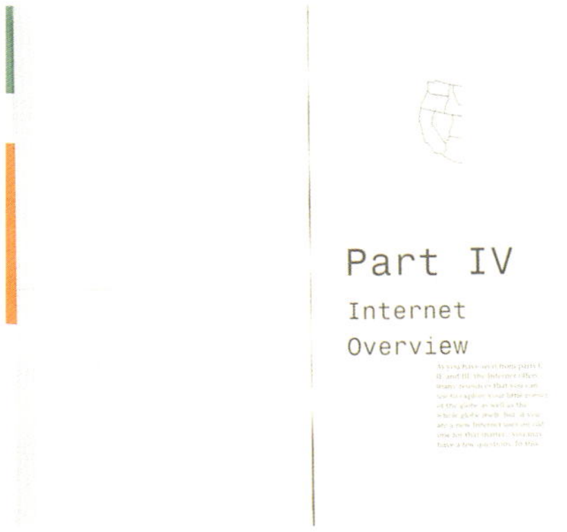

Internet Guides

BOOKLETS

Designer : Fred Bower
Writers : Brad Miser, Adam Engst
Client/Publisher : Hayden Books

marlene mccarty

entrant's comments

The Asyst Lab Book, which is generously filled with quotes by notables in the fields of science and technology, tables of symbols and values, a periodic chart of elements, diagrams of energy consumption and temperature variation, and calculations of cleanroom efficiency, was fashioned as a giveaway for the attendees of the Fall 1994 Semicon Show. It was intended for use as a notebook to collect and capture thoughts, inventions, and other important data that course through the daily lives of the scientists and engineers who are the users of Asyst's technology.

THE ORGAN ZATION OF TYPE AS GUIDE TO THE INNER SANCTUM

The design of this book is sublime, it's truly that kind of sensitive, dainty design that I can only lust af:er. My only desire left unfulfilled by this object is that it is not a rea life lab book. The fact that it is a "look-alike" leaves me a little sad. I wish real technicians could have such a beautiful thing in their life. I naively picked this piece thinking that it was in fact a lab book. –mm

Asyst

LAB BOOK

Designers : Steven Tolleson, Jean Orlebeke
Design Director : Steven Tolleson
Design Firm : Tolleson Design
Client/Publisher : Asyst Technologies
Typographer : Tolleson Design
Printer : Digital Engraving
Paper : Tissue Canary, Mead Offset

entrant's comments

Monday, February 14, 1994, was the fifth anniversary of the Iranian decree calling for the death of British writer Salman Rushdie. On this day, 4,000 participating bookstores inserted the Rushdie flyer into all books sold. In total, 450,000 flyers were distributed throughout the United States. In this way, the organizers and supporters of the statement asked all those who care about books, writers, and freedom of expression to renew their determination to free Rushdie from the trap of the *fatwa*.

marlene mccarty

also selected by Jan van Toorn, see p.131

THE ORGANIZATION OF TYPE AS GUIDE TO THE INNER SANCTUM

This piece is clever. It's probably very successful if it's distributed correctly. The piece is so correct, all the rough edges are gone. I think that has to do with the fact that this is following in the footsteps of a lot of activist work that has been done in the past few years. And, of course, when you're following in those footsteps, you have the chance to polish off all the rough edges. –mm

Rushdie

FLYER

Designer : Stephen Doyle
Creative Directors : Stephen Doyle, William Drenttel
Writer : Don De Lillo
Design Firm : Drenttel Doyle Partners
Printer : Red Ink Productions
Project Initiators : Nan Graham, Paul Auster, Oren Teicher, William Drenttel

also selected by Jan van Toorn, see p.138

THE ORGANIZATION OF TYPE AS GUIDE TO THE INNER SANCTUM

This is another one of those wonderful pieces that you could write an essay about. It sort of takes us back to the 1980s and the whole art theory discussions of what's real and what's not real – what is a rearticulation of itself. It's nice to see design that is more than making things look pretty. –mm

entrant's comments

The Information is a book about books, a writer writing about writers, a product of publishing about publishing. Under the circumstances of such relentless self-referral, it was tempting to proceed with a jacket about jackets, especially since one of the main characters has written a wildly successful utopian novel (though what one should look like is beyond even my imagining). Too trite. Instead, I thought it would be better to make it look like the jacket is missing, thus forcing the viewer to plunge into the text before he or she even picks it up.

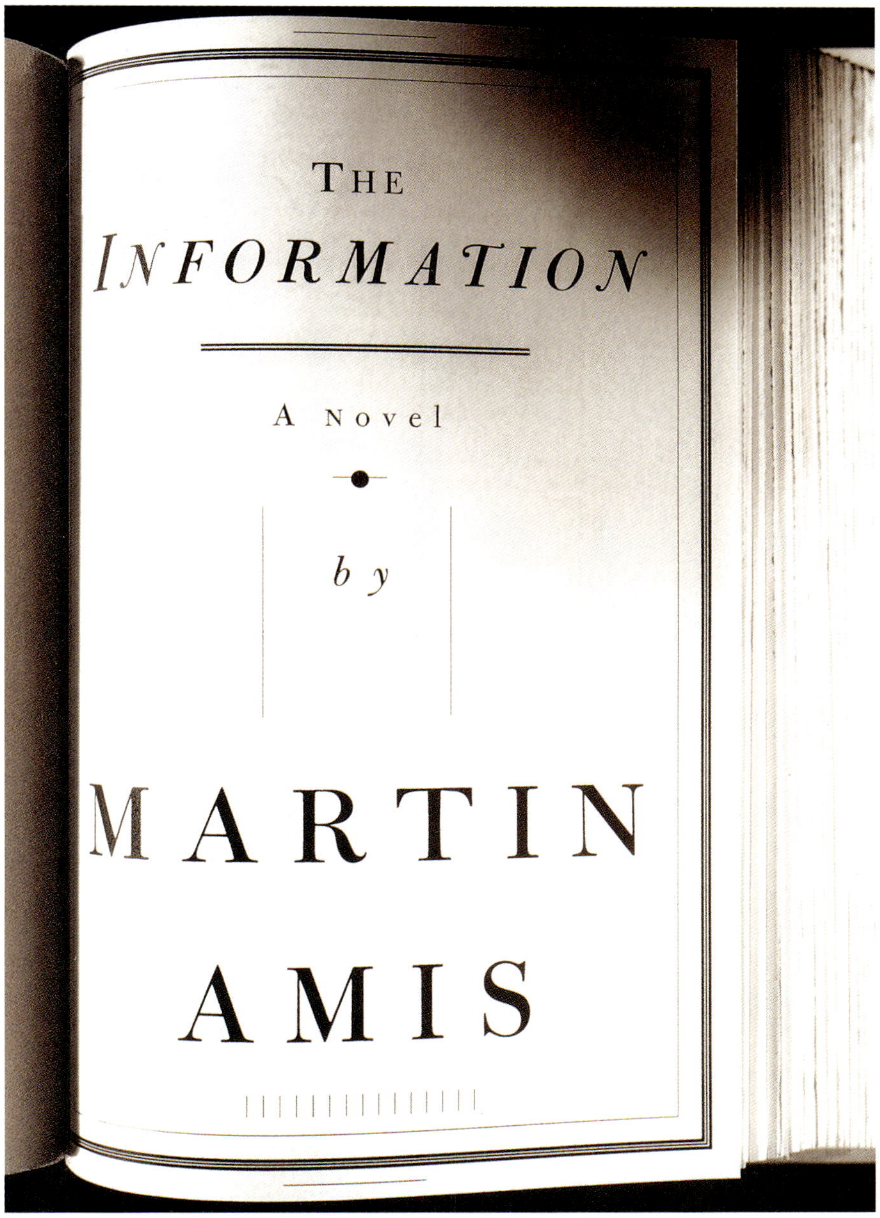

The Information

BOOK COVER

Designer : Chip Kidd
Design Director : Rick Pracher
Writer : Martin Amis
Photographer : Chip Kidd
Design Firm : Chip Kidddesign
Client/Publisher : Harmony Books
Typographer : Chip Kidd
Printer : Coral Graphics

marlene mccarty

also selected by
Jan van Toorn, see p.128

THE ORGANIZATION OF TYPE AS GUIDE TO THE INNER SANCTUM

This is probably one of the most straightforward pieces in the whole show as far as design is concerned anyway. It's sort of a paradigm piece. It's very straightforward. It deals with social issues in a matter-of-fact way. It has beautiful photography through which a great respect for the subjects is reflected. It gives the whole program of UNIFEM validity. Most socially engaged, politically oriented, nonprofit organizations need serious visual validation to propel themselves out of marginal obscurity.

–mm

entrant's comments

The United Nations Development Fund for Women (UNIFEM) annual report highlights the Fund's commitment to provide financial and technical support to women from developing countries. Emerson, Wajdowicz Studios has designed the UNIFEM annual reports for four consecutive years. The book is pure emotional communication. It is unique, different, and very powerful. We developed a restrained, deceptively simple, almost minimalist design approach incorporating original photos by Sebastião Salgado.

UNIFEM 1993
ANNUAL REPORT

Designers : Lisa LaRochelle, Jurek Wajdowicz
Design Director : Jurek Wajdowicz
Photographer : Sebastião Salgado
Design Firm : Emerson, Wajdowicz Studios, Inc.
Client/Publisher : United Nations Development Fund for Women
Typographer : Emerson, Wajdowicz Studios, Inc.

marlene mccarty

THE ORGANIZATION OF TYPE AS GUIDE TO THE INNER SANCTUM
Instead of the typical school strategy of using graphics that look or feel like entertainment graphics, graphics have been used that look and feel like art-world graphics. It is an interesting masquerade of art school catalog as art catalog. –mm

entrant's comments

From Laurence Dreiband's introduction to Artwork, "The aim of this book is to offer current and prospective fine art students a range of realistic options and practical advice and to show that a life in art can be a source of financial support as well as creative gratification. Many students and parents assume that fine art offers only struggle and deprivation and no security of future employment." My approach to this design focused on communicating solidity and trust. The model employed as an aesthetic frame for the book was the visual language of a governmental institution. Size, cover material, and rounded corners specifically reference the passport. Information about art presented through this aesthetic reveals, at a very subtle level, inherent tensions between an individual and an institution: surrender/control, freedom/confinement, flesh/metal, art/work.

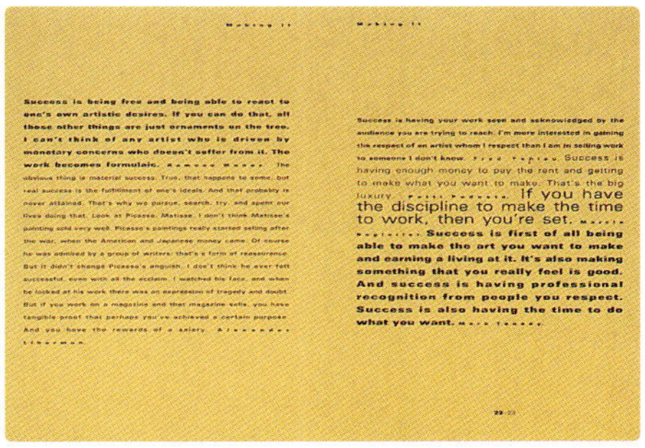

Artwork

BOOK

Designer : Rebeca Mendez
Design Director : Rebeca Mendez
Text and Interviews : Laurence Drieband, Wendy Adset
Copy Editing : Karen Jacobson
Photographers : Cathy Ascar, Arthur Elgort, Megan Feeney, Doris Jew, Steven A. Heller, Pierre Picot, Merlin Rosenberg
Production Manager : Ellie Eisner
Design Firm : Art Center Design Office
Client/Publisher : Art Center College of Design
Typographer : Rebeca Mendez, Macintosh
Printer : Typecraft, Inc.
Paper : Matrix Matte, Lexatone Karnak

marlene mccarty

also selected by Jan van Toorn, see p.123

IT HAS SOMETHING TO DO WITH SEMIOTICS

Well of course I was going to pick this piece. It has a beaver and hoot owls on it. In other words, a beaver, hooters, and a cock. It's a really funny piece.

–mm

entrant's comments

Here are just a few entries from this indispensable little treasury: Bald-headed hermit, Bazoongas, Beat-the-bishop, Best leg of three, Clapper-clangers, Dance-the-mattress-jig, Doctor Johnson, Eat-at-the-Y, Exercise-the-ferret, Firkytoodle, Flesh-cushions, Flip-Flaps, Flog-the-log, Flopper-stoppers, Gamahoochie, Glory hole, Go-trom-boning, Gorilla salad, Lapland, Mazola party, Nookie-bookie and Hairburger. Form follows content. Hubba-hubba!

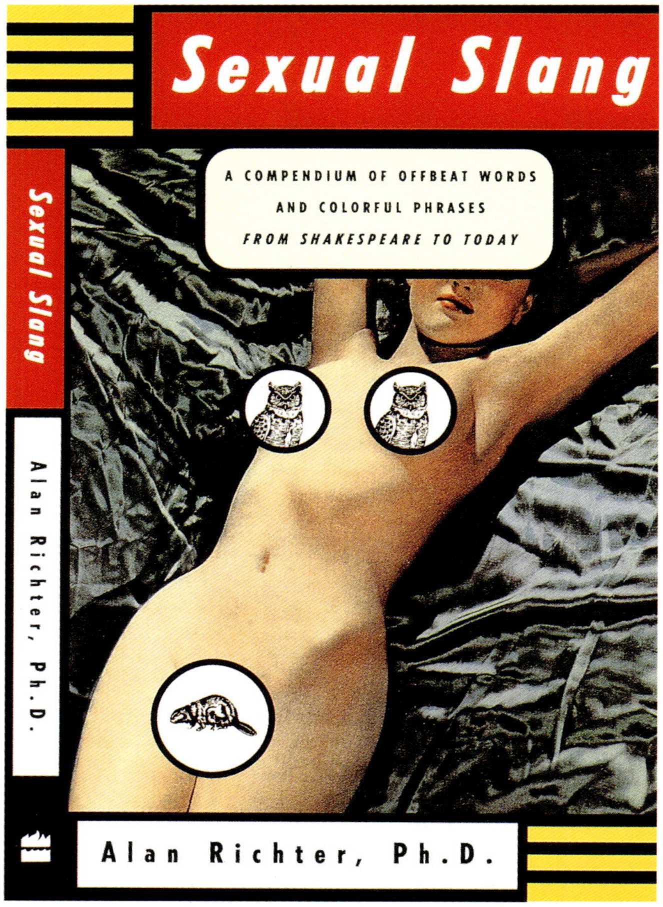

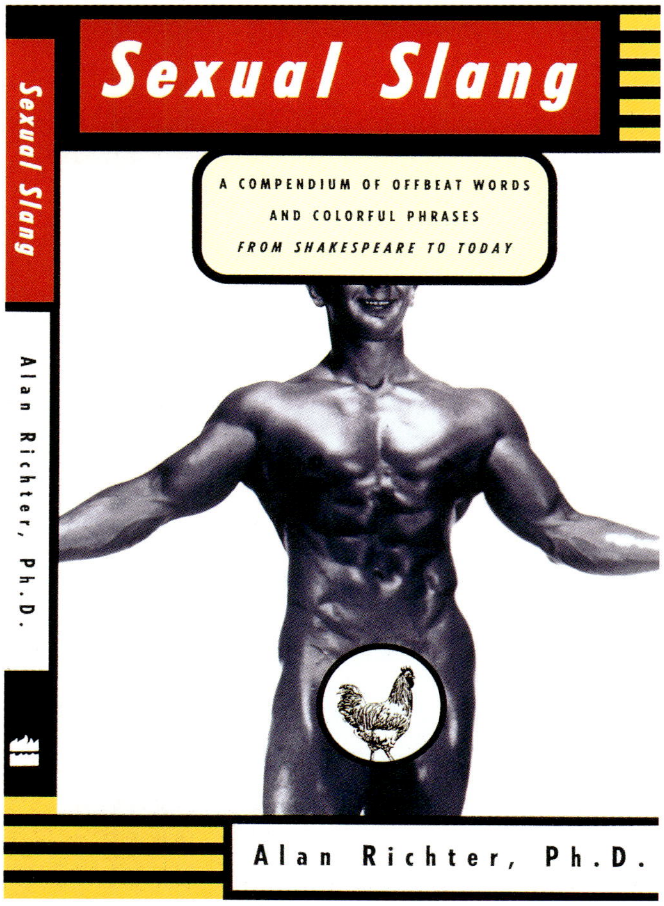

Sexual Slang

BOOK COVER

Designer : Chip Kidd
Design Firm : Chip Kidddesign
Client/Publisher : HarperCollins
Printer : Coral Graphics

marlene mccarty

also selected by Jan van Toorn, see p.124

IT HAS SOMETHING TO DO WITH SEMIOTICS

Not boring it is. The thing that attracted me to this piece was that the imagery is not being used as a texture – the imagery is not being used as a mere rearticulation of reality. In fact, the imagery is itself a concept, and there is very careful consideration given to the text, which is involved with the imagery. It's a model solution for an annual report. –mm

entrant's comments

Reinsurance is about as interesting to most people as incontinence products and frozen peas. It's not terribly different for investors and analysts, who see it as a highly cyclical business, and, worse yet, as a commodity product. The Zurich Reinsurance Centre (ZRC) annual report is designed as a sledgehammer to break down this wall of preconceptions and position our client as an innovative, dynamic growth company in a milquetoast industry.

ZRC Not Boring

ANNUAL REPORT

Designer : James Pettus
Design Directors : James Pettus, David Dunkleberger, Frank Oswald
Writer : Frank Oswald
Photographers : F. Scott Schafer, Christopher Hawker
Design Firm : WYD Design, Inc.
Client/Publisher : Zurich Reinsurance Centre
Typographer : James Pettus
Printer : Allied Printing Services, Inc.
Separator : Allied Printing Services, Inc.
Paper : Simpson Kashmir

marlene mccarty

IT HAS SOMETHING TO DO WITH SEMIOTICS

I love this CD. To be really honest, I have a love/hate feeling for the cover. I mean look at this weird illustration. On the one hand, it makes my skin crawl. On the other hand, it totally sucks me in. It is effective. The contrast with what's going on inside is important. You open this weird, repellent illustration and you have these wonderful, full, close crops of Karen Carpenter and her brother. Very conceptual. Very, very. Just crops. The box houses a collection of singles. The cover for each single has a picture of Karen on the front and her brother on the back, or vice versa, depending on which one you prefer and which way you take it out of the box. The idea of this passage of time, this memorial to the past – to this dead person – is a case where there is absolutely no typography and the pictures are left to carry the message. We, the viewers, who are used to being spoken to, have to delve into these images and try to figure them out. -mm

entrant's comments

I think this was the culmination of way too many teenage hours spent sifting through thrift-shop bins full of sad-eyed Keene paintings; paint by numbers; hook rug kits; Frampton "Comes Alive" albums (record missing); oil portraits of family pets; bean, pea, and macaroni clowns; Herb Alpert eight-tracks; etc., etc. Four years of art school can't push out a childhood of "bad" art influence.

If I Were A Carpenter

7-INCH RECORD SET

Designer: Sunja Park
Design Director: Sunja Park
Illustrator: Andrew Brandou
Design Firm: A&M Records Art Department
Client/Publisher: A&M Records
Typographer: Sunja Park
Printer: A.G.I.
Separator: Color Service

entrant's comments

Ange Leccia uses the term "arrangements" for all his projections and installations. He creates new "arrangements" from existing materials and images, from which they derive a second meaning. "I want to demonstrate that you can make poetry from simple objects," he says. "It should be seen as an invitation and challenge to look at everyday things in another light." By bringing the objects in contact together in a harmonious setting, they are neutralized. They lose their dangerous side. Hulks that generally produce a lot of noise and power appear hypnotized.

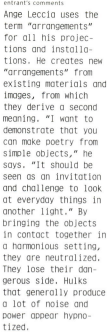

marlene mccarty

IT HAS SOMETHING TO DO WITH SEMIOTICS

This book speaks for itself. This is an entire book of imagery based on Ange Leccia's work, which, in a nutshell, is about constructions of sight and thought through objects and the techno-qualities of those objects (a lot of cars). This book is a very clever interpretation of that. The full-bleed images fold in and out of each other in a simple but deceiving way – in a way that American bookbinders would not even attempt. ("Lady, go home.") Unwrap the dust cover and you will find the entire text for the book. The artwork speaks for itself. It's an amazing feat for a designer to push the edges of design and still not interfere with the artwork being framed. –mm

Arrangement

BOOK

Designer: Irma Boom
Photographer: Ange Leccia
Design Firm: Irma Boom
Client/Publisher: Stroom hcbk
Printer: Rosbeek
Separator: Rosbeek
Paper: Beda Litho

entrant's comments

At Harley-Davidson, the focus has been and will continue to be on long-term growth. It's a journey of evolution, progress, and continuous improvement that began over 90 years ago. The 1994 annual report features dramatic, full-color portraits of real customers, dealers, and employees from all over the world. The information was organized into short stories that keep the reader engaged throughout the book. With the use of organic form, a classic color scheme, and bold typography, the book uniquely represents Harley-Davidson, Inc.

EVEN BIGGER CONCEPT

This piece just blows my mind. The whole concept of this piece is worthy of a "theory" essay. As an annual report goes, it's straight. It's good design. Hot imagery. There are handsome black-and-white financials on pale yellow pages. It's an embodiment of extremities. On the one hand, an annual report goes to stockholders – to people who have invested money into the project. It has to show responsibility. At the same time, Harley-Davidson is a multimillion dollar company whose image is based on the bad boy. Fuck the establishment. Fuck every day life. Hit the road. I'm interested to see that image – that concept – packaged as a stable money-making power. –mm

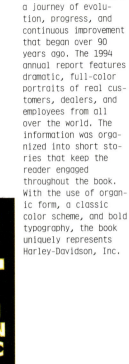

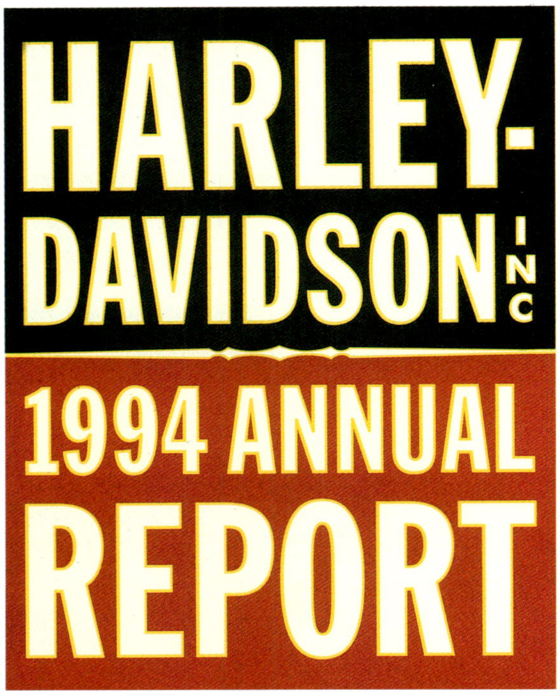

Harley-Davidson, Inc. 1994

ANNUAL REPORT

Designer : Curt Schreiber
Design Director : Dana Arnett
Writer : Ken Schmidt
Photographer : James Schnepf
Design Firm : VSA Partners, Inc.
Client/Publisher : Harley-Davidson, Inc.
Typographer : VSA Partners, Inc.
Printer : George Rice & Sons
Separator : George Rice & Sons
Paper : Mead Papeterie, Mead Escanaba

marlene mccarty

also selected by Caryn Aono, see p.24

EVEN BIGGER CONCEPT
I had to laugh out loud. I was totally sucked in by the simple promises of a product catalog, just like the million we get at work. But, as you're looking at it, it lures you right over the edge with some kind of weird, beautiful touch. There is a twisted, nostalgic stance that this product takes on. (I usually *hate* nostalgia, but this is so loopy.) A certain irony develops: This product is so new, it cannot own nostalgia. There were no snowboards when Herbert Bayer's weird tint-shift history was being made. There is no history of that age for this product. It is humorous in its adoption of the whole ski product arena and history. I thought this was one of the best pieces in the show. –mm

entrant's comments

Since snowboarding is such a trend-driven industry, the catalogs can't be even one second behind what's hip at the moment. And something that's cool one week is a joke the next. What's difficult is that you need to be able to forecast the cool stuff one year or more in advance. We kept a close eye on snowboard trends and attitudes, and decided to follow the muse of Sears, summer of '72. But we didn't want it to look too kitschy or tongue-in-cheek. Just fun, yet taking itself somewhat seriously.

K2 Snowboard

CATALOG

Designers : Michael Strassburger, Vittorio Costarella, George Estrada
Design Director : Michael Strassburger
Writers : Michael Strassburger, Vittorio Costarella, George Estrada
Illustrators : Michael Strassburger, Vittorio Costarella, George Estrada
Photographers : Eric Berger, Jeff Curtes, Jimmy Clarke, Aarron Sedway, others
Design Firm : Modern Dog
Client/Publisher : K2 Snowboards
Typographers : Michael Strassburger, Vittorio Costarella, George Estrada
Printer : Valco
Separator : WY'east
Paper : Simpson Evergreen

EVEN BIGGER CONCEPT

A comic book. The *National Enquirer. Road and Track*. A Wheaties box. *Sports Illustrated.* A real-estate catalog. This piece is art. The academics of design have been replaced by a web of reified vernacular-referencing (and we're not talking about "nostalgic longing for simpler times" as the vernacular!) It is interesting because the discussion of masquerade is not being evaluated through a high-art/low-art (or rather high-design/low-design) construction. –mm

entrant's comments

The premise was that the audience for this job, namely toy buyers, were inundated with toy catalogs. Humor seemed like a great way to get their attention. The literal product sell was equal to the entertainment value. Hunt Weber Clark Associates and Galoob's creative team developed six spoof catalogs to represent each one of the product lines. To sell MicroMachines, we did a spoof of *Road and Track* magazine, Mutant League spoofed *Sports Illustrated*, and Biker Mice from Mars satirized the *Hollywood Reporter*. My Little Doll House became an upscale real-estate brochure and Sky Dancers became a Disney-like comic book. My favorite was Z-Bots' spoof of the *National Enquirer*. I was a little disappointed though, when they killed my original cover story idea, "How Do you Know When Your Z-Bot is Gay?"

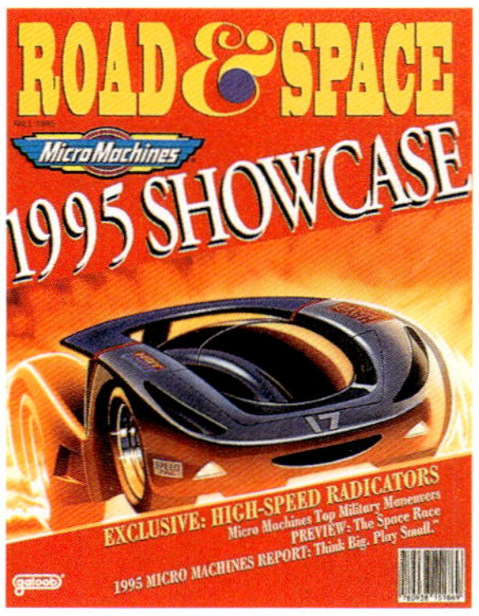

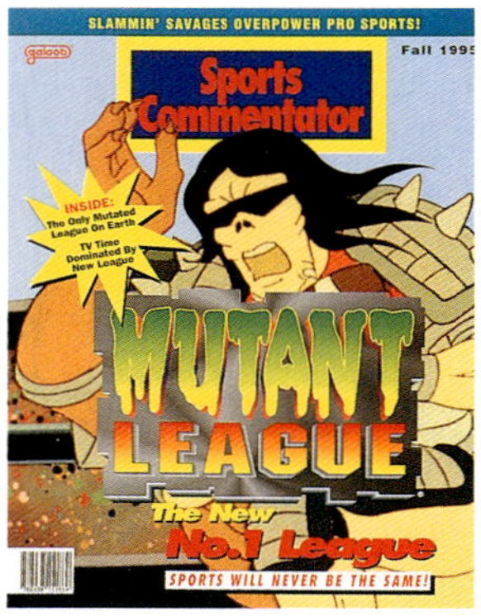

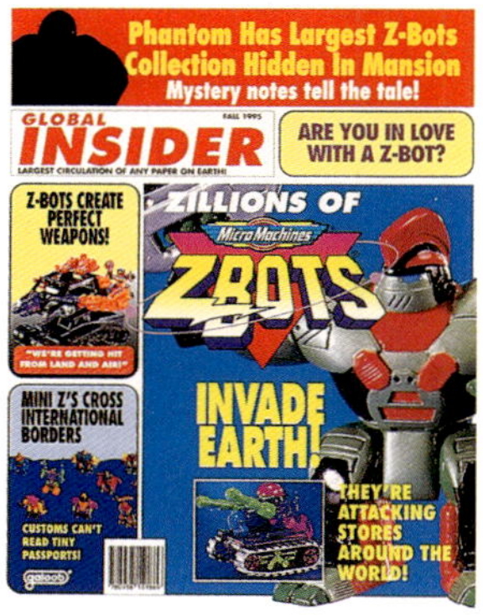

Lewis Galoob Toys, Inc. 1995 Toy Fair

CATALOGS

Designers : Nancy A. Hunt-Weber, Alan Adler, Gary Williams, Virginia Sanders
Design Directors : Nancy A. Hunt-Weber, Alan Adler
Writer : Paul Heydt
Photographer : Pacific Image/Tom McAfee
Design Firm : Hunt Weber Clark Associates
Client/Publisher : Lewis Galoob Toys, Inc.
Printer : New World Colour Printing
Paper : 100 lb. Centura Book

marlene mccarty

also selected by
Jan van Toorn, see p.125, and Caryn Aono, see p.26

EVEN BIGGER CONCEPT/ IF IT AIN'T BROKE DON'T FIX IT

This piece blows my mind. Talk about "Entertainment Sells!" A women's college produced its admission catalog in the genre of *Sassy* magazine. What a call! It's like an art piece. There is so much meaning dying to be excavated. It's really, really smart design. It's really funny design. And I bet it's really successful design.

–mm

entrant's comments

In response to a gradual drop-off in enrollment, Pine Manor College was looking to make a radical departure in how its viewbook read and looked. The viewbook was reeingineered to appeal to the prospective student rather than the parent. It takes into consideration the profile of the typical PMC student, both academically and socially. The viewbook uses the layout and writing style of teen magazines, such as *Sassy* and *Seventeen* as its model.

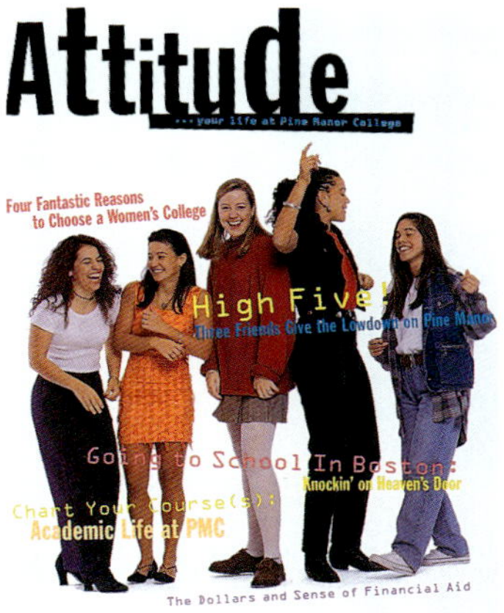

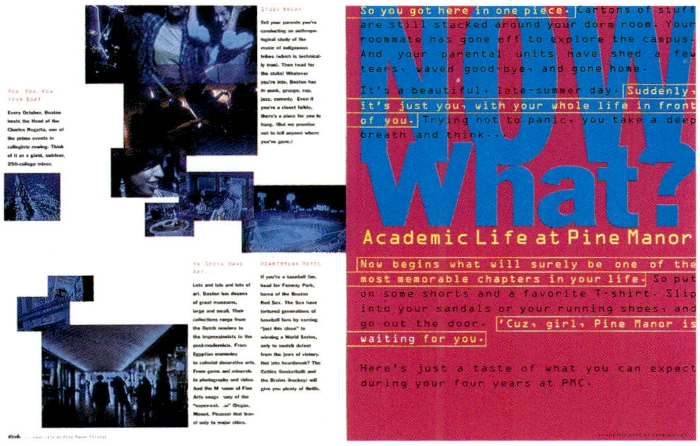

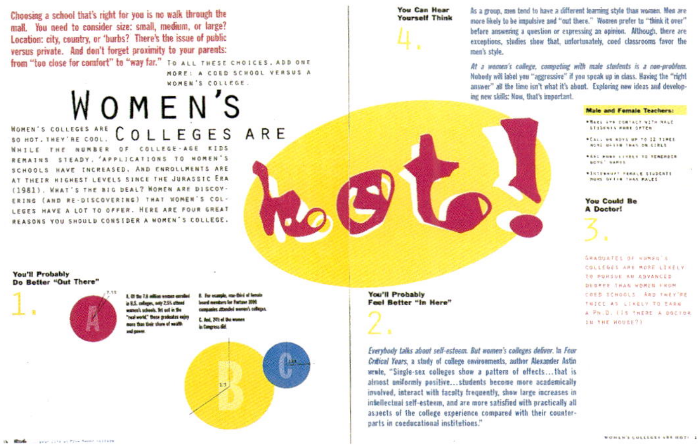

Attitude – Pine Manor College

VIEWBOOK

Designer : Lee Allen Kreindel
Design Director : Lee Allen Kreindel
Writer : Christine Kane
Photographers : Molly Lynch, Charles Barclay Reeves
Illustrators : Diane Bigda, James Kraus, Jeff Tate
Design Firm : Lee Allen Kreindel Graphic Design
Client/Publisher : Pine Manor College
Typographer : Lee Allen Kreindel
Printer : Dynagraf, Inc.
Separator : Dynagraf, Inc.
Paper : Repap Multiffect Gloss Text and Cover

marlene mccarty

EVEN BIGGER CONCEPT/
IF IT AIN'T BROKE
DON'T FIX IT

I'm a sucker. Of course I'd pick something with a pierced tongue on it. (Note: school thing again.) –mm

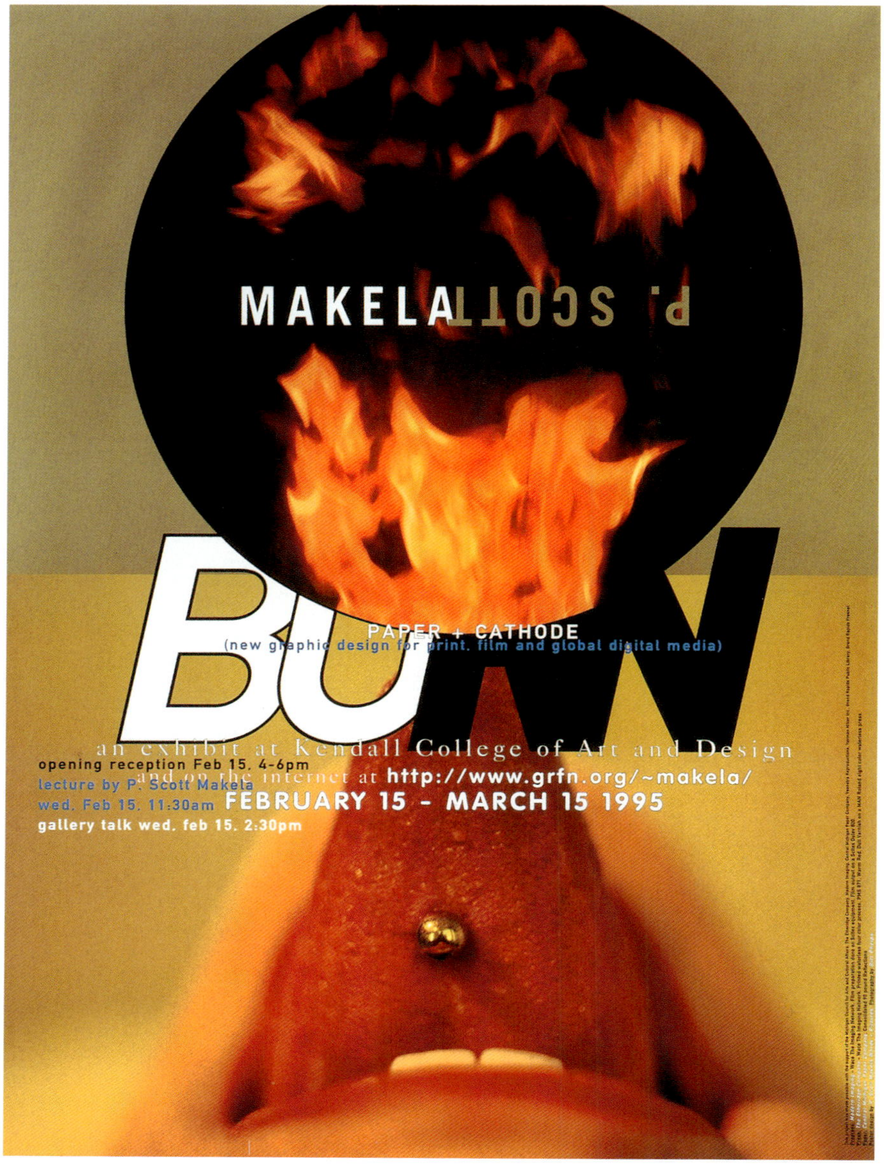

entrant's comments

The digital realm of visual communication was best represented here by the "flaming upward tongue" of spoken, passionate, and powerful language. What is born will burn and will be born again. The poster was created for the opening of my first one-person show of graphic design for print, film, and new media. These varying surfaces are as active and volatile as wet human flesh and the ridge tips of a liquid fire. Before we are conceived into this world, we are only an intention, not unlike a flame before it builds. They are very much like the linguistics of our words, which are, again, only an intention until they are spoken.

Burn/Born

POSTER

Designer : P. Scott Makela
Photographer : Bill Phelps
Design Firm : Words + Pictures for Business + Culture
Client/Publisher : Kendall College of Art and Design
Typographer : P. Scott Makela
Printer : The Etheridge Company
Separator : Modern Imaging
Paper : Central Michigan Paper Co., Consolidated 90 lb. Reflections

marlene mccarty

EVEN BIGGER CONCEPT/
IF IT AIN'T BROKE
DON'T FIX IT

It's that school thing – traditional academic design. This one is pretty. (Yes. I said pretty!) –mm

entrant's comments

Cranbrook design students are hired by the Cranbrook Art Museum to design exhibition announcements, which gives the students an opportunity to implement studio experiments and ideas. This museum invitation announces a show that is on view all summer displaying works of the school's graduating class. Two images are combined to make a visual pun, drawing on allegory and cliché to create a visual game that offers various reads and provides the audience the latitude to construct their own interpretations.

Graduate Summer Exhibition

ANNOUNCEMENT

Designer: Geoff Kaplan
Design Director: Katherine McCoy
Writer: David D.J. Rau
Photographer: Geoff Kaplan
Design Firm: Cranbrook Academy of Art
Client/Publisher: Cranbrook Art Museum
Typographer: Geoff Kaplan
Printer: KTD Printing Associates
Separator: Key Tech
Paper: Carnival White 80 lb. Cover

marlene mccarty

EVEN BIGGER CONCEPT/
IF IT AIN'T BROKE
DON'T FIX IT
School Days. -mm

entrant's comments

The primary objective of the Summer of Art 1994 poster was to get the attention of high school students in order to inform and encourage inquiry regarding summer programs offered at Otis College of Art and Design. The imagery shows a nebula in which students are in their own orbits, highlighting the experiences one could encounter throughout the summer. Along the bottom edge, perforated cards were meant to be torn away and mailed back to the college.

Summer of Art 1994

POSTER

Designer : Lisa Nugent
Design Director : Lisa Nugent
Photographer : Dennis Keeley
Design Firm : ReVerb
Client/Publisher : Otis College of Art and Design
Typographers : Lisa Nugent, Dave Ho
Printer : Monarch Litho, Montebello, California
Separator : Digtal Pre-press International, San Francisco

marlene mccarty

also selected by Jan van Toorn, see p.143

EVEN BIGGER CONCEPT/
IF IT AIN'T BROKE
DON'T FIX IT

This is one of those seminal pieces, which goes back to the discussion of schools and how they present (sell) themselves. CalArts perpetuated much of this design strategy. This piece s masterful, and probably has more refined qualities than some of the other pieces in this "school" genre. –mm

entrant's comments

After the Northridge earthquake rendered our campus useless, a moth-balled facility once used by Lockheed Corporation for weapons and space shuttle development was donated to CalArts. It was an unusual example of the art community benefiting from post-war weapons hypnosis. The facility was a lifeless, dreary research facility hidden in the desert hills north of Los Angeles. It was difficult to design this brochure. How was I to entice prospective students from around the world to come to "Lockheed Art School" replete with fires, earthquakes, landslides, and droughts? What you see is CalArts (and L.A. in general) represented through a once-off veneer: high-tech nerdy disguised by Los Angeles Googi; a brochure masquerading as a poster; retro as future. Or is it the other way around?

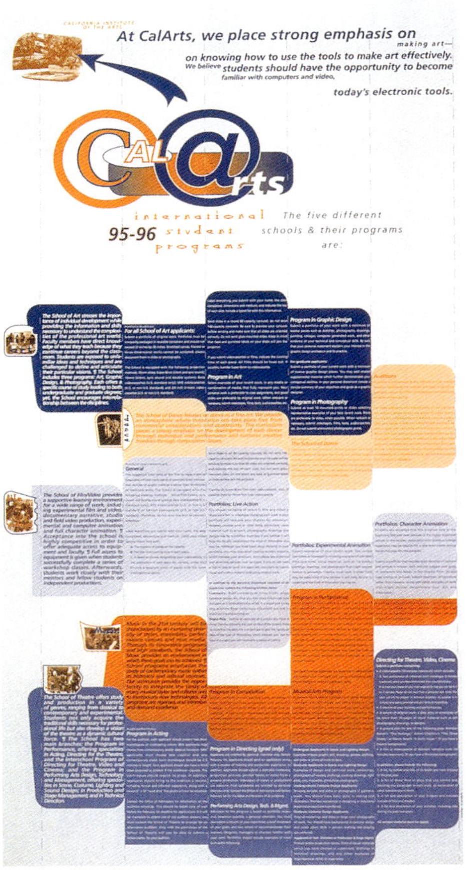

CalArts International Student Programs

POSTER

Designer : Richard Sienkiewicz Shanks
Design Firm : California Institute of the Arts
Printer : CP Graphics
Separator : Icon West
Paper : Cis Label

marlene mccarty

EVEN BIGGER CONCEPT/
IF IT AIN'T BROKE
DON'T FIX IT

Nice flower. I find the discussion of these types of materials more interesting en masse than as single pieces. They all look good. They all represent good, solid, learned design. The college look. –mm

entrant's comments

The San Francisco Art Institute's community outreach includes the Summer Young Artist Program, a series of classes and activities for high school students who want to explore new, mature venues at college level. The Institute's location and environment are unique. The structure is full of surprises and is especially exciting to young people. For the promotional poster, our goal was to capture the array of possibilities such a place and program offers through images freely connected to both art and summer. We purposely kept the connections provocative and playful to entertain our audience and encourage their own interpretations. We were thus allowing the students a subtle, creative gesture and a hint of what is to come.

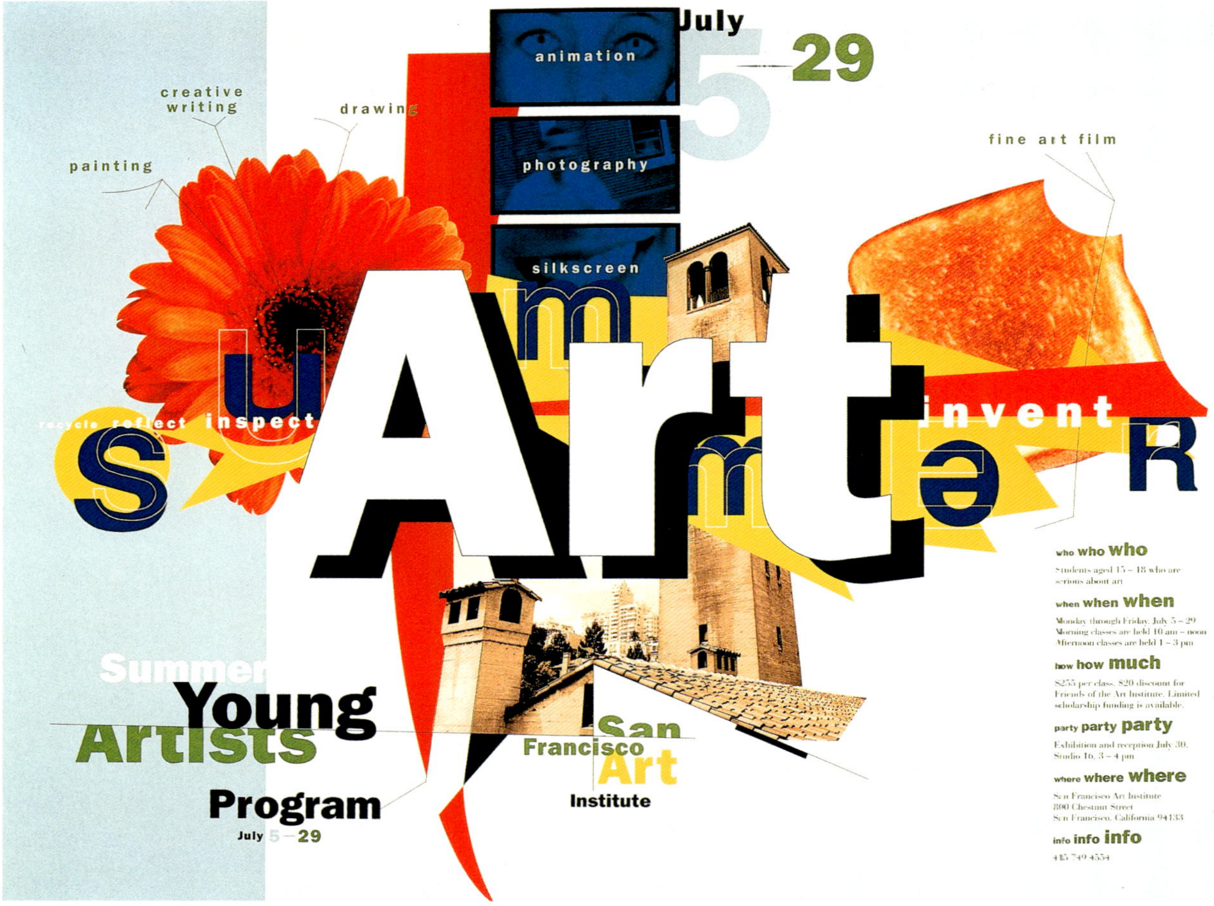

San Francisco Art Institute

POSTER

Designers: Raul Cabra, Martin Venezky
Design Director: Raul Cabra
Writer: Patricia Quill
Photographers: various
Design Firm: Cabra Diseño
Client/Publisher: San Francisco Art Institute
Typographer: in-house
Printer: Alonzo Printing
Separator: The Prepcenter
Paper: 80 lb. Recovery Gloss

marlene mccarty

also selected by Caryn Aono, see p.25

EVEN BIGGER CONCEPT/ IF IT AIN'T BROKE DON'T FIX IT

This piece belongs to my self-constructed category of "the computer look for schools." CalArts and Cranbrook have been groundbreakers in this territory. Now we have this whole association of colleges in Ohio adopting this strategy. It's revealing that this school-propagated, entertainment-industry-looking design is being claimed by many different kinds of schools to sell the school to the students. (Entertainment sells.) It's also interesting that now it is the students who are being catered to as the ones who will be deciding where they go to school, whereas 20 or 25 years ago, the school catalogs catered to the parents.

–mm

entrant's comments

Each year, the same necessary, but dry and basic, information about colleges and universities in Ohio is presented to high school juniors and seniors. We try to wake it up. A quote from our client, "Realizing that TCIO (Toward College in Ohio) must also be user-friendly to parents and counselors, we may have felt that some of the graphics and text designs were a bit 'far out.' We are willing to forego personal likes and dislikes because the evidence indicated that the design is working."

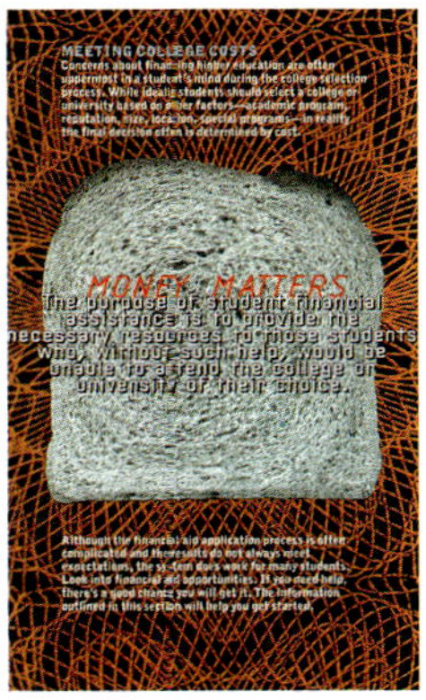

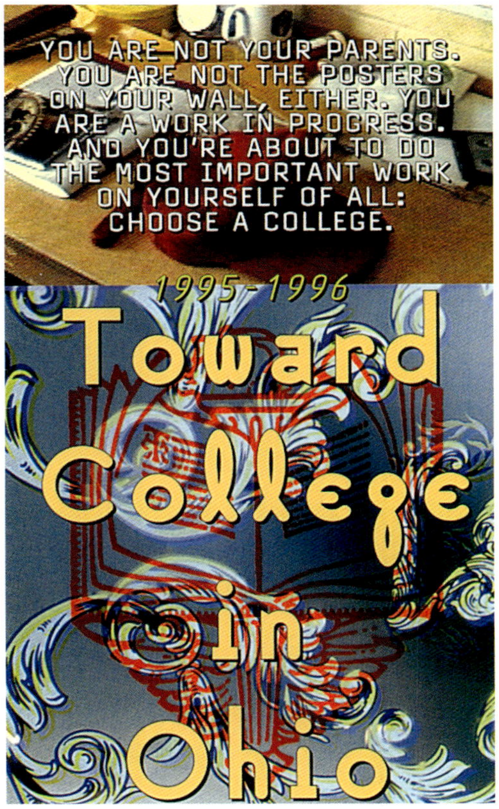

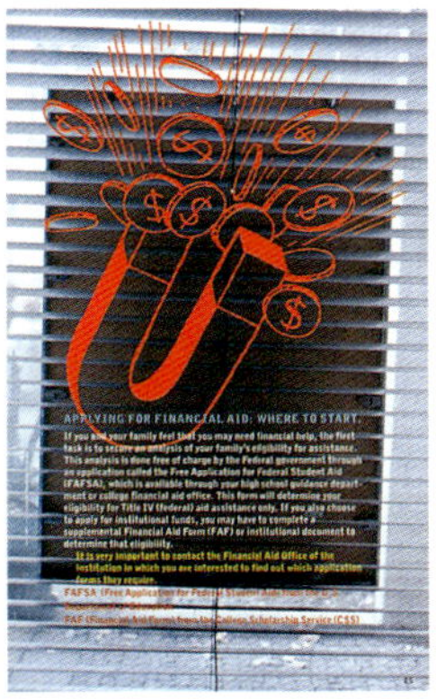

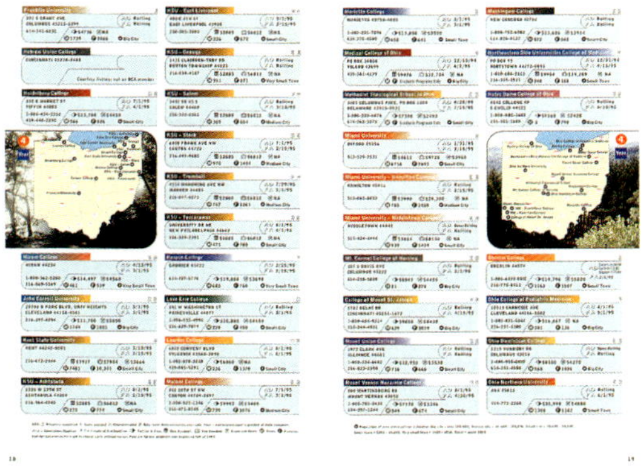

Toward College in Ohio 1995–1996

BROCHURE

Designer : Crit Warren
Design Director : Crit Warren
Writer : George Felton & Others
Photographer : Crit Warren
Design Firm : Schmeltz + Warren
Client/Publisher : The Ohio College Association
Typographer : Schmeltz + Warren, Macintosh
Printer : West-Camp Press
Separator : West-Camp Press
Paper : Futura Matte 70 lb. Text

marlene mccarty

EVEN BIGGER CONCEPT/
IF IT AIN'T BROKE
DON'T FIX IT

None of that "It's a serious political issue; it's got to be ugly" attitude here. Social issues and politics suddenly seem like a part of our world, not some weird shadowy marginal thing that we once heard about on the six o'clock news. ~mm

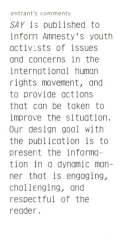

entrant's comments

SAY is published to inform Amnesty's youth activists of issues and concerns in the international human rights movement, and to provide actions that can be taken to improve the situation. Our design goal with the publication is to present the information in a dynamic manner that is engaging, challenging, and respectful of the reader.

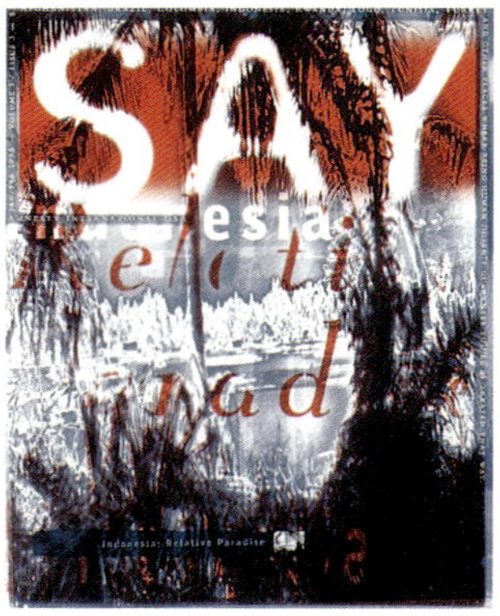

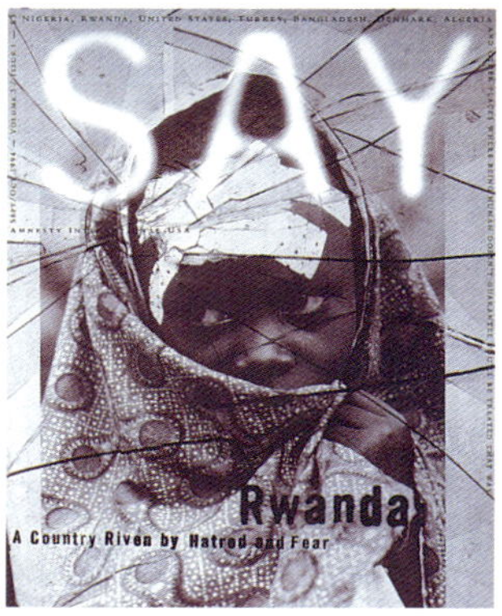

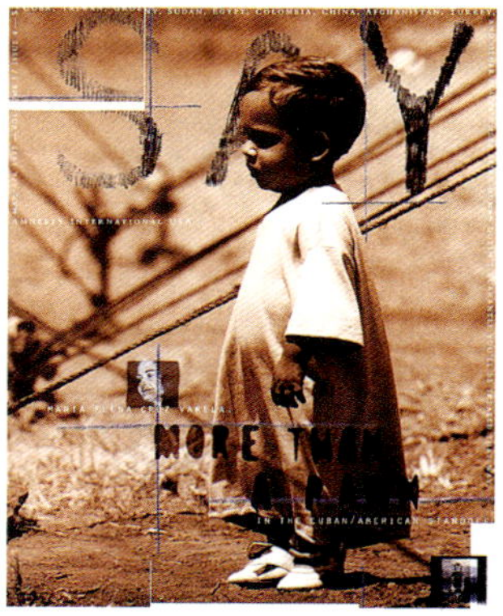

SAY
MAGAZINE

Designers: Hal Wolverton, Geoffrey Lorenzen, Kat Saito, Pamela Racs, Robin Muir
Design Directors: Alicia Johnson, Hal Wolverton
Photographers: Stephen Dupont, Various
Illustrators: Geoffrey Lorenzen, Pamela Racs
Design Firm: Johnson and Wolverton
Client/Publisher: Amnesty International
Printer: The Irwin Hodson Company
Paper: Resolve Matte

marlene mccarty

EVEN BIGGER CONCEPT/ MUSIC INDUSTRY

This piece is part of the bigger conversation about the music industry – how the music industry reveals itself graphically and how that, in turn, fuels a large segment of the graphic design world. Yes, I'm saying the music industry drives graphic design and not the reverse. This is a striking example of the music industry using graphic design in a wonderful way. It's also interesting that this is an annual report. –mm

entrant's comments

The RIAA is a trade association whose members create, market, and distribute approximately 90 percent of all sound recordings produced in the United States. To show its member companies that the RIAA was on the cutting edge with its mission to lead them into a future powered by digital technology, they wanted an annual report that felt fresh and hip. A free-form format was adopted that keeps each spread completely different from the last. To save time and money, the photography was done in black and white, then colored in Photoshop. Emigre's Dogma font, a typeface caught somewhere between '70s groove and '90s rave, seemed to suggest the paradoxical situation the music industry faces as it enters the revolution/evolution of the digital age.

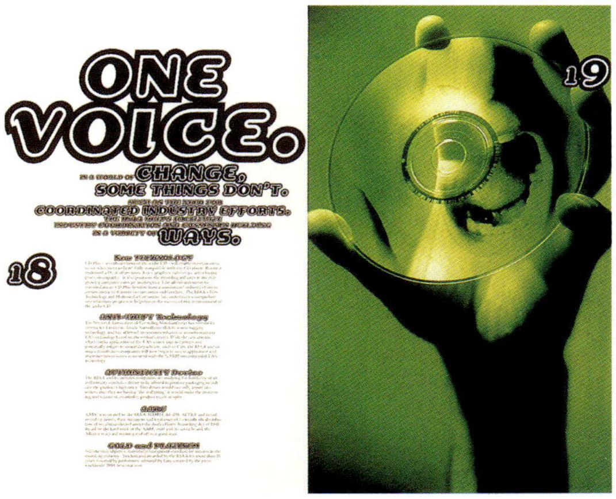

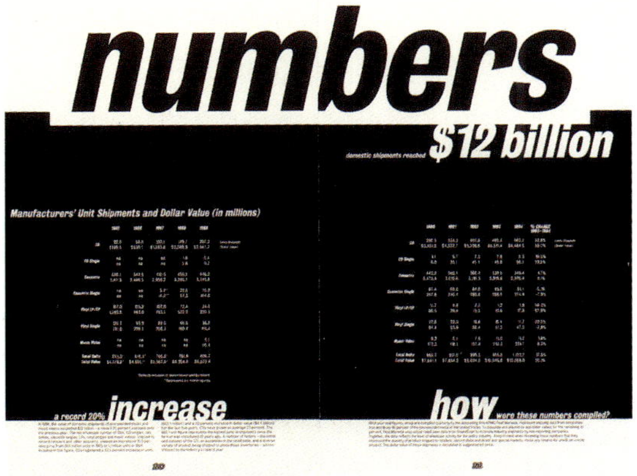

(r)evolution – Recording Industry Association of America 1994

ANNUAL REPORT

Designer : Neal Ashby
Design Director : Neal Ashby
Writers : Neal Ashby, Fred Guthrie
Illustrator : John Moore
Design Firm : Recording Industry Association of America
Client/Publisher : Recording Industry Association of America
Typographer : Neal Ashby
Printer : Steckel
Separator : Steckel
Paper : Starwhite Vicksburg
Photographer : Kevin Irby

marlene mccarty

EVEN BIGGER CONCEPT/
MUSIC INDUSTRY

There were many CDs entered into the 100 Show. I chose this one because I think the way it looks most embodies how CD packaging has to work. It has to be very tactile. It has to be totally visceral. It has to function in a world of Tower Record sensory overload. This cover made my skin crawl. It's like hair and some kind of red body part with a 3D spew that's kind of slimy. Its visceral character is its function.

–mm

entrant's comments

Like anyone, I have always wanted my face on a record cover. I also like the idea of an image that seems disturbing and naughty at first glance, but is actually simple and quite innocent. Two for the price of one.

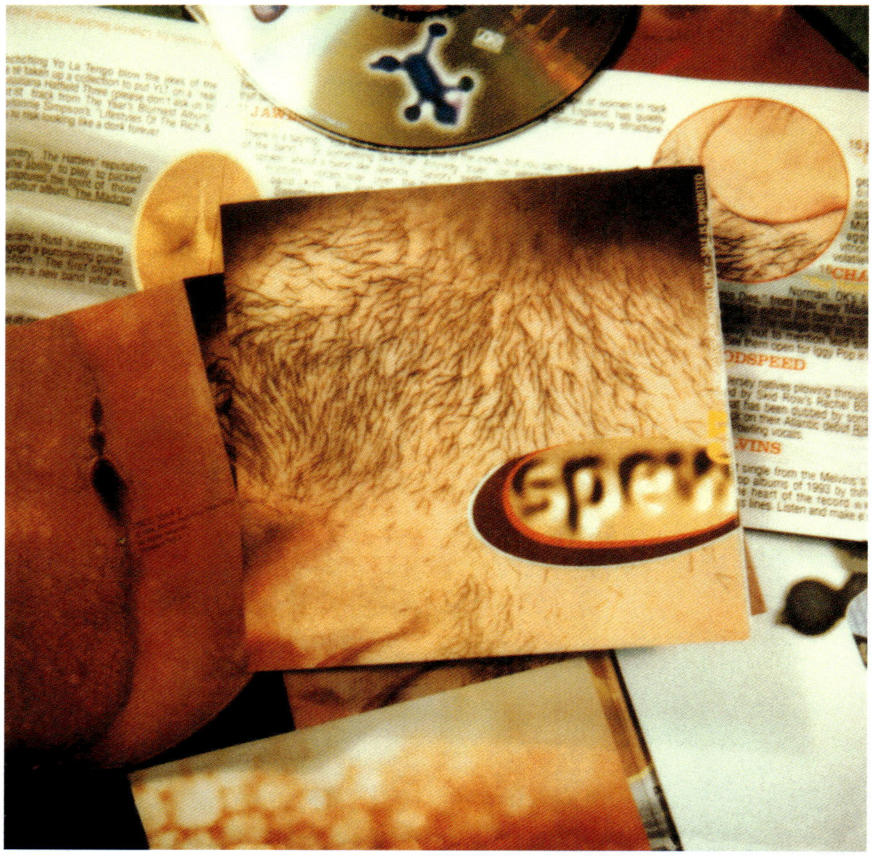

Spew 5

CD PACKAGING

Designer: Charlie Becker
Design Director: Melanie Nissen
Writer: Jeff Dandurand
Photographer: Charlie Becker
3-D Computer Illustrator: Rob Eberhardt
Client/Publisher: Atlantic Records
Printer: Ivy Hill
Separator: Color Service

marlene mccarty

entrant's comments

Retro-fanaticism, computer hysteria, wordplay, personal hygiene. I think that's kinda where this was coming from.

EVEN BIGGER CONCEPT/ MUSIC INDUSTRY

I do feel that the music industry is driving a lot of graphic design. I just liked this piece. I know it's so easy just to say that. I liked it. I liked the pink can. I liked the yellow background. -mm

Fresh, Always

AD

Designer: Charlie Becker
Design Director: Melanie Nissen
Writers: Frank Gargiulo, Valerie Wagner
Photographer: Charlie Becker
Illustrators: Rob Eberhardt, Charlie Becker
Client/Publisher: East West Records
Separator: Progress Graphics

EVEN BIGGER CONCEPT/
MUSIC INDUSTRY

This piece is so simple, and yet it's still up to par in this music industry category I made. It made me relish simple design decisions. –mm

entrant's comments

Pell Mell is an instrumental rock band. "Interstate" is their first album for a major record label. Our goals for the graphic design were to be clear, direct, and smart (like the music) and to stand out from the sea of slick, obtuse record covers. As for the imagery, we took our cues from the title, the hypnotic, driving music, and our fondness for American roadside vernacular.

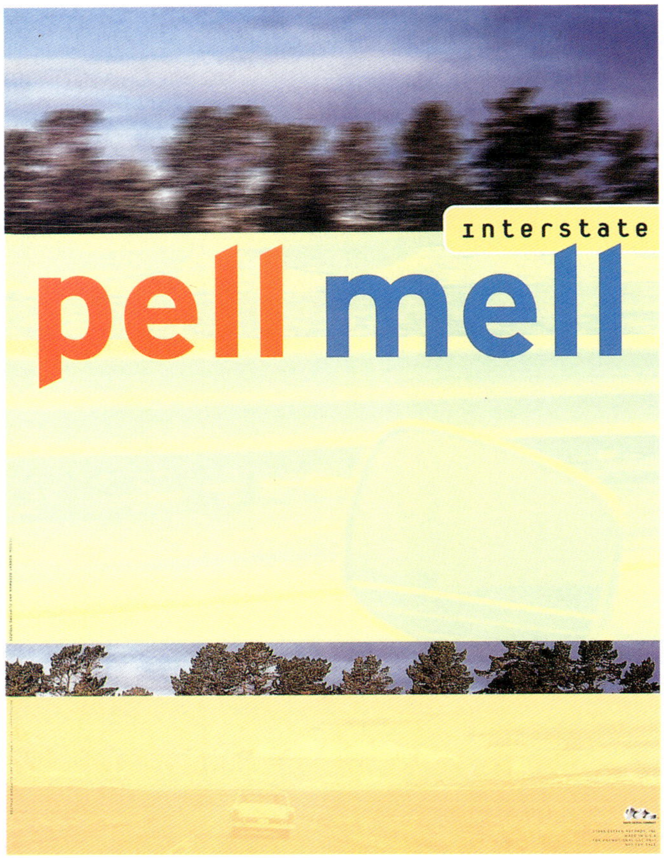

Pell Mell

ALBUM COVER AND POSTER

Designers : Robert Beerman, Clifford Stoltze
Photographers : Kelly Spalding, Clifford Stoltze
Design Firm : Stoltze Design/Sametz-Blackstone
Client/Publisher : DGC (Geffen Records)
Typographer : Stoltze Design
Printer : Westland Graphics
Separator : Continental Color

marlene mccarty

EVEN BIGGER CONCEPT/ MUSIC INDUSTRY

I chose this piece as a representative piece in the same way that I chose the white *Wired* as an embodiment of all *Wireds* (see p.109). This piece is an embodiment of MTV and reflects so much work that MTV has done. MTV has exerted an enormous amount of influence on the design world. This piece is indicative of the irony that MTV has pushed for years and years. It's interesting that MTV can still pull it off. –mm

entrant's comments

This project is a celebration of all things superficial and fun in life, thus the title, "Fluff." In an attempt to counter the stress faced by so many young adults today, "Fluff" expresses the idea that it's okay to waste time, and that wasting time well is an art form. But that doesn't mean we should ever forget those who die at an early age at the barrel of a gun or from the HIV virus. The design, creative aspects, and art direction of this project are all secondary to the overall concept. We dedicate it to those who could not enjoy its celebration of life.

Video Music Awards

PROGRAM GUIDE

Designers: Stacy Drummond, Jeffrey Keyton, Tracy Boychuk, David Felton, Johan Vipper

Design Directors: Stacy Drummond, Jeffrey Keyton, Tracy Boychuk, David Felton, Johan Vipper

Design Firm: MTV Off-Air Creative

Client/Publisher: MTV: Music Television

Printer: Northstar

marlene mccarty

EVEN BIGGER CONCEPT/ MUSIC INDUSTRY

I picked this piece because it's sweet. It's very sweet. It's very lovable. And it has a little pillow. It's very poetic. A nice contrast to most of the work submitted this year – work which is very market-driven, very industry-driven. There seemed to be very little room for the quieter, more poetic version of graphic design. (And I don't mean graphic interpretation of poetry, yuck.) –mm

entrant's comments

Sleepwalkers neither slumber silently nor stay put in their beds. They literally follow their dreams, prowling the twilight between waking and subconscious. This fetishistic collaborative project chronicles one's somnambulist nocturnal wanderings, compulsions, and secrets – *c'mere,* let me whisper in your ear – all nestled in with a compilation of instrumental compositions to dream by.............. Sleep tight.

Dreaming Out Loud

EMIGRE MUSIC SAMPLER

Designer : Gail Swanlund
Writer : Amy Gerstler
Design Firm : Emigre Graphics
Client/Publisher : Emigre Graphics
Printer : Cal Central
Separator : Cal Central
Paper : Gilbert Esse White Red

marlene mccarty

EVEN BIGGER CONCEPT/ MUSIC INDUSTRY

This is an example of a good, solid, content piece that still makes me want to scream, "HOW COME POLITICAL GRAPHICS HAVE TO LOOK LIKE SUCH A DOWNER?" –mm

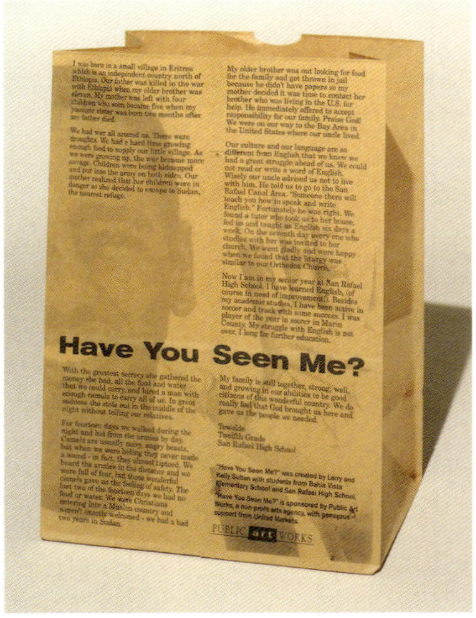

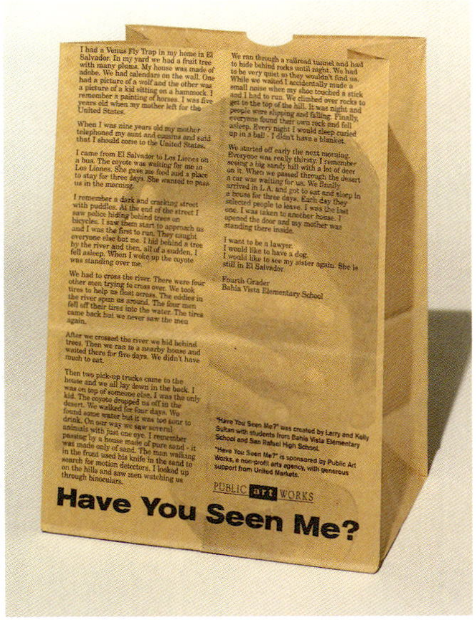

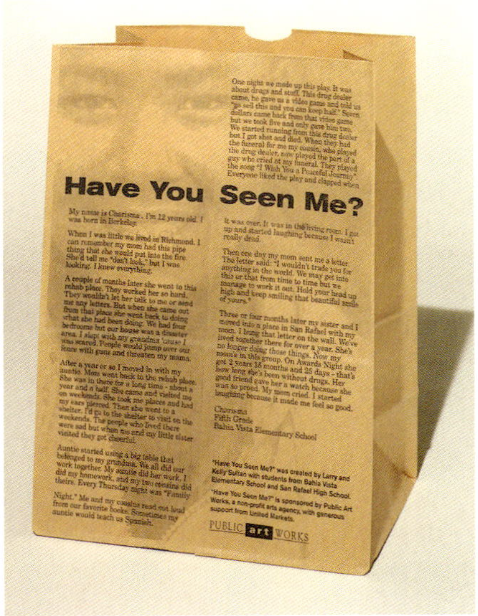

entrant's comments

The objective of the project was to create visibility for youths by publishing their writings, poetry, and artwork. Initially, it was a project between Larry and Kelly Sultan and students in the San Rafael area, and I was asked to design on the most common canvases of our culture: grocery bags and milk cartons. The crudeness of the printing/assembly and the limited choices (none) of inks presented several challenges. In lieu of press checks or proofs, I hoped for the best. But the biggest surprise was how politicized the bags became once in distribution. On one bag, a Salvadoran student described his journey across the border. The sponsoring grocery market was accused of supporting illegal immigration and pulled the bag from circulation to avoid a threatened boycott by one patron. "Have You Seen Me?" became the center of a heated debate over Proposition 187, which denies rights and services to illegal immigrants, and the role of public art and its responsibility to create discourse, inspire action, and, in this case, to tell a story. Collaborative projects that blur graphic design and fine art are few and far between. I wish to do more.

Have You Seen Me?

BAGS

Designer: Brian Scott
Design Director: Brian Scott
Writers: Students of Bahia Vista Elementary School and San Rafael High School
Photographer: Larry Sultan
Design Firm: Boon
Client/Publisher: Larry and Kelly Sultan, Public Art Works
Typographer: Brian Scott
Printer: Pt. Townsend
Papers: Kraft

entrant's comments

We were called the day before. Limited to two colors. Our idea was to encourage people to vote or they'll "lose their voice." Jill's Video Scream was perfect for adding urgency and emphasis to the headline. And we made our deadline.

EVEN BIGGER CONCEPT/ MUSIC INDUSTRY

What interests me about the music industry is that, at times, it actually allows graphic design to have power — to speak. These pieces are often produced at a breakneck pace and, consequently, some of their rough edges show.

–mm

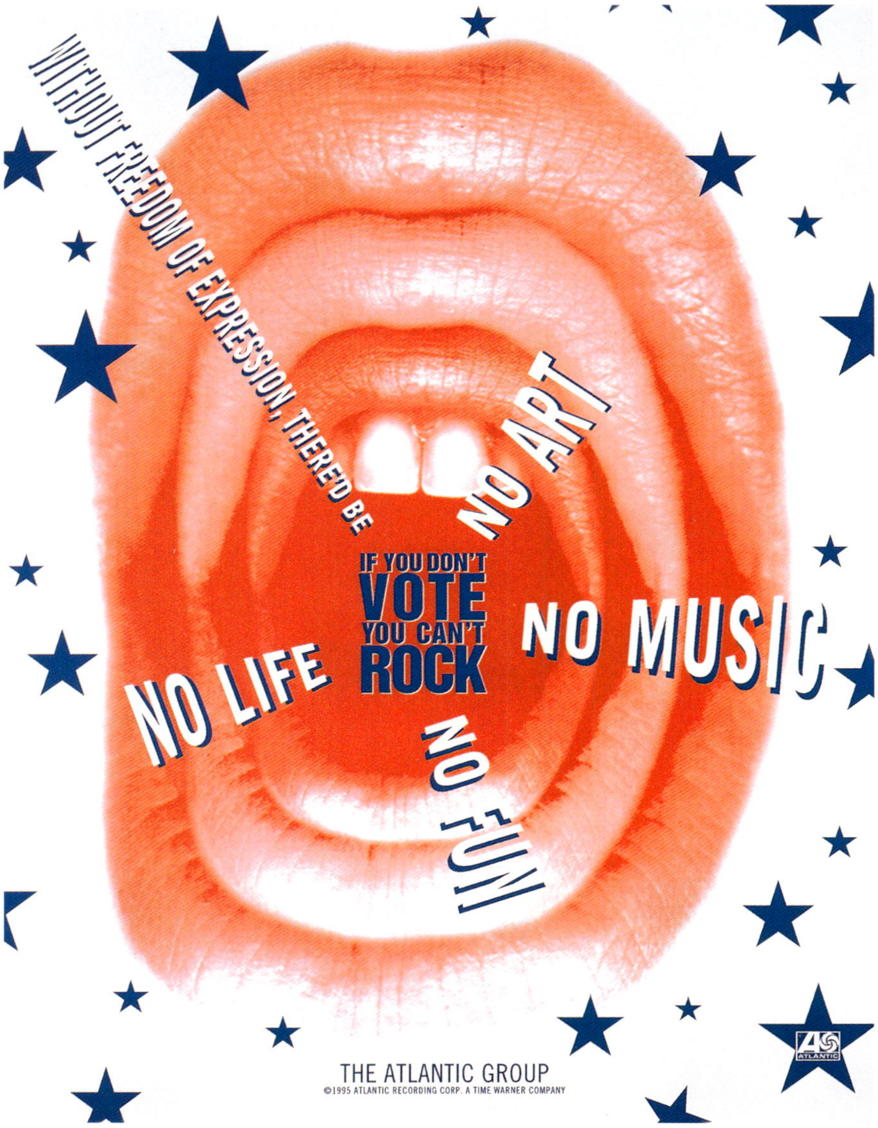

Rock the Vote

BULLETIN

Designer : Benjamin Niles
Design Director : Richard Bates
Writer : Eve Hartman
Photographer : Jill Greenberg
Design Firm : Atlantic Records
Typographer : Benjamin Niles

marlene mccarty

EVEN BIGGER CONCEPT/
MUSIC INDUSTRY

A certain level of truthfulness and humor is reached through very limited and straightforward means. It's wonderful to see projects that can be so unelaborate and still be so successful. –mm

entrant's comments

We thought using the military's own imagery and copy in the context of a holiday greeting could help point out some of the military's inconsistencies and hypocrisies (don't ask, don't tell; use of aircraft for private purposes). Bold holiday colors and a large format were selected to attract attention. Images from the Marine Training Manual were found and used to contrast sharply with traditional holiday messages. The military's hypocrisy was further underscored by tiny type (again from military manuals) along the bottom, which informs us of the military's ongoing interest in new ways to address problems.

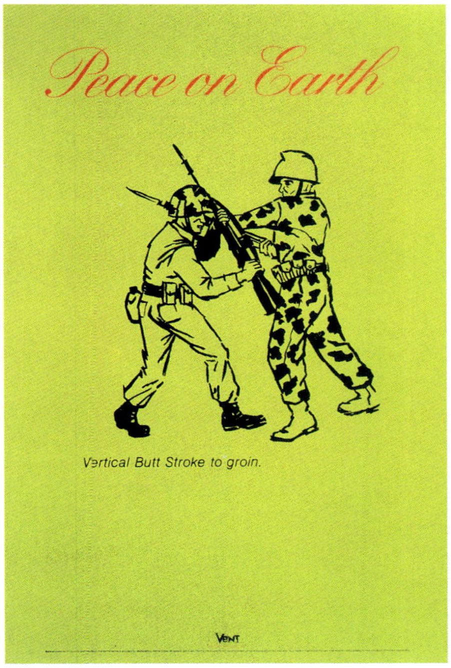

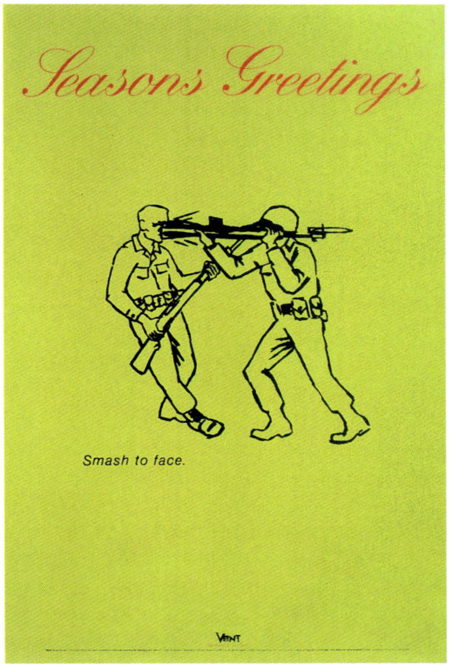

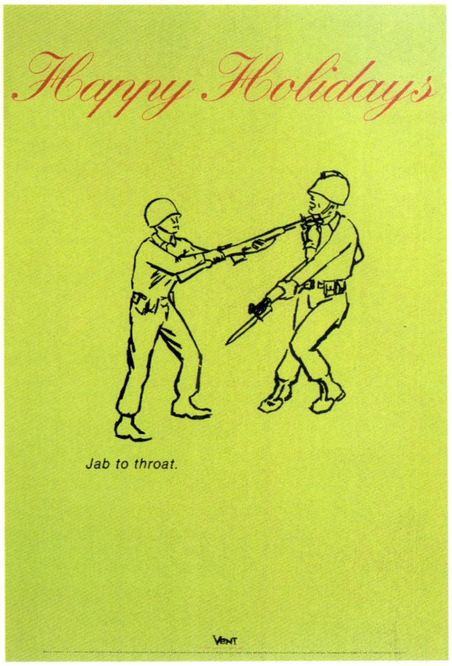

Vent

HOLIDAY POSTERS

Designer : After Hours Creative
Design Director : After Hours Creative
Writer : After Hours Creative
Illustrator : U.S. Marine Corps
Design Firm : After Hours Creative
Client/Publisher : Vent
Typographer : After Hours Creative
Printer : Metro Screen Print

marlene mccarty

EVEN BIGGER CONCEPT/
MUSIC INDUSTRY

In the same sense as the Tom Recchion posters (see p.66 and 67), I was drawn to this one. It's hard to separate these choices from the context within which they were seen at the 100 Show. This poster has such a presence in this land of computer layering that I couldn't help but take it for just being different. It did appeal to me (once again) as a hand-drawn interpretation of typography and image. Though I do have to be honest and say that I don't feel any immense attempt at "looking forward" in this piece.

–mm

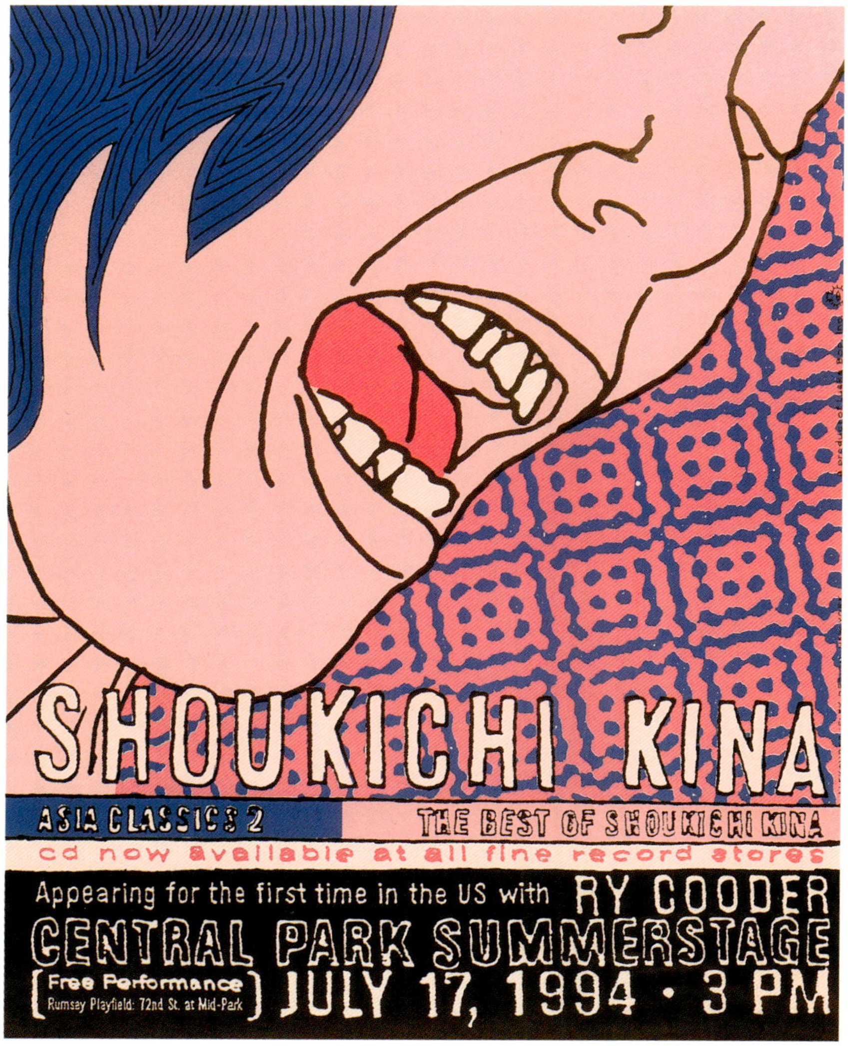

entrant's comments

This poster was for a concert in New York's Central Park, promoting the music of what can best be described as an Okinawan funk band. No good imagery of the band or its leader was available, so we took it upon ourselves to illustrate the poster, which follows the look of a CD cover that we had previously designed for the band. Equipment used: pilot razor-point pen, photocopier.

Shoukichi Kina

POSTER

Designer : David Albertson
Art Director : Alexander Isley
Illustrator : David Albertson
Design Firm : Alexander Isley Design
Client/Publisher : Luaka Bop Records
Printer : Masterpiece Printers

marlene mccarty

EVEN BIGGER CONCEPT/ MUSIC INDUSTRY

The label alone for this piece is sc warm and fuzzy (metaphorically, not really) that it deserved a prize. We looked at a number of interactive disks in this competition, and frankly, they were disappointing. Then, I stumbled upon this disk. "Wow, this is the best interactive thing we've looked at in the whole show. I'm giving it a prize." It breaks the boring constraints of print work that most interactive work still falls into. –mm

entrant's comments

The Poster Children interactive press kit was designed to a be a companion piece to the band's fifth album, "Junior Citizen." The graphics were inspired by Japanese *anime* and the CD was designed in the spirit of a fireworks package. Our goal was to make a demo that people would look at more than once. We believe that there is more to the concept of "interactivity" than pressing a button and watching a quick-time movie. To us, the only true interactivity nowadays occurs in computer games, in which random elements force audience-generated outcome.

We believe that the first step to the next level of interactive multimedia begins with the employment of random events. We are a techno-peasant outfit (our only computer is a Macintosh Quadra 650), and this is our first excursion into the world of multimedia. Working with our limited resources, we decided to make a statement equating interactivity with television, since presently, the most interactive of all small demos still doesn't hold attention quite as well as a television set.

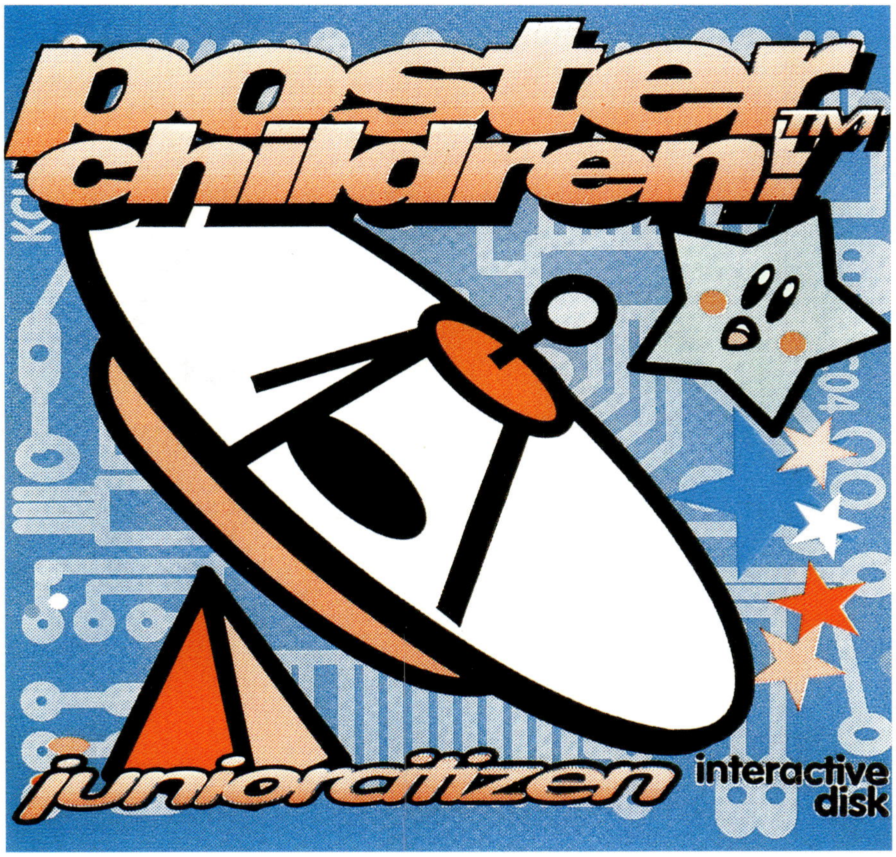

Poster Children "Junior Citizen"

INTERACTIVE PRESS KIT

Designer : Rose Marshak
Art Director : Rose Marshak
Client/Publisher : Sire/Reprise

marlene mccarty

TOUCH THE FUTURE
Nike is really big, and these pieces actually deserve a lot of discussion, which a comment on them can hardly do. What drove my decision to accept these pieces was their very, very specific target market, and the way that, by targeting such a tight, specific audience, Nike has allowed itself to develop a very rich and very varied design-driven marketing, which we do not see in most of the larger companies.
–mm

entrant's comments
The Trash Talk campaign is a part of Nike's NYC integrated effort. The quotes feature witty examples of on-court intimidation from past and present street legends. Players are cast from playgrounds, and as a sign of respect and recognition of their uniqueness, the NYC campaign only appears in New York City.

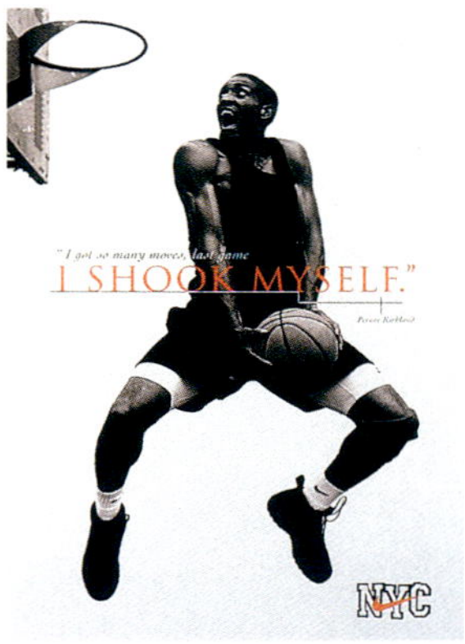

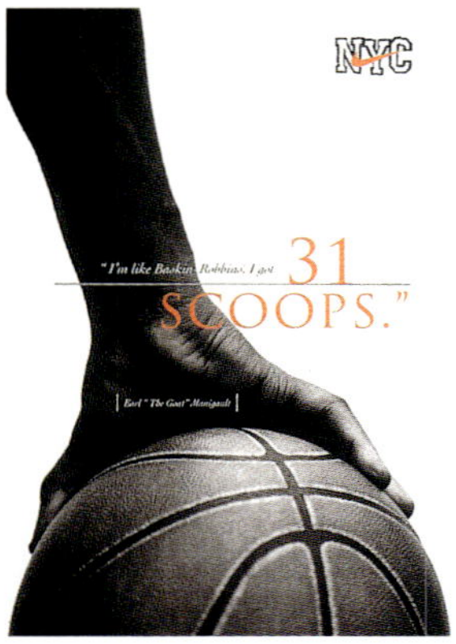

Nike NYC Trash Talk

BILLBOARDS

Designer : Imin Pao
Art Director : John Jay
Writer : Jimmy Smith
Photographer : John Huet
Design Firm : Wieden & Kennedy
Client/Publisher : Nike
Typographer : Imin Pao
Creative Directors : Dan Wieden, Susan Hoffman, Jamie Barrett, Jim Riswold

marlene mccarty

TOUCH THE FUTURE

This poster is very odd because it does have a resonating sense of old Swiss posters. There's a certain kind of, as the Swiss would say, "translation quality." It's driven by a simple image, as opposed to being driven by 80,000 images. It radiates a sort of surreal dramatic power. Thirst was at the forefront of establishing "the computer-design look." That look then solidified into a set of boundaries. Now Thirst is beginning to break their own boundaries. Admirable. –mm

entrant's comments

"Hello. How are you? Won't you tell me your name?" The digital messages whisper an end to paper while it sleeps. "But will I awaken in another (world)?" Shifting the consciousness of Gilbert's technology from "just paper" to "platform-independent storage" was part of the design mission. To enhance the awareness of Gilbert as the surface for archiving digital experiences in an engaging manner was the essence of the artifact. Working surfaces for the 21st century designed for the technology-driven work that lies ahead.

Wired

POSTER INSERT

Designers : Rick Valicenti, Mark Rattin
Design Director : Rick Valicenti
Writers : Lynn Martinelli, Rob Witting
Photographer : William Valicenti
Digital Illustrators : Rick Valicenti (poster image), Mark Rattin (intro images)
Design Firm : Thirst
Client/Publisher : Gilbert Paper
Typographer : Rick Valicenti
Printer : Dixon Web
Separator : Electronic Prepress Services
Paper : Gilbert Neutech

TOUCH THE FUTURE

Speaking of computerland, in the same way that the Babes in Toyland poster just leaps out of one side of every prescribed category (see p.66), there is a body of Rick Valicenti's work which leaps out the other. So okay . . . there's a bunch of computer-layered-looking design. So much so that one can almost call it a tradition. However, there's this work from Rick Valicenti that, although it's dealing with this tradition, it's also breaking those prescribed bounds in ways that are very unexpected. I'm specifically referring to the Gilbert paper ads in *Wired* magazine. These are really wonderful ads. One in particular – the one with the muscleman genie – is so ironic. It's over-the-top tasteless but it's not camp. It's a web of meaning aimed at the computer geek, the premiere audience of *Wired* magazine. We (even the uninitiated) see the heroicizing of the computer nerd and his (or her?) dream of the giant power that will be added to the soul upon purchase of the kerjillion-gigabyte drive. I guess my only question is . . . Who cares about paper? –mm

entrant's comments

Realize Change. All bets are off. What was black is now turning white. What is Now is Then. Work becomes Play. David provokes Goliath. Realize Change. Characters like Corporate Clark Kent and Athena 90210 look like icons we've become familiar with or have pretended to be while online. The maze of technology is the landscape. A vortex of shedded information yields to resurrection. Realize Change. Stairways of Golden Keyboards reach to digital heaven. Purple mountains emerge in virtual reality.

Wired

AD CAMPAIGN

Designer : Rick Valicenti
Design Director : Rick Valicenti
Writer : Thirst
Photographer : William Valicenti
Digital Illustrators : Mark Rattan/Rick Valicenti
Design Firm : Thirst
Client/Publisher : Gilbert Paper
Typographers : Rick Valicenti/Mark Rattan
Printer : *Wired* Magazine/Danbury Press

marlene mccarty

TOUCH THE FUTURE
Of course this was a very clever idea for *Wired* – an entire black-and-white issue. I must say it's almost successful. The advertising makes it a little problematic (or maybe I'm slow). It is amazing – the widespread influence that *Wired* has had on designers, on people in the design field, and on the audience that designers speak to. The appearance and success of this magazine has shifted everyone's expectations – everyone's desires . . . So I chose it. I chose it based on its importance in the real world rather than for the particular design of any one cover or spread. I figure it's bigger than that. –mm

entrant's comments

For *Wired*'s second anniversary, we decided to play off the reader's expectations and produce the entire issue in black and white. We wanted to make the point that *Wired*'s vision of the future is not dependent on the six-color production values we normally make use of. While it was easy to decide to produce a black-and-white issue, the blank white cover was more of a gamble. The logo was blind-embossed and a match-gray shadow was added to aid the illusion of depth. The monthly "Get Wired" message, which is usually produced in a foreign language, was rendered in Braille. This issue, with no words or pictures on the cover, has turned out to be our biggest seller.

Wired 3.01

ENTIRE ISSUE

Designers: John Plunkett, Thomas Schneider, Eric Courtemanche, Andrea Jenkins
Design Directors: John Plunkett, Thomas Schneider
Design Firm: Plunkett + Kuhr/*Wired* Magazine
Client/Publisher: *Wired* Magazine
Printer: Danbury Printing and Litho

selections by

jan van toorn

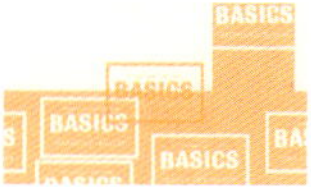

RADIO LISTENER'S WARNING
EFT OF THE DIAL
PUMA
Sexual Slang
Alan Richter, Ph.D.
SCHOOL OF DESIGN
LANDSCAPE ARCHITECTURE
THE INFORMATION
MARTIN AMIS
COLORS
AIDS
ASIA
The Crystal Goblet
Spit
MORE PARTNERS
LESS WASTE
Out of the Mouths of Babes
Women's humor is a tradition
TAX
The Los Angeles Experiment
Attitude
High Five
MONEY
IS JUST A TYPE OF INFORMATION
Morphosis
reinsur-
ance is
boring
Go
ON

jan van toorn

My continuing fascination with communication design is related to the intellectual challenge that I recognize in all forms of public communication. In fact, I have never been interested in design for its own sake. What fascinates me is the way it relates information and what it engenders within the social and symbolic contexts of society. For me, the most important motive behind creating a product is that it should, as much as possible, live up to my ideas about the function of the public sphere as a collective interest.

I am curious about the way designers tackle this issue in a media situation that is more in keeping with global reality, and that curiosity led me – a "spoiled" Dutch designer – to agree to be a member of the jury of the Eighteenth Annual 100 Show. The task was anything but disappointing. The submissions, as well as my discussions with the staff of the American Center for Design and fellow jury members, have given me a much clearer picture of contemporary design approaches in the United States, although I noticed that quite a number of interesting colleagues were not represented.

While I was judging, I found myself directly confronted with the new ways by which the information economy is altering the delicate balance between the makers of products and the consumers of these products. That is, design is a product, and as a product, it affects cultural signification and the formation of political opinion – often with disastrous consequences. Interestingly, during the judging, I was able to look at the extent to which designers can still satisfy the yearning to insert their own voices in the work – voices that often make an oppositional contribution to the public debate on social and cultural reality.

In the Netherlands, government funding in the public sector allows us to nurture the dream of a purely aesthetic and/or functionalist counter-symbolism, separate from the spectacular "void" of the culture industry. Conversely, the naked reality of the United States makes it very clear that, for a long time now, this orientation has fallen short. We can no longer express a critical distance with respect to the commodity culture in this way. We are too close. Virtual hype has accelerated the adoption of new forms at such a speed that these forms are hollow almost from their inception. This is the current paradox of design. In my view, the media provide a public forum for debating the common interest – a sphere in which images could be constructed that counteract or expose the images created by powerful social groups and special interests. Yet the dominantly commercial "production relationships" of those very same media (i.e., the changed relationship between producers and intellectual mediators) lead to the degeneration of all forms of visual information.

That realization led me to make selections that are interesting, in my view, for formal aesthetic reasons but about whose content and approach to the public I have misgivings. The selections encompass a spectrum of "good design." Some are noncritical contributions (i.e., they attempt to design without trying to engage in the relationship between client and audience.) Others are attempts at imminent criticism that choose positions based on social consciousness. To clarify the considerations that played a role in my selection process, I arranged the pieces in three categories.

The first category (pp.114–125) consists of designers whose craftsmanship is quite admirable but who are, in my opinion, not sufficiently aware of the significance of their work within a broader cultural context. Although these pieces seemingly incorporate a controversial aesthetic or theme, the programmatic attitude is largely formally aesthetic or technological, and the designers do not question the meaning of their own mediation in social and symbolic terms. The formal quality of this type of design gives it a significant role in the creation and reinforcement of affirmative images of the world, in the manufacture of consent, and in the positioning of established economic, political, and institutional interests.

The second group (pp.126–131) is important because I wish to emphasize that the public services offered by governments and nonprofit organizations provide real opportunities to take nonauthoritarian, reflexive approaches. Clients from this sector are more likely to be socially motivated, even if they, like many designers, are generally unfamiliar with the practical possibilities of a dialogic approach – an approach which engages both designer and audience.

The third group (pp.132–143) consists of deliberate individual quests to escape the one-dimensional rhetoric of the profession and the media, as seen in the attention paid to the content of the message and the attempt to confront the audience in a more argumentative fashion.

The problem encountered by the second and third categories holds the key to a design that aspires to go beyond the culture of total publicity that imprisons designers in the first category. It is important to remember that design has profited to an unbelievable extent from the capitalist economy's ingrained culture of aesthetic consumption. The dissemination of ideas and goods emphasizes the image of the product and producer, instead of emphasizing the idea's or good's production and underlying intentions. As a result, professional mediation has adapted to the ideological and strategic considerations of the client, so that the real space for making the world readable is being restricted to the attractive staging of commerce and power. A primarily economic orientation has penetrated deeply into the content and form of the symbolic, and design appears to have forgotten the conditions, methods, and means of critical practice.

The pieces in the last two categories of my selection can be viewed as attempts to escape this condition. They show a willingness "to share fate, a mentality that replaces the politics of cultural differentiation by a politics of sociality."[1] For designers, the only possibility of revitalizing such a "utopian" position indeed does lie in a more realistic relationship with the world and in the more autonomous role of mediation. That means politicizing one's own actions, about which most practicing intellectuals are ambivalent. Such ambivalence primarily arises from a general lack of reflection on the conditions that create opportunities for politicizing humanistic and democratic intentions. That is why designers do not realize that the politicization of design is entirely different from a political design or designer but instead has everything to do with a critical attitude toward the process of cultural signification — a field currently dominated by constant institutional and disciplinary intervention.

Design needs to recover a serious and contemporary orientation toward the public interest, allowing the designer to develop communicative strategies for a more democratic functioning of the public sphere. These strategies must be based on a personal and/or collective oppositional agenda. That implies accepting the idea that you have to place yourself within the triangular relationship formed by the interests of the client, professional action, and the public, taking into account the dialectics of innovation and tradition in the social context. Only when designers accept these responsibilities can we overcome the fictions of objectivity and subjectivity, of neutral mediation and authoritarian interference, and of individual action as an act of personal hermetic creation. We forget that individual beliefs and desires are governed by social and cultural fabrications, by regimes of power, by economy, by law, by education, by language, etc.

By articulating an independent position within the trialectic of the commission situation, designers can create a distance between themselves and the content and intentions of the client, thereby changing the character of the message entirely. Depending on the nature of the information and the situation, such a point of view allows the mediator to embed commentary at multiple levels. Unlike the pursuit of harmony or agreement between the various interests, the designer's intervention in this case must be seen as narrative interaction[2], making it possible to experience the interaction between the mediator's perspective and the client's. This non-neutral but polyphonic cohesion invites the receiver to interpret the message actively.

It is only through this form of operational criticism that designers truly become co-authors and editors (or, in the event that they are working for themselves, authors and directors), and that design can play a role in opening up new public space in the media. This approach unavoidably leads to a more meaningful use of visual language, because that is what the multidimensionality of the position demands. It will teach us how to deal with more differentiated modes of communication, like the complementary use of language within the pictorial and literary reflexive traditions, now almost forgotten by design. What is perhaps equally important is that it can contribute to a new public symbolism in which, at last, the visual and conceptual are once again viewed as equivalent forms of human communication.

1 Scott Lash, during the symposium "Toward a Theory of the Image," Jan van Eyck Akademie, Maastricht, 1995.

2 Compare Berthold Brecht's "epic theater" and the narrative structure of the New Journalism.

jan van toorn

CATEGORY 1

I have arranged my selections into three categories. The first group, starting with *Colors*, is about my schizophrenia as a designer. I'm fascinated, on the one hand, by the highly professional and aesthetic aspects of good design, and irritated, on the other hand, by the complete lack of any realistic orientation of design to the complexities of the world today. *Colors*, for me, is exemplary of how the acceptance of the simplistic representations of market, politics, and bureaucracy has paralyzed design's dialectical notion of socio-political innovation and tradition. –jvt

entrant's comments

Ignorance is dangerous. The purpose of the AIDS issue was to give young people in 80 countries the facts about HIV, which they need to protect themselves and others from AIDS and from the prejudice that too often comes with it. The first section explains AIDS, HIV, and how to avoid infection in a simple, almost clinical way. Next is a collection of more magazine-like stories, which directly and indirectly talk about the culture of AIDS. Working with Tibor [Kalman, editor-in-chief], we developed a design for the four bilingual editions, which was guided both by the life-and-death information being conveyed and respect for our readers' intelligence.

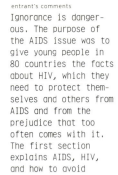

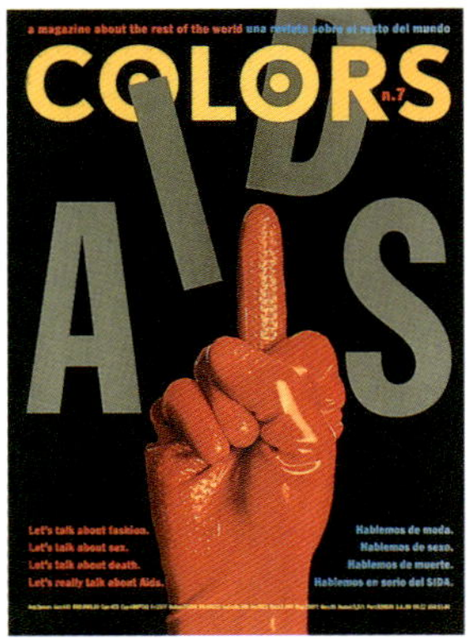

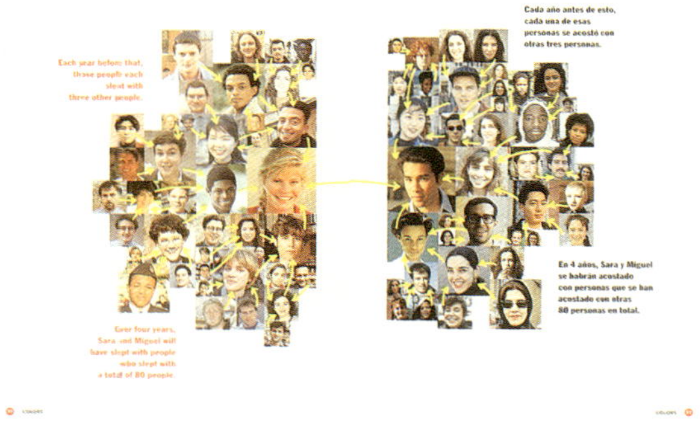

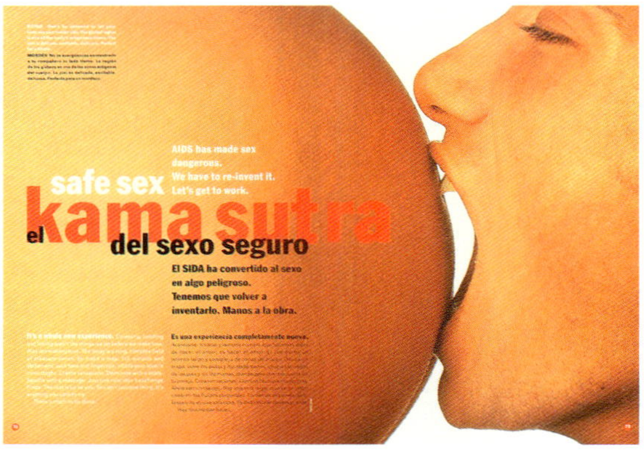

Colors 7: AIDS

MAGAZINE

Art Director : Scott Stowell
Associate Designer : Leslie Mello
Writers : Danny Abelson, Alex Marashian
Photographers : various
Client/Publisher : Colors Communications Srl
Typographers : Scott Stowell, Leslie Mello, Jose Luis Castilla Civit, Uta Thomeczek
Printer : Elcograph SpA, Como
Separator : Adda, Como

jan van toorn

CATEGORY 1

As a designer, I'm jealous of the creativity and smart "connoisseurship' of this piece by Allen Hori. The unexpected combinations in the montage of images, texts, and forms make it intriguing to look at. However, the paradoxical possibilities for interpretation of its own message, "calculated to reveal rather than to hide the beautiful thing which it was meant to contain," do not go beyond the formal aesthetic level. As long as you continue to see the world as something harmonious, there is no need to escape from the classical coherence of the form.

–jvt

entrant's comments

The biggest intrigue in responding to something that has had, and continues to have, such a long life of its own is the observation of a cycle becoming nearly complete in and of itself – similar to the formation of a vacuum, where its seal of containment allows for no further exchange. The following list outlines my movement around this vacuum:

functioning
  discrepancies
containing, revealing illusiveness,
  transparency
obviated gender
anomaly
cloaked critiques
  of connoisseurship
quixotic assumptions
knowing palate
bitter tonic
salt, spit

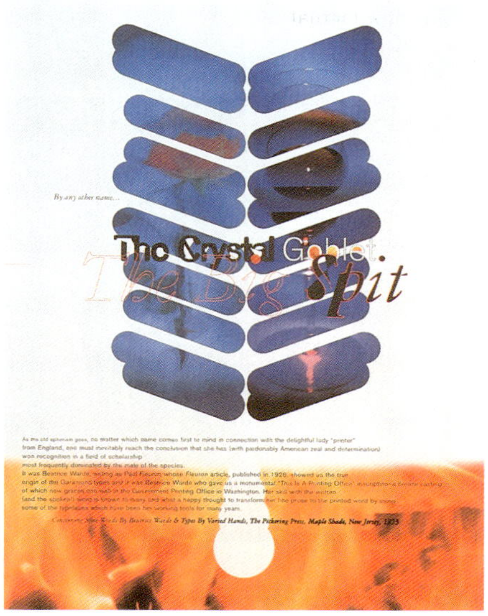

The Crystal Goblet – The Big Spit

AD

Designer: Allen Hori
Photographer: Christopher Weil
Design Firm: Bates Hori
Client/Publisher: Mohawk Paper
Typographer: Allen Hori
Printer: Diversified Graphics
Paper: Mohawk Vellum

CATEGORY 1

These booklets are done perfectly. The extent to which their "new form" fits in with the more conventional typography of the cassettes is striking. At the same time, they are sufficiently distinctive in terms of style and illustrations to briefly draw our attention as consumers to the product again. After all, that is what they are meant to do. There is hardly any new factual information. –jvt

Team TDK #2 – Magnetics

BOOKLET

Designer : Kirk James
Design Director : Steve Farrar
Writer : in-house
Illustrators : various
Photographers : various
Design Firm : Jager Di Paola Kemp Design
Client/Publisher : TDK
Typographer : in-house
Printer : DePalma Printing
Creative Director : Michael Jager
Paper : Potlatch Vintage Gloss 70 lb. Text

entrant's comments

TDK – The Truth Promos. These booklets are designed to educate readers about the features and benefits of TDK's companion tape products in a way that makes the typically stale information dynamic and memorable. Targeted retail managers and salespeople in music stores tend to be young, hip, and have a heightened awareness of design. In order to cut through the clutter of images found in these stores and to secure the attention of opinion leaders on the sales floor, the design details and production quality had to rise far above the stream of typical promotions and industry junk mail. Education, distinction, and brand loyalty are our ultimate goals.

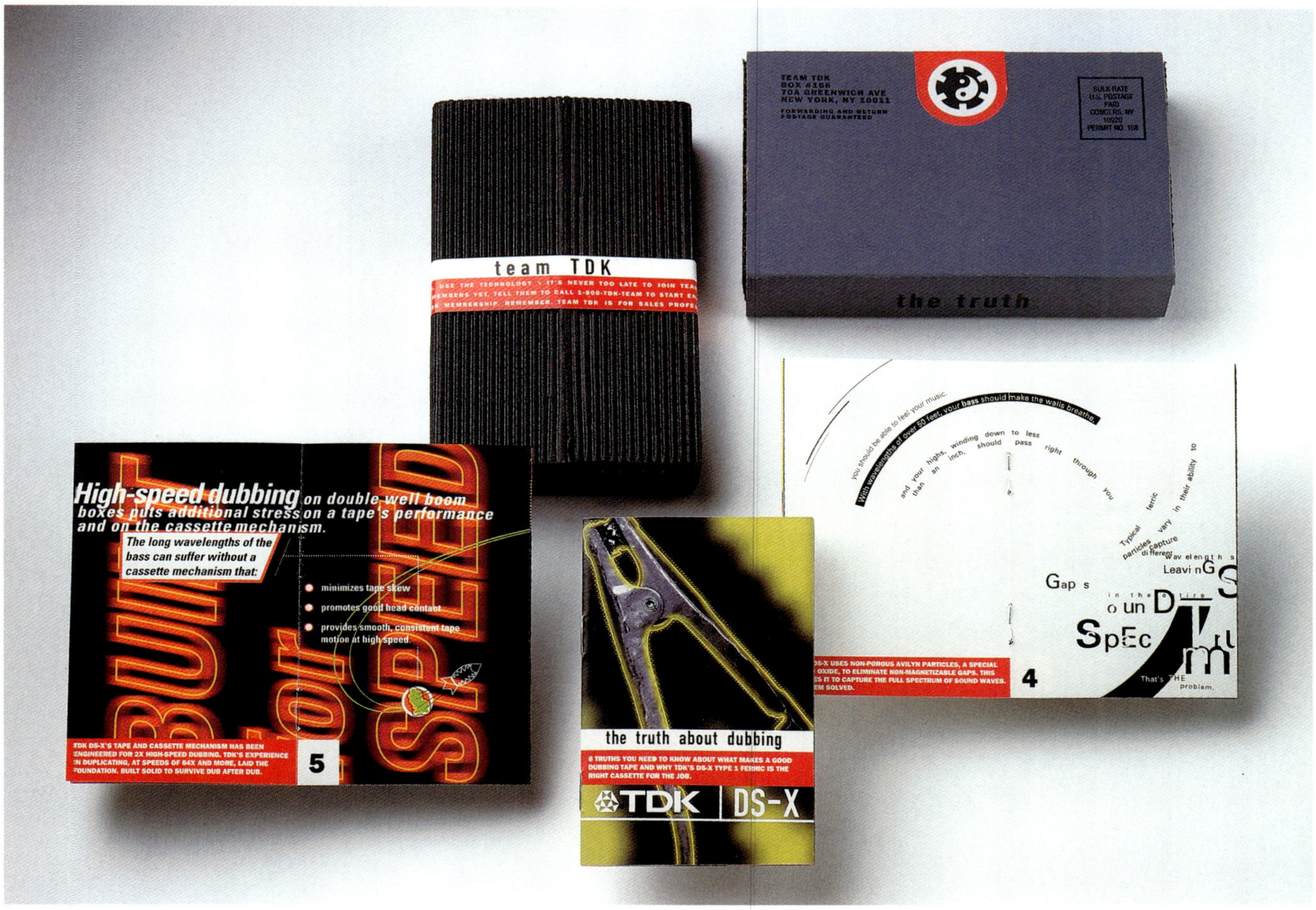

Team TDK #3 – Dubbing

BOOKLET

Designer: Richard Curren
Design Director: Steve Farrar
Writer: in-house
Illustrators: various
Photographers: various
Design Firm: Jager Di Paola Kemp Design
Client/Publisher: TDK
Typographer: in-house
Printer: DePalma Printing
Creative Director: Michael Jager
Paper: Potlatch Vintage Gloss 70 lb. Text

jan van toorn

CATEGORY 1

The layout and photography of the Premark annual report establish a clear and convincing identity. They are a perfect response to the product-positioning theme that guides the company's product development, "extraordinary design for everyday living." All the same, the designers' preoccupation with formal quality has prevented them from including any measure of significant distance from that approach. As a result of the lack of a wider cultural perspective, the design fits in precisely with the company strategy, "leveraging a high worldwide brand awareness."

–jvt

entrant's comments

Premark manufactures and markets major brand-name products: Tupperware, Hobart, Wilsonart, Florida Tile, West Bend, to name a few. That's its story. The products are very recognizable and often well-designed. Make the product the hero and let the design be simple.

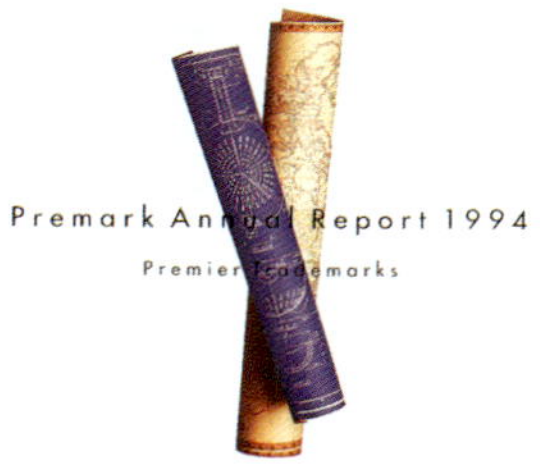

Premark 1994

ANNUAL REPORT

Designers : Greg Samata, Dan Kraemer
Design Director : Greg Samata
Writers : Isabelle Goossen, Christine Hanneman
Photographer : Sandro Miller
Design Firm : SamataMason Inc.
Client/Publisher : Premark International Inc.
Typographers : Dan Kraemer/SamataMason Inc.
Printer : Anderson Lithograph
Separator : Anderson Lithograph
Paper : Simpson Kashmir, Champion Benefit Squash

jan van toorn

CATEGORY 1

What applies to this *Wired* Intro and Electric Word spreads (next page) applies to the whole magazine. They are beautifully made, with great craftsmanship and a genuine engagement in the exploration of the possibilities of the electronic revolution. Nevertheless, the question of the meaning of the images that are produced reminds me of some words by Jean-Luc Godard: "There are hardly any images left today, only clichés. There are even fewer images nowadays than in the Middle Ages." In this respect, many designers for multimedia practice a form of self-censorship with regard to content. Their fascination with the technology is generally expressed in a closed, harmonious vernacular.

–jvt

entrant's comments

Each issue of *Wired* begins with a quote that strikes us as the single-most important or provocative idea in that issue. We design these pages as highly visual "advertisements for ideas" in the hope that readers will be led to a story they might otherwise have missed. This quote is from a story on two physicists who apply their ideas regarding chaos theory to predicting market trends – hacking Wall Street, so to speak.

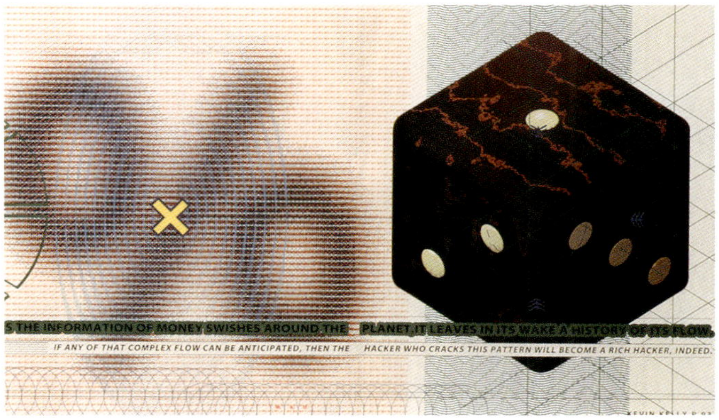

Wired 2.07 Intro

MAGAZINE SPREAD

Designers : John Plunkett, Erik Adigard
Writer : Kevin Kelly
Design Directors : John Plunkett, Thomas Schneider
Illustrator : Erik Adigard M.A.D.
Design Firm : Plunkett + Kuhr/*Wired* Magazine
Client/Publisher : *Wired* Magazine
Printer : Danbury Printing & Litho

jan van toorn

also selected by

Caryn Aono, see p.23

CATEGORY 1

See previous page.

entrant's comments

"Electric Word" is a monthly department of late-breaking news and gossip. (We call it "bulletins from the frontlines of the digital revolution.") We use this section to try to reflect in print the feeling of navigating through the Net by experimenting with a less-linear-than-normal presentation of information. Text is not anchored to a grid and headlines are not necessarily where one expects to find them. In addition, the gossip column slices horizontally through the pages and stories, so that, in the end, we have a collection of seemingly random bits floating across a series of pages.

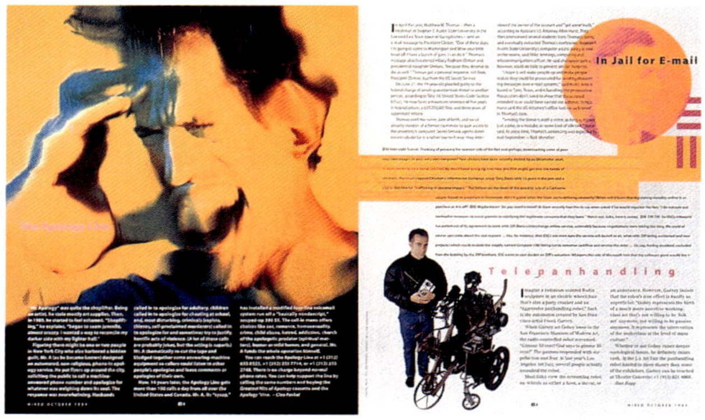

Wired 2.10 Electric Word

MAGAZINE SPREAD

Designer : John Plunkett

Design Directors : John Plunkett, Thomas Schneider

Design Firm : Plunkett + Kuhr/*Wired* Magazine

Client/Publisher : *Wired* Magazine

Printer : Danbury Printing & Litho

jan van toorn

CATEGORY 1

A well-made campaign in every respect. It is interestirg because it combines functionalist elements with elements of a more everyday style. Still, I was struck by the ncn-pictorial syntax of the form. The visual apɔroach is a typical product of the rational and descriptive tradition of design, so that the designers do not have to ask themselves what they think of the subject. –jvt

entrant's comments

After a two-year hiatus, the Minnesota chapter of the American Institute of Graphic Design brought back its regional design show. The goal of the show was to re-evaluate all aspects of the typical design-show process. "Back to Basics" was the theme. The Duffy team's task was to convey this idea in all of the show's support materials. We did this by using imagery inspired by children's schoolbooks and art education texts. For example, the evolution of a designer is shown in a chart illustrating the progression from simple scribbles in kindergarten to books and logos as professionals. Spontaneous illustrations, simple paper, bold typography, rudimentary printing techniques, and sometimes awkward compositions were just a few of the ways we reinforced the "Basics" concept and depicted the process of design.

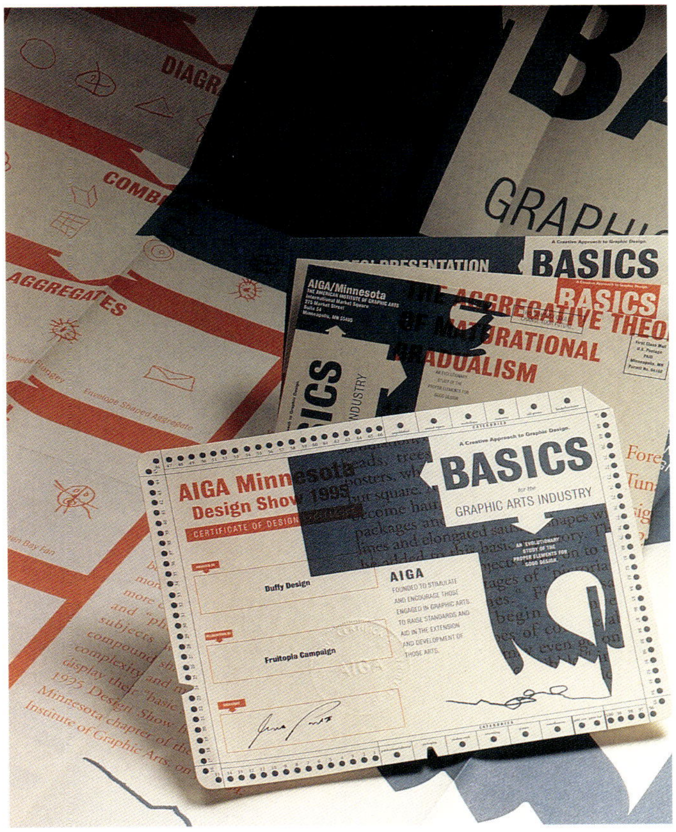

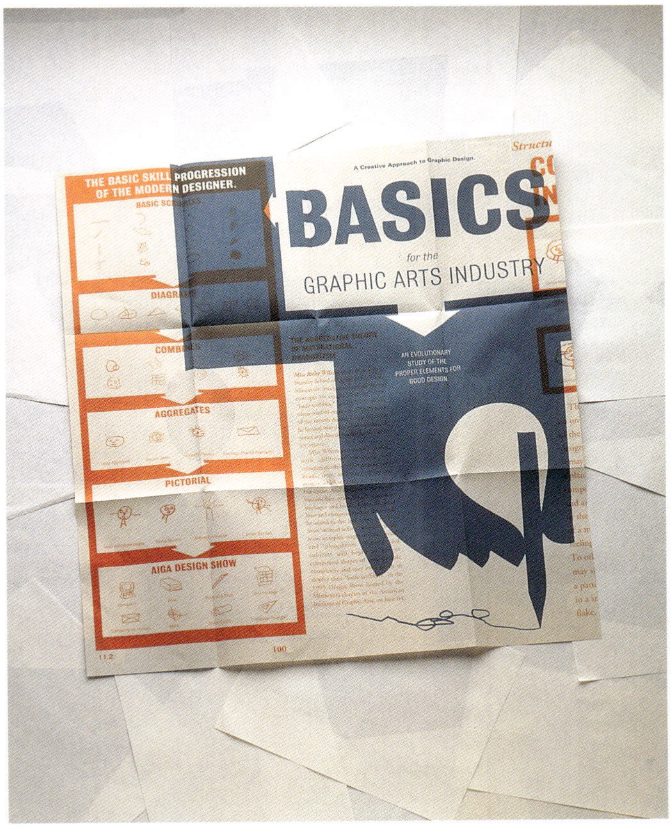

AIGA Back to Basics

CAMPAIGN

Designer : Duffy Team
Design Firm : Duffy Design
Client/Publisher : American Institute of Graphic Arts, Minnesota
Printer : various

jan van toorn

CATEGORY 1

This poster appeals to me because of the meticulous way it deals with images and text. The smaller text reads, "Radio listener's warning. Listening to this new and improved half hour of alternative music, exclusive interviews and performances may reverse the flow of enzymes in your body." Somewhat later I discovered that MTV published this poster, which made it questionable for me. The alternatives of MTV, like those of a magazine such as *Colors*, with their simple representations of difference as a means for social improvement, devoid of political content and implications, make me hesitate.

–jvt

Left of the Dial

POSTER

Designer : Christopher Davis
Writer : David Lanfair
Design Firm : MTV Off-Air Creative
Client/Publisher : MTV: Music Television
Printer : Manhattan Color Graphics

entrant's comments

The "alternative nation's" poster posed a design problem that was social in context. The idea of "alternative" has been largely accepted by mainstream culture. So the word no longer means what it did in the '80s. Likewise, current so-called "cutting-edge" design has become increasingly familiar. To some insiders, this genre has become a stereotype, thereby losing its power to position itself as "alternative." So I approached the problem inversely, poking fun at mainstream images and satirizing middle-class values. The problem for me became less about design and more about social identity.

jan van toorn

also selected by Marlene McCarty, see p.80

CATEGORY 1

A lot of fun went into making this appealing cover. I like the directness of this kind of design, though I believe that sexual slang goes much further than what the cover shows. Yet another piece of evidence that it is high time for designers to break out of the mental world which is confined to universal stereotypes. -jv:

entrant's comments

Here are just a few entries from this indispensable little treasury: Bald-headed hermit, Bazoongas, Beat-the-bishop, Best leg of three, Clapper-clangers, Dance-the-mattress-jig, Doctor Johnson, Eat-at-the-Y, Exercise-the-ferret, Firkytoodle, Flesh-cushions, Flip-Flaps, Flog-the-log, Flopper-stoppers, Gamahoochie, Glory hole, Go-trom-boning, Gorilla salad, Lapland, Mazola party, Nookie-bookie and Hairburger. Form follows content. Hubba-hubba!

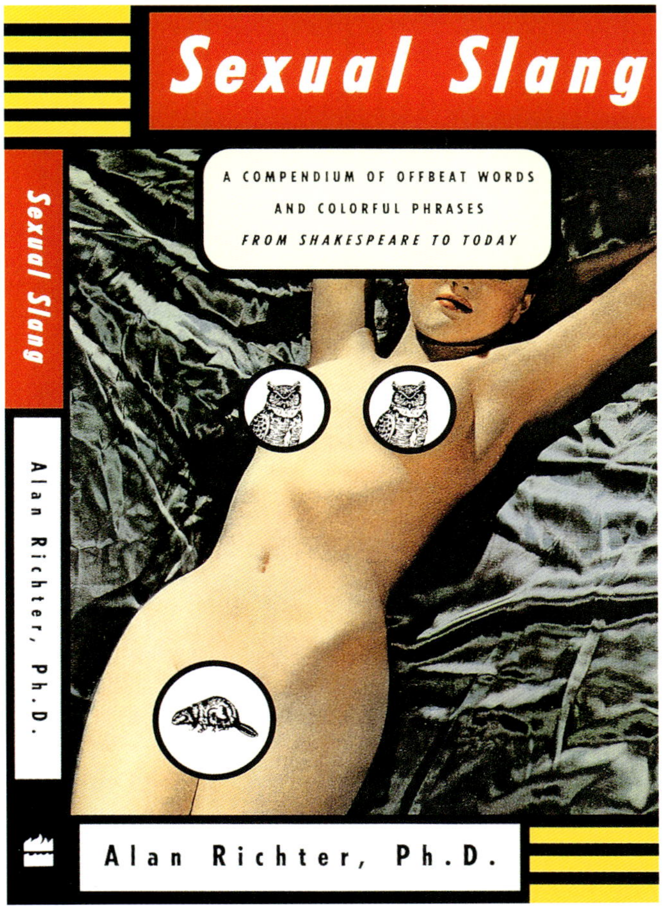

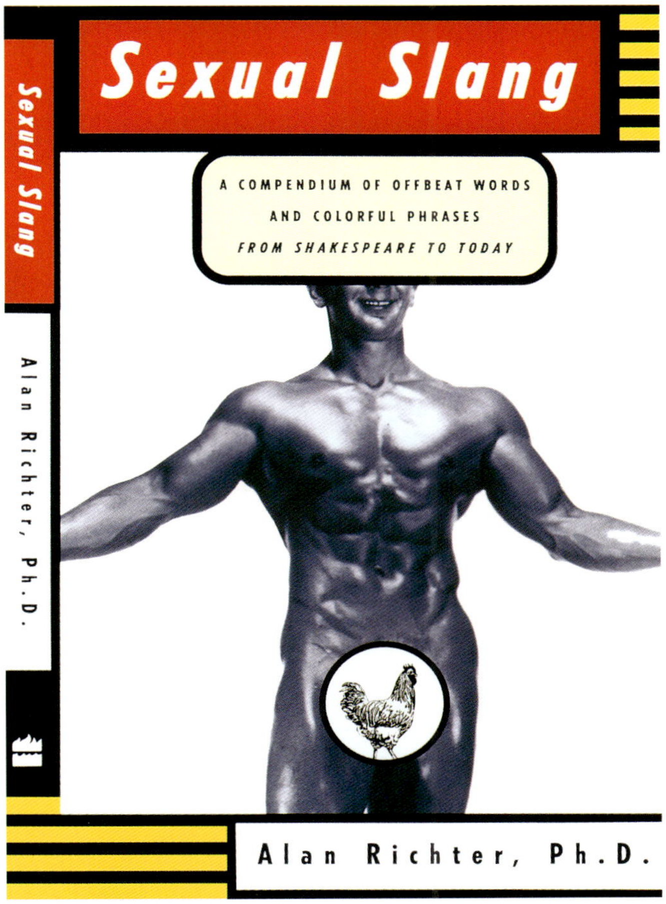

Sexual Slang

BOOK COVER

Designer : Chip Kidd
Design Firm : Chip Kidddesign
Client/Publisher : HarperCollins
Printer : Coral Graphics

jan van toorn

also selected by Marlene McCarty, see p.81

CATEGORY 1

An annual report that appeals to me because it is rather cheeky. The design is straightforward in its handling of photography, diagrams, and other typographic elements, such as borders, etc. It continually goes a bit further than you would expect on the basis of purely stylistic grounds. The designer displays a certain irony, and is evidently also exploring the limits of the content of the commission. –jvt

entrant's comments

Reinsurance is about as interesting to most people as incontinence products and frozen peas. It's not terribly different for investors and analysts, who see it as a highly cyclical business, and, worse yet, a commodity product. The Zurich Reinsurance Centre (ZRC) annual report is designed as a sledgehammer to break down this wall of preconceptions and position our client as an innovative, dynamic growth company in a milquetoast industry.

ZRC Not Boring

ANNUAL REPORT

Designer : James Pettus
Design Directors : James Pettus, David Dunkleberger, Frank Oswald
Writer : Frank Oswald
Photographers : F. Scott Schafer, Christopher Hawker
Design Firm : WYD Design, Inc.
Client/Publisher : Zurich Reinsurance Centre
Typographer : James Pettus
Printer : Allied Printing Services, Inc.
Separator : Allied Printing Services, Inc.
Paper : Simpson Kashmir

jan van toorn

also selected by
Caryn Aono, see p.26 and Marlene McCarty, see p.87

CATEGORY 1

I hesitated for a long time before I chose this. I did it all the same because the design is so enthusiastic and departs considerably from the orthodox way in which colleges present themselves. It is freer and targets the (female) students instead of the parents. With regard to meaning, the design and the pictures conform pretty much to *petit bourgeois* education geared to the status quo. To quote the brochure, "Yet out in the 'real world' those graduates enjoy more than their share of wealth and power."

–jvt

entrant's comments

In response to a gradual drop-off in enrollment, Pine Manor College was looking to make a radical departure in how its viewbook read and looked. The viewbook was reeingineered to appeal to the prospective student rather than the parent. It takes into consideration the profile of the typical PMC student, both academically and socially. The viewbook uses the layout and writing style of teen magazines, such as *Sassy* and *Seventeen* as its model.

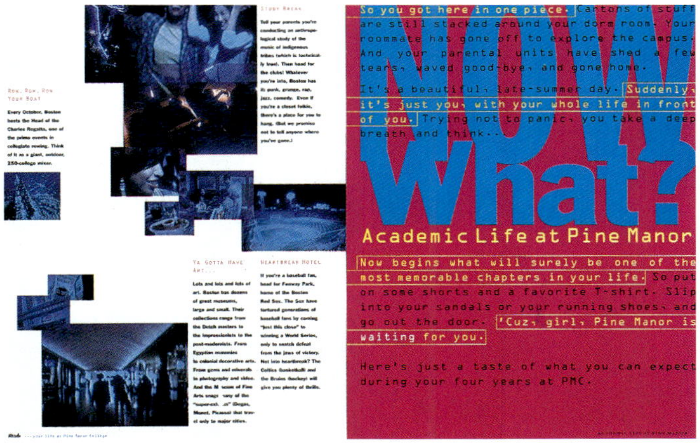

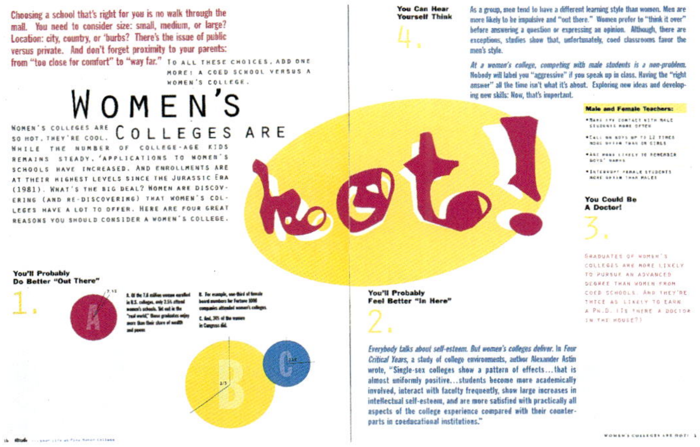

Attitude – Pine Manor College

VIEWBOOK

Designer : Lee Allen Kreindel
Design Director : Lee Allen Kreindel
Writer : Christine Kane
Photographers : Molly Lynch, Charles Barclay Reeves
Illustrators : Diane Bigda, James Kraus, Jeff Tate
Design Firm : Lee Allen Kreindel Graphic Design
Client/Publisher : Pine Manor College
Typographer : Lee Allen Kreindel
Printer : Dynagraf, Inc.
Separator : Dynagraf, Inc.
Paper : Repap Multiffect Gloss Text and Cover

jan van toorn

CATEGORY 2

My second category includes projects that serve a common interest. I have grouped them together here because, in one way or another, they deliberately tackle the mentality and meaning of the subject. They are all modest in their formal solutions, but display a good deal of variety in the way they display their designers' commitment. The latter is convincingly conveyed by the design for the annual report of the United Nations Office of Project Services. In particular, the selection and distribution of the photographs indicate that the designers see their own intermediary role as witnesses, rather than as the providers of an alibi for institutional policy.

–jvt

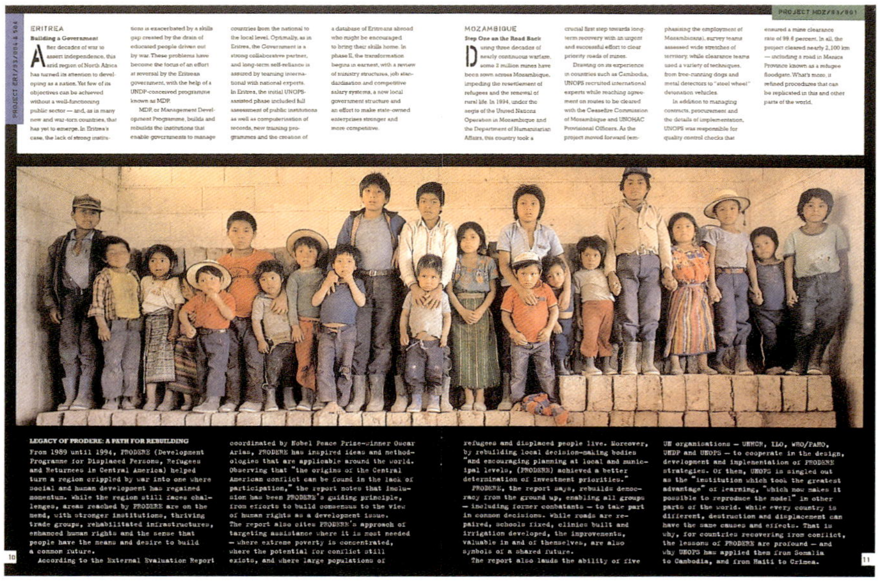

entrant's comments

The United Nations Office for Project Services (UNOPS) 1994 Annual Report is a powerful and extremely energetic book. The objective was to produce an exciting, colorful annual report that would tell about the global efforts of UNOPS through which, with limited funds, local needs are effectively matched with the right national and international expertise. Emerson, Wajdowicz Studios art-directed, designed, and produced an unexpected book (in three languages). Its rhythm and original photojournalistic design approach feature powerful, sometimes astonishing photos, and the appropriate, unpretentious typography of a report from the front.

United Nations Office for Project Services 1994

ANNUAL REPORT

Designers : Lisa LaRochelle, Jurek Wajdowicz

Design Director : Jurek Wajdowicz

Photographers : various

Design Firm : Emerson, Wajdowicz Studios, Inc.

Client/Publisher : United Nations Office for Project Services

Typographer : Emerson, Wajdowicz Studios, Inc.

jan van toorn

CATEGORY 2

As in The United Nations Office for Project Services 1994 annual report, this report also shows where the designers stand. Without an exaggerated propensity toward form, they articulate their support by means of typographic accents determined by the content, and by the selection, framing, and graphic treatment of the photographs. –jvt

entrant's comments

The 1994 global report for the Trickle Up Program has elegance, effectiveness, and beautiful simplicity that mirror the elegance of the practical solutions, simplicity of structure, and effectiveness of the Trickle Up Program. A non-governmental international organization, it is one of the world's proven programs to defeat poverty. The format and content of the global report feature real achievements and beneficiaries of the worldwide program. Its *modus operandi* is clearly presented. Appropriately, there is nothing superfluous or wasted in the design of this report.

Trickle Up Program 1994

GLOBAL REPORT

Designers : Lisa LaRochelle, Jurek Wajdowicz
Design Director : Jurek Wajdowicz
Photographers : various
Design Firm : Emerson, Wajdowicz Studios, Inc.
Client/Publisher : Trickle Up Program
Typographer : Emerson, Wajdowicz Studios, Inc.
Printer : H. MacDonald Printing

also selected by
Marlene McCarty, see p.78

CATEGORY 2

This annual report, by the same designers as the Trickle Up Program 1994 global report and the United Nations Office for Project Services 1994 annual report (see previous two pages), shows that it is not always necessary for design presence to establish an identity for a subject you believe in. Of course, the appeal that this holds for me is a reaction to the fact that the aesthetic overload of design meditation stands in the way of much more comprehensive and unbiased provision of information. –jvt

entrant's comments

The United Nations Development Fund for Women (UNIFEM) annual report highlights the Fund's commitment to provide financial and technical support to women from developing countries. Emerson, Wajdowicz Studios has designed the UNIFEM annual reports for four consecutive years. The book is pure emotional communication. It is unique, different, and very powerful. We developed a restrained, deceptively simple, almost minimalist design approach incorporating original photos by Sebastião Salgado.

UNIFEM 1993
ANNUAL REPORT

Designers : Lisa LaRochelle, Jurek Wajdowicz
Design Director : Jurek Wajdowicz
Photographer : Sebastião Salgado
Design Firm : Emerson, Wajdowicz Studios, Inc.
Client/Publisher : United Nations Development Fund for Women
Typographer : Emerson, Wajdowicz Studios, Inc.

jan van toorn

CATEGORY 2

This booklet tries to raise awareness among Michigan families to care about their physical condition. It is a good example of the public provision of information in the service of the common good. This is realized by the design and photography in a clear manner that is accessible to all. Still, it is a pity that the design remains tied to a rather conventional idiom, so that the booklet has acquired a more official and detached character than necessary. It seems as if such a good piece of advice does not apply to designers or their clients. -jvt

entrant's comments

This brochure initiated the Michigan Fitness Foundation's capital fundraising efforts. The organization was formed to address the poor health of Michigan residents by raising funds to support fitness programs around the state. Bold colors and typography are used to express both the urgency of the problem and the excitement of a solution: "Stop and Think" (red), "Then Go" (green). This stop/red, go/green motif leads into a problem/solution format, whereby statistical information about poor health is presented in red, and the Foundation's initiatives that can address these issues are presented in green. Color photography shows how anyone can participate in healthful activities.

Michigan Fitness Foundation

BOOKLET

Designer : Kevin Dean Budelmann
Writer : Polly Hewitt
Photographer : David Banta
Design Firm : Square One Design
Client/Publisher : Michigan Fitness Foundation
Typographer : Kevin Budelman
Paper : Consolidated Futura 100 lb. Text
Printer : Superior Colour Graphics
Separator : Superior Colour Graphics

jan van toorn

CATEGORY 2

This small report of the Metro Waste Authority is successful in explaining to everyone in a simple and clear manner what kinds of public services it provides. The design is highly professional. It is particularly endearing because it shows that form can be information and argument, instead of a carrier of institutional goods and services that creates a dependency among the consumers. –jvt

entrant's comments

Flash cards emphasize the role that long-term education has in changing attitudes about waste and its impact on the environment. It was also an effective way to describe the Metro Waste Authority and its role in the community, as well as the goals we're all working to achieve. To further make the point, the report was mailed with a pre-labeled envelope and a request to forward it to a local school.

Metro Waste Authority

ANNUAL REPORT

Designers : Steve Pattee, Kelly Stiles
Design Director : Steve Pattee
Writer : Mike Condon
Illustrator : in-house
Design Firm : Pattee Design
Client/Publisher : Metro Waste Authority
Typographers : Steve Pattee, Kelly Stiles
Printer : Holm Graphic
Separator : Holm Graphic
Paper : chipboard, French Dur-o-tone

jan van toorn

entrant's comments

Monday, February 14, 1994, was the fifth anniversary of the Iranian decree calling for the death of British writer Salman Rushdie. On this day, 4,000 participating bookstores inserted the Rushdie flyer into all books sold. In total, 450,000 flyers were distributed throughout the United States. In this way, the organizers and supporters of the statement asked all those who care about books, writers, and freedom of expression to renew their determination to free Rushdie from the trap of the *fatwa*.

also selected by Marlene McCarty, see p.76

CATEGORY 2

This flier reminds us that Salman Rushdie is still a man without a fixed address. For me, the message is so important that I did not even think about its form when I saw it for the first time. After "ON" you immediately start to read. The typography has a great classical perfection, but I have objections to the lack of emotion that it produces. The designer refuses to get involved and conceals his own commitment behind the usage of a fine and universal vocabulary. "NO" instead of "ON" would have been a very different start. –jvt

Rushdie

FLYER

Designer : Stephen Doyle
Creative Directors : Stephen Doyle, William Drenttel
Writer : Don De Lillo
Design Firm : Drenttel Doyle Partners
Printer : Red Ink Productions
Project Initiators : Nan Graham, Paul Auster, Oren Teicher, William Drenttel

entrant's comments

We as readers and designers found the text "pink." Therefore, to our minds, a subtle yet slick, leftist pink cover begets analogous readers. The interior of the book was designed to be straightforward, but also typographically fetishistic. In other words, the design of the book is meant to act as Pepto-Bismol to an important but potentially threatening message.

CATEGORY 3

The third category that I've selected concerns work by designers who approach the subject matter of the assignment from a topical and/or realistic social perspective, and who provoke the imagination in doing so. They are generally to be found in the cultural and educational sector, which provides scope for the development of oppositional strategies and alternative means of expression beyond the official language of design, which is dominated by commerce and the media. It is remarkable that this mentality has little connection with stylistic preferences, but much more with the designer's understanding and interpretation of the theme. In the case of "Building Paranoia," at first sight this seems to be a simple booklet. But the attentive reader and viewer will note how carefully the typography articulates. The selection and framing of the images are equally significant and shed light on the subtle mediation of the author-designer. -jvt

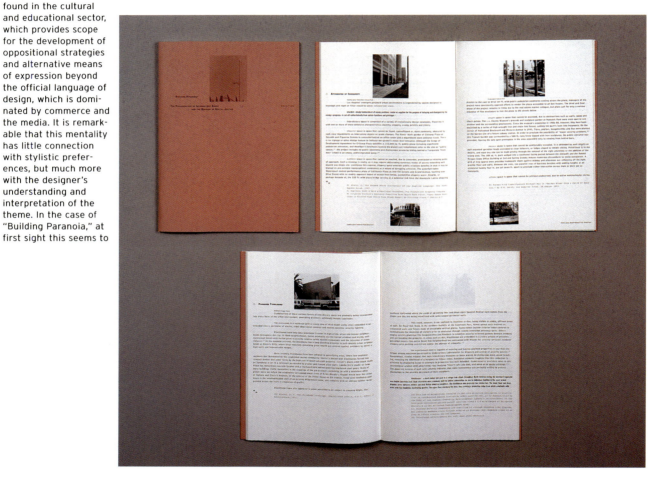

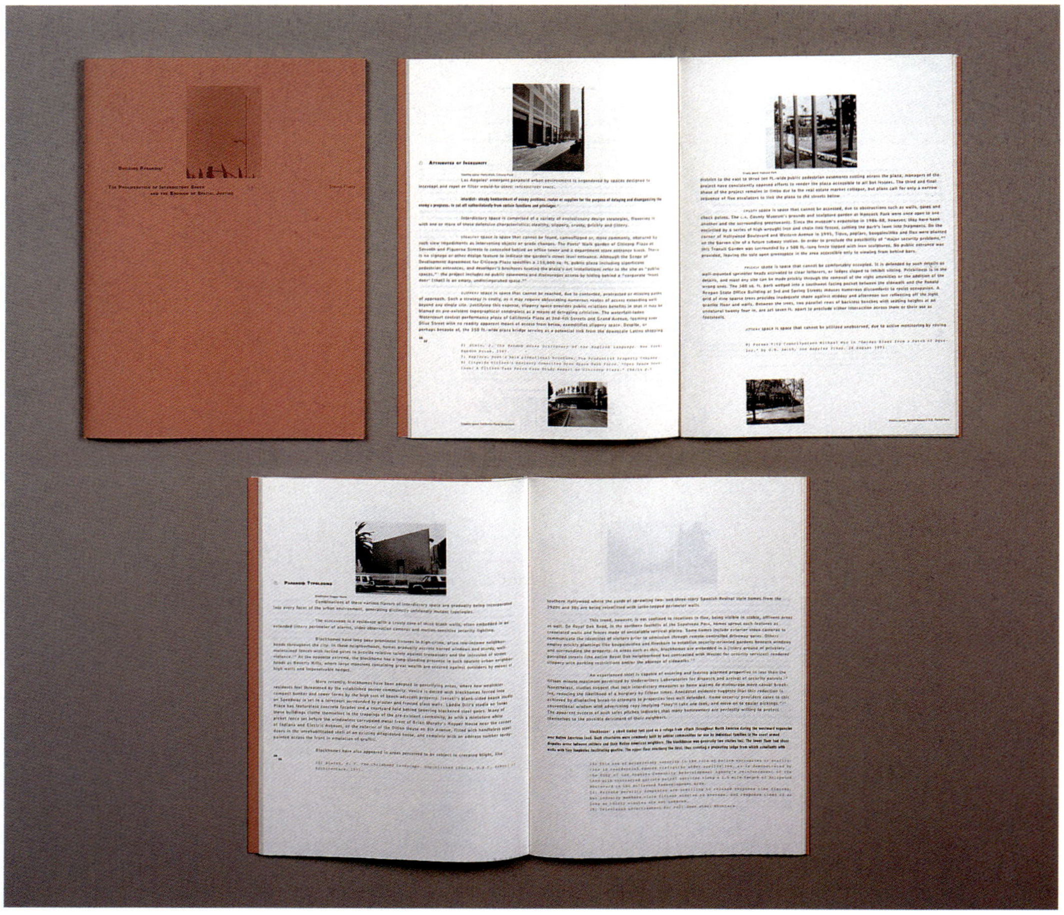

Building Paranoia

BOOKLET

Designers : Nicholas Lowie, Sheridan Lowrey
Design Directors : Nicholas Lowie, Sheridan Lowrey
Writer : Steven Flusty
Photographers : Benny Chan, Patrick Ramsey, Steven Flusty
Design Firm : Lowie, Lowrey Design
Client/Publisher : Los Angeles Forum for Architecture and Urban Design
Typographers : Nicholas Lowie, Sheridan Lowrey
Printer : Typecraft, Inc.
Paper : Matrix Dull 80 lb. Jacket: Ikonofix Matte Mauve 78 lb.Text

jan van toorn

CATEGORY 3

This book is marked by a strong logical orthodoxy, which is expressed in typographic conventions. In its most conventional form, it has a strictly one-dimensional structure and the information is arranged in a fragmented fashion. This idea is largely thrown overboard in this book, which I like very much. It has a complementary structure. In other words, "legible" connections are made at a number of levels without doing violence to the separate functions of reading and viewing. By meaningful intervention, the design offers all kinds of approaches to the content – discursive, pictorial, aesthetic, etc. Through a clever and painstaking montage of the visual material, the individual projects are clearly presented. It is also characteristic that visual comprehension precedes the reading stage, and that the reading stage in turn offers different ways of comprehending the images. Only an empirically trained intuition can handle such a complex communication structure so successfully and enjoyably. –jvt

entrant's comments

At first glance, this book appears to be highly stylized, but all of its formal graphic moves function to enhance the subject matter. This book is about the design process of Morphosis, so photographs are sequenced and positioned to draw attention to architectural composition. Sketches are reproduced on vellum and interleaved between signatures to remind the reader both of the complexity of design development and the expression of architectural ideas through different design phases. Fissures and shifts in typography (between different fonts of Monotype Grotesque) echo visual composition in the photographs, which visually connects the architect's verbal descriptions to the physical phenomena of the architecture depicted in the photographs.

Morphosis: Buildings and Projects, 1989–1992

BOOK

Designers : Lorraine Wild, Whitney Lowe, Andrea Fella
Editor : David Morton
Writers : T. Mayne, R. Weinstein
Photographers : various
Design Firm : ReVerb
Client/Publisher : Rizzoli International Publications
Typographers : Lorraine Wild, Whitney Lowe, Andrea Fella
Printer : Rizzoli

CATEGORY 3

This book is an interesting attempt to breach established disciplinary rules of book typography. Like the subject of the book, it tries to deal with the complexities of freedom and experiment. "In L.A. experimentation can be easy. Doing things you have never done before . . . Freedom is the issue, but so is necessity and structure." The design is an accurate representation of the questions and concerns about the qualities and character of the art of space. All the same, the typography shrinks from accepting the challenge of the creative risks of the architectural project. As a last resort, the designer has given in to formal aesthetic concerns.

–jvt

entrant's comments

The Los Angeles Experiment documents a summer workshop conducted at Southern California Institute of Architecture during the tumultuous period following the Rodney King verdict in 1992. Author and workshop participant Mick McConnell kept a diary of the events happening at these daily sessions and the upheaval exploding in L.A. I sought to visually weave McConnell's personal journal, juxtaposing it against the essay contributions of the professional architects. I found a rich textural base within the student work. I created graphic screens and photo montages to emulate this evocative visual experience within the workshop and events of this time.

LAX: The Los Angeles Experiment

BOOK

Designer : Ron Bartels
Design Director : Ron Bartels
Writers : Mick McConnell, Others
Photographers : Ron Bartels, Mick McConnell, Others
Design Firm : Ron Bartels Design
Client/Publisher : Dennis L. Dollens, SITES/Lumen Books
Typographer : Pickering Boe Graphics
Printer : Thompson-Shore, Inc.
Separator : Pickering Boe Graphics
Paper : Mead 70 lb. Moistrite Matte

jan van toorn

CATEGORY 3

This book is about art in the public space – about art as social intervention. The design reports the project with enthusiasm and commitment. Without denying its structuring role, the typography makes this engagement clear by its visual interference in the formal structure of the book. Photographs and documentation of each project are handled in a different specific manner, which is primarily motivated in terms of substance. A solid attempt to do justice to the content without concealing the designer's own intervention. -jvt

entrant's comments

Culture in Action documents eight, Chicago-based, public art installations. Activist, adventurous, and community-based, the book and the projects within espouse the same ideals – irresolution, collaboration, mutilingualism. Text and images can be read in any order; pictures are fragmented; narratives are typographically varied; and the cumulative effect is an intricate weaving of word and image. Reflecting the project's collaborative process, the equal voices of curator, editor, artist, and designer merge here to create an amalgam greater than the individuals involved.

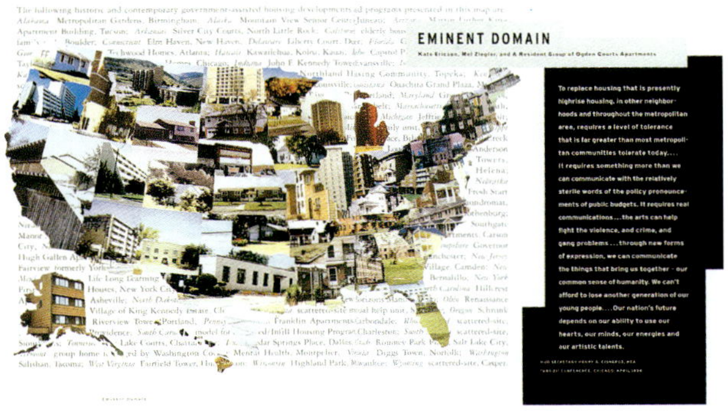

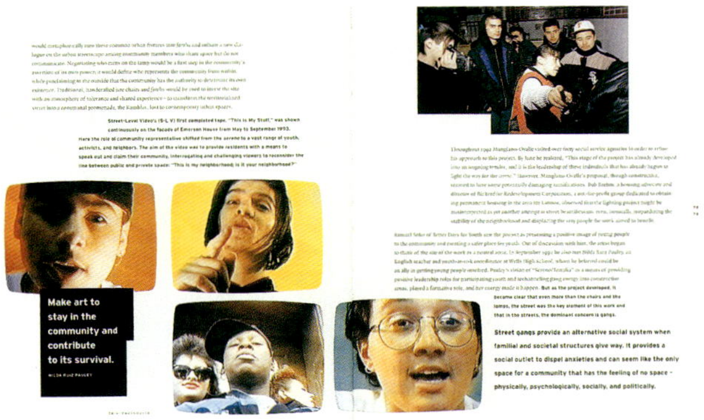

Culture In Action

BOOK

Design Firm : studio blue
Designer : Cheryl Towler Weese
Production Consultant : Katherine Fredrickson
Typographers : Cheryl Towler Weese, JoEllen Kames
Client/Publishers : Sculpture Chicago and Bay Press
Writers : Mary Jane Jacob, Michael Brenson, Eva Olson
Editor : Terry Ann R. Neff
Printer : Toppan, Hong Kong
Separator : Toppan, Hong Kong

jan van toorn

CATEGORY 3

I chose this book because of the cautious but refined treatment of the formal conventions of the novel The limited opportunities to expose the typographic concept of the book are used in a subtle way. The well-considered editing and framing of the photographs on the cover and in the book are essential in this respect, as is the positioning of the columns of text on the page. The designers' modest interaction is just what you would not expect, accompanying the book with an intriguing comment. -jvt

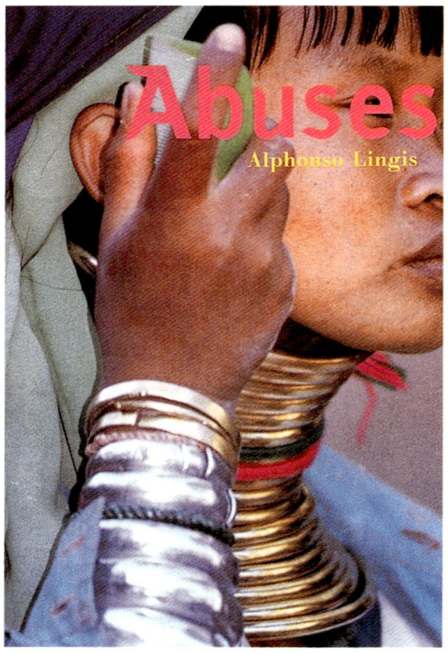

entrant's comments

Lingis juxtaposes the beautiful with the horrific in his essays and photographs, which record and reflect on the sometimes discordant juncture of meetings between himself, a philosopher who teaches in Pennsylvania, and the inhabitants of the diverse non-Western countries that constituted his itinerary. The design attempts to be elegant, yet slightly off, with an asymmetrical grid and the combination of Walbaum – clear and graceful – with Barry Deck's Truth, which is uneven in "color" and menacing in its geometry. The ornamental device that appears on the title page and part titles suggest a boundary – barbed wire, stitches. The cropping and type placement on the jacket show how framing and language intervene between object and gaze.

Lust

The Calypso. It's the biggest theater on Thanon Sukumvit, Bangkok's Fifth Avenue. It has seats for two thousand; expensive seats for the well-heeled and upwardly mobile: Germans and Japanese and Americans and French and Saudis and Kuwaitis and Chinese from Hong Kong and Singapore. There is a cast of a hundred, a different show each night. Palaces, skyscrapers, desert oases drop upon the huge stage in outbursts of electric lightning. The Empress of China appears, seated on the uplifted hands of muscular men whose naked bodies have been metallized in gold greasepaint. Gongs and the *shakuhashi* propel the advance of the traditionally transvestite dancer of Japanese Kabuki theater. Now the stage fills with ballerinas spinning out adagios and minuets from Swan Lake. Mahalia Jackson with rapturous voice sees the sweet chariot comin' to take me home. Mae West comes sashaying in with a chorus line of nuns. Marilyn Monroe resurrects with puckered lips to coo for diamonds; your incredulous fingers want to feel for the wound to be sure. Divas, grande dames, vamps, pop superstars, they are all, of course, men in their early twenties. Now there is the stripper. With rose-blushed complexion, under a sunny cascade of Farrah Fawcett hair, clad in a silver-sequined gown, she uncoils in the cone of a spotlight. She slinks toward you on spike heels, her lips tremble and part, her sultry eyes fix you, her silvered fingernails clutch

Abuses

BOOK

Designers : Somi Kim, Lisa Nugent
Design Director : Somi Kim
Writer : Alphonso Lingis
Photographer : Alphonso Lingis
Design Firm : ReVerb
Client/Publisher : University of California
Typesetting : Braun-Brumfield, Inc.
Printer : Edwards Bros.

jan van toorn

also selected by Caryn Aono, see p.31

CATEGORY 3

The cover of this book does not conform to the norm in terms of design. With respect to content, however, it is very interesting because of the way in which the notion of cultural identity is interpreted. The paradoxes of the Asian-American condition are presented through its straightforward combination of images and of the logo. A substantial introduction to the book by the designers.

–jvt

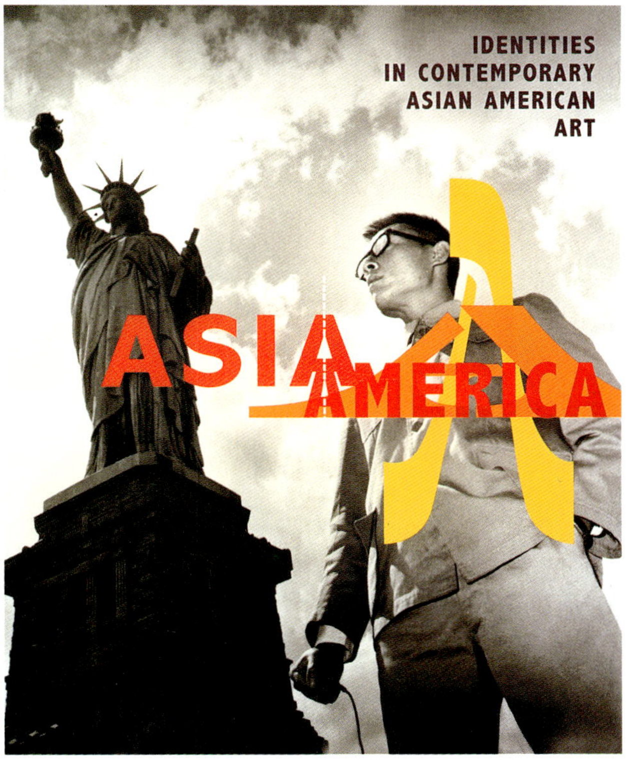

entrant's comments

The artists included in this exhibition show in their work the negotiations that they have undertaken in their respective journeys across a constantly shifting bicultural landscape. Because there are no clear divisions or boundaries, but, rather, multiple perspectives across cultural, historical, and artistic issues, we set up a page grid with a central horizon line defined by certain typographic details, while other elements hug either the top or the bottom of the page. The typefaces used are all sans serifs, playing into the idea of visual difference with a superficial similarity at first glance, which is loosely analogous to the use of one geographic term to describe so many widely varying cultures. Each of the three essays is treated differently, with the typography of the opening spreads referring to border crossings and the multiple voices that shape one's identity. In the cover typography, we tried to refer to non-Western alphabet forms without using stereotypical "thematic" typefaces that mostly derive from Chinese or Japanese characters. A shift occurs in the title treatment in the front matter, reiterating the impossibility of representing the relationship between Asia and America as a fixed form.

Asia/America

BOOK

Designers : Somi Kim, Lorraine Wild, Andrea Fella
Publication Director : Joseph Newland
Writers : M. Machida, V. Desai, J. Tchen
Photographer : assorted
Design Firm : ReVerb
Client/Publisher : The Asia Society Galleries, New York
Typographers : Somi Kim, Lisa Nugent, Andrea Fella
Printer : Typecraft
Separator : Typecraft

also selected by Marlene McCarty, see p.77

CATEGORY 3

A book jacket displaying the book as an object, opened at the title page. It is a familiar alienating photographic effect that allows the viewer to experience the object as object by means of an unusual interaction. Given the title of the book, *The Information,* it may be an understatement regarding the artificial character of reportage. –jvt

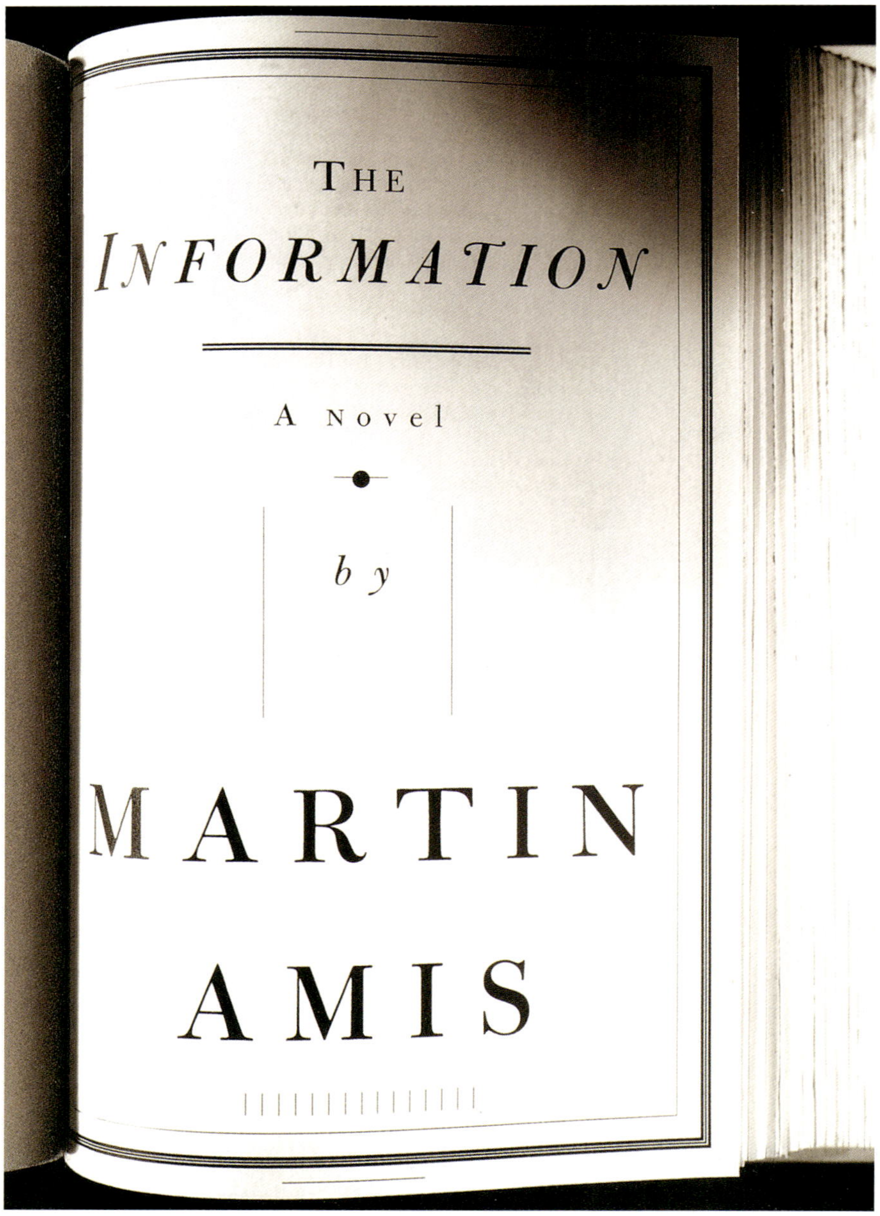

The Information

BOOK COVER

Designer: Chip Kidd
Design Director: Rick Pracher
Writer: Martin Amis
Photographer: Chip Kidd
Design Firm: Chip Kidddesign
Client/Publisher: Harmony Books
Typographer: Chip Kidd
Printer: Coral Graphics

entrant's comments

The Information is a book about books, a writer writing about writers, a product of publishing about publishing. Under the circumstances of such relentless self-referral, it was tempting to proceed with a jacket about jackets, especially since one of the main characters has written a wildly successful utopian novel (though what one should look like is beyond even my imagining). Too trite. Instead, I thought it would be better to make it look like the jacket is missing, thus forcing the viewer to plunge into the text before he or she even picks it up.

CATEGORY 3

This poster is about women's humor as an independent tradition, which is felt to be essential to the understanding of women's experience and self-possession. In a way, the form tries to represent the liberating power and politics of women's humor. I do not think that this is entirely successful. The approach remains stuck, to some extent, in the form, and there is a lot to be read. As a result, the poster is more detached than it was intended to be.

-jvt

entrant's comments

"Out of the Mouths of Babes: The Power and Politics of Women's Humor" campaign is a poster and mailer designed to promote the cultural events for Women's History Month sponsored by the university's Women's Studies Department. The events for the 1995 Bowling Green State University's Women's History Month revolved around humor and feminism. The challenge, as I saw it, was to set up non-condescending settings for humor. The first setting uses imagery from cinema and theater marquees, television, and neon signs. (I selected the typeface Burnout specifically because it is a reference to old neon signage.) The second setting for the poster was comic books. In order to refer to comic books, I used a voice bubble for the title. I selected two process colors, cyan and magenta, to suggest four-color process printing yet stay within a two-color budget. Lastly, I used the naturally colored French Speckletone paper to look like cheap, pulp comic book paper.

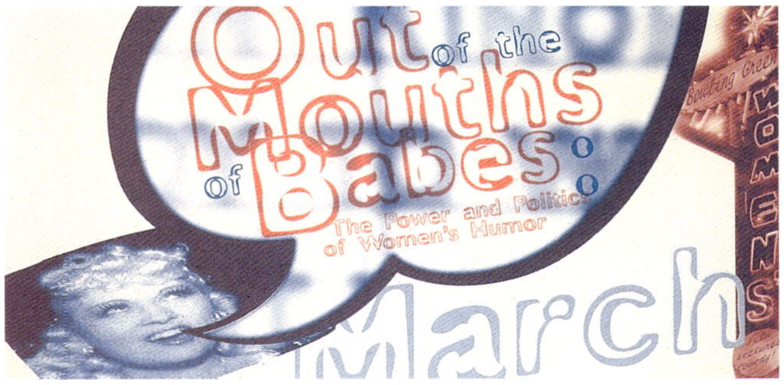

Out of the Mouths of Babes: Women's History Month

PROMOTIONAL CAMPAIGN

Designer : Todd Childers
Design Director : Todd Childers
Writer : Jacqui Nathan
Photographer : uncredited photos from press kit
Illustrator : Todd Childers
Design Firm : Todd Childers Graphic Design
Client/Publisher : Bowling Green State University Women's Studies Department
Typographer : Todd Childers
Printer : Post Printing
Separator : Post Printing
Paper : French Speckletone

jan van toorn

CATEGORY 3

A promotional campaign for graduate studies from a well-intentioned institute, where a serious and adventurous countercurrent has emerged as an alternative to the flood of triviality in disciplines such as design. Although the design is well organized, I am once again struck by the extent to which American critical practice is determined by the discursive tradition. It is primarily the word that is expected to get the message across. The visual structure has an equally literary character. I would like to advocate investing in empirical research on the pictorial traditions. The intellectual integrity and cultural heresy of a place like North Carolina State University can also find its expression in the image. –jvt

entrant's comments

To promote the graduate programs at the School of Design, we developed a versatile and economical system using both sides of a press sheet to produce a poster and a composite brochure. The designers were challenged to visually and verbally articulate each program's philosophy and to negotiate the scale shifts and fragmentation of the poster image within the booklet. The architecture poster-brochure evokes the problematics of space, place, and structure inherent to that discipline. The landscape architecture poster-brochure utilizes the micro/macro theme of humans and the natural environment. The graphic design poster-brochure journeys through different communicative environments – street, text, and video monitor.

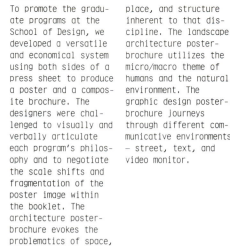

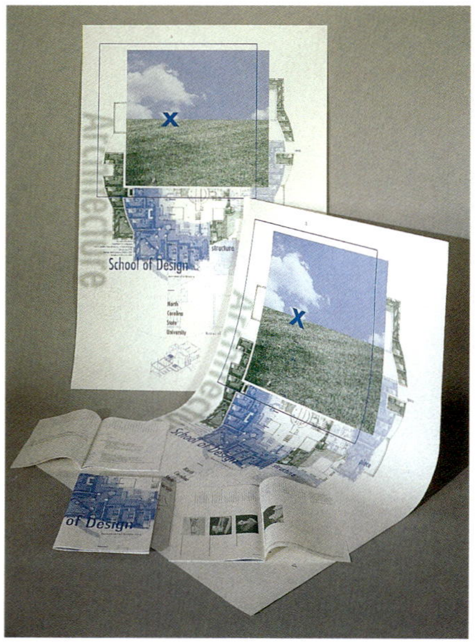

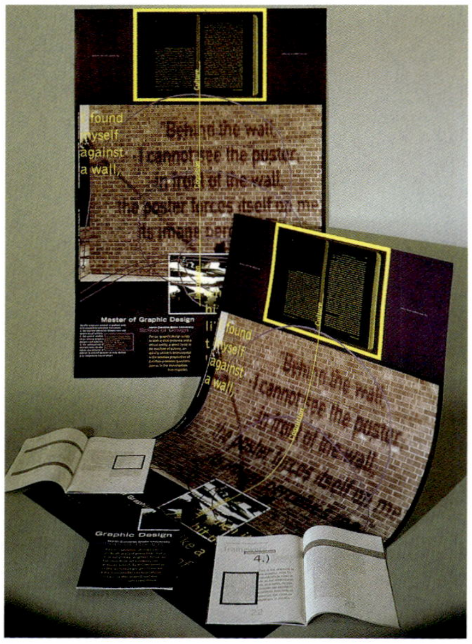

Graduate Studies in Design

PROMOTIONAL CAMPAIGN

Designers : Regina Rowland, Michelle Mar, Andrew Blauvelt, Brad Brechin, Matthias Brendler
Design Director : Andrew Blauvelt
Writers : various
Photographers : various
Design Firm : North Carolina State University Graduate Studio
Client/Publisher : School of Design, North Carolina State University
Typographer : Macintosh
Printer : Theo Davis Sons
Paper : Vintage Velvet Remarque, Hopper Oyster Text

jan van toorn

CATEGORY 3

An interesting attempt to evade the unnecessary detachment of the professional vocabularies in social documentation and reporting. The authors/designers create a plurality of approaches to the material and set it against a background that they have formulated. As a result of this confrontation with the contradictions of the subject, the viewer/ reader is deliberately urged to take a stand. Here, as in Graduate Studies in Design promotional campaign (see p.140), I think the use of images should certainly have been as strong as the treatment of the text. –jvt

entrant's comments

Unspoken is a collaboration between artist Kim Yasuda and me, in a format we call page-specific installation. With the advantage of hindsight, we question the privileged lens of Ansel Adams, whose postcard portraits of interned Japanese-Americans operate in the same propagandist spirit as *Reifenstahl* and contemporary American media. This points to how design and photography often deny accountability in their portrayals. Ain't no reparations for the indignities that graphic design traffics. From Aunt Jemima to O.J. to Michael Jordan, designers deploy stereotypes more efficiently, and more vividly, than ever. And we buy it.

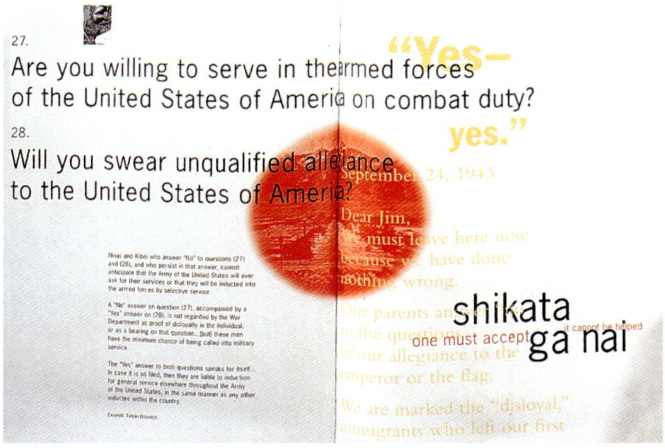

Unspoken

SPREADS

Designer : Garland Kirkpatrick
Design Director : Garland Kirkpatrick
Writer : Kim Yasuda
Photographers : Ansel Adams, Dorothea Lange
Design Firm : Helvetica Jones, Venice, California
Publisher : The Friends of Photography, San Francisco
See: Journal of Visual Culture
Typographer : Garland Kirkpatrick
Printer : C & C Offset, Ltd., Hong Kong
Separator : C & C Offset, Ltd., Hong Kong
Paper : Chrome Coat

jan van toorn

also selected by
Caryn Aono, see p.60

CATEGORY 3

This document is about a promising interactive digital project that tries to develop more expressive and intuitive interfaces for multimedia. The experiment is an exploration of the possibilities of a more fluid syntax for navigation in interactive communication. The design of the document could be labeled "the new informality." It is a successful reinterpretation of a style that was in vogue in the '40s and '50s. I wish that the promising character of the project it describes had a clearer influence on the structure of the printed work in its dealings with the reader. –jvt

entrant's comments

This is a California Institute of the Arts MFA thesis consisting of two complementary parts. First, I wrote and designed the book *Print is Dead* as a way to organize the research I amassed about interface design. Through it, I raise issues such as, What makes a fluid, intuitive interface design? What constructs exist in multimedia interfaces today that can be built upon or should be dropped? And what new constructs should be developed to make navigation through digital spaces more customizable and expressive? The digital companion "Flicker" implements many of these issues. It is a proposal interface for an on-line B-movie service. Using Flicker, customers would be able to access menus listing available cult-classic movies, view a clip of the movie, receive information about the film on screen or by fax, and then instantly download the film to their televisions to view. The interface I've designed explores different levels of navigability from simple point-and-click buttons to hot type and scrolling lists. Interface design will need to become more expressive and intuitive to reflect the many different voices that interactive television will introduce.

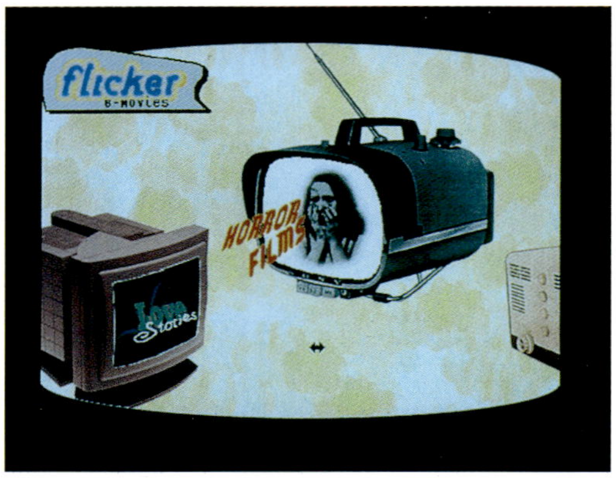

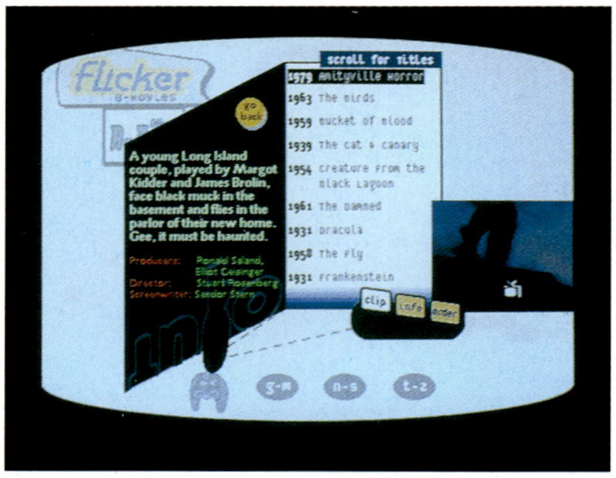

Print is Dead – Or So It Seems

THESIS PROJECT

Designer : Richard Sienkiewicz Shanks

jan van toorn

also selected by Marlene McCarty, see p.91

CATEGORY 3

I like the more or less deliberate anarchical design style of the program. The CalArts designers use this unconventional approach in an attempt to distinguish themselves and liberate themselves from the traditional vocabularies of official design. It suggests space for experiment and the independent development of creativity to future students. The tone of the text in the brochure, by contrast, is highly institutional. This is often the fate of the designer. In the case of such a discrepancy between the ideas of the designer and the client, I would like to see this difference between management and artistic staff brought out into the open instead of being concealed behind a form idiom that is convincing in itself. –jvt

entrant's comments

After the Northridge earthquake rendered our campus useless, a moth-balled facility once used by Lockheed Corporation for weapons and space shuttle development was donated to CalArts. It was an unusual example of the art community benefiting from post-war weapons hypnosis. The facility was a lifeless, dreary research facility hidden in the desert hills north of Los Angeles. It was difficult to design this brochure. How was I to entice prospective students from around the world to come to "Lockheed Art School" replete with fires, earthquakes, landslides, and droughts? What you see is CalArts (and L.A. in general) represented through a once-off veneer: high-tech nerdy disguised by Los Angeles Googi; a brochure masquerading as a poster; retro as future. Or is it the other way around?

CalArts International Student Programs

POSTER

Designer : Richard Sienkiewicz Shanks
Design Firm : California Institute of the Arts
Printer : CP Graphics
Separator : Icon West
Paper : Cis Label

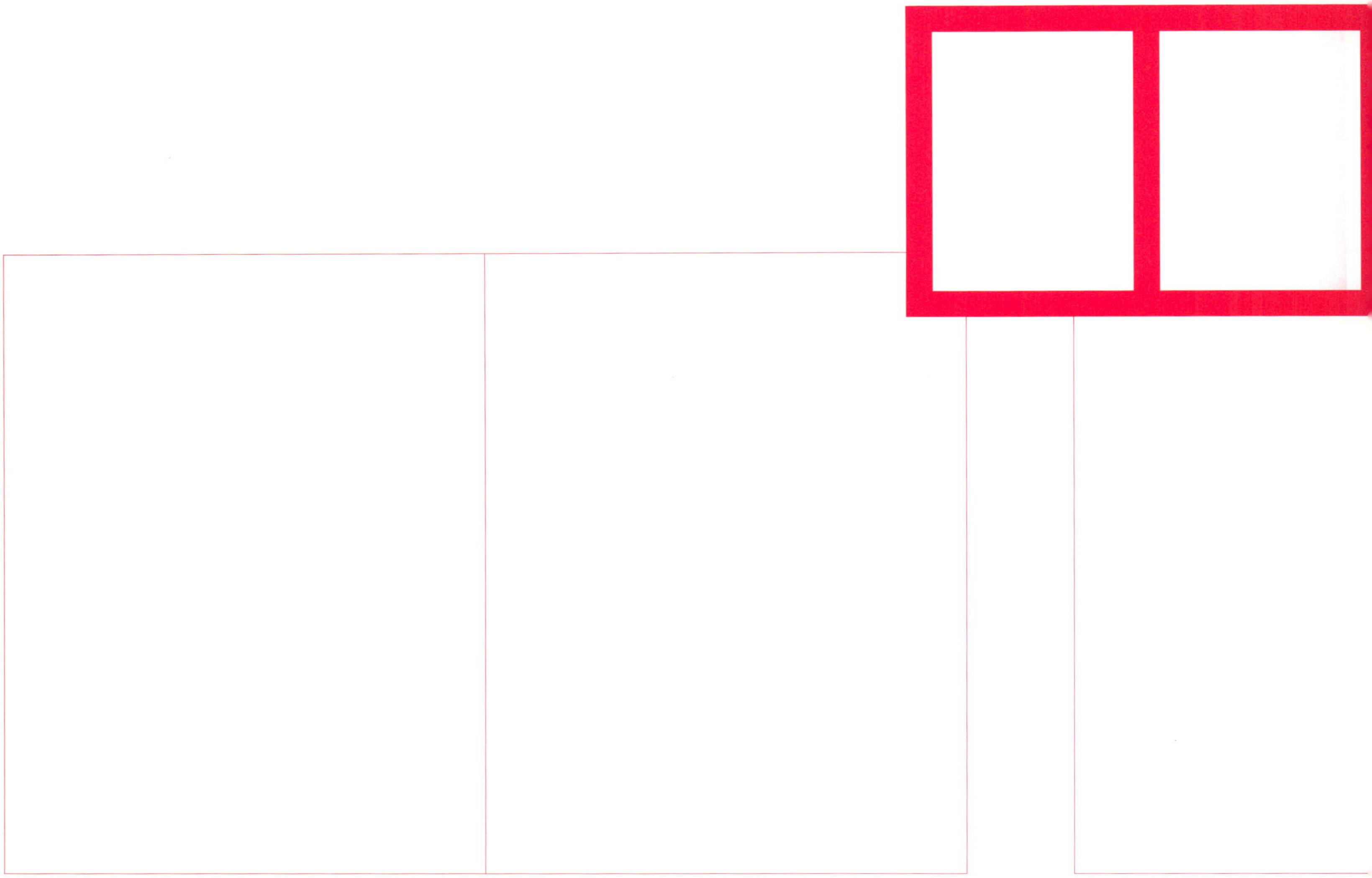

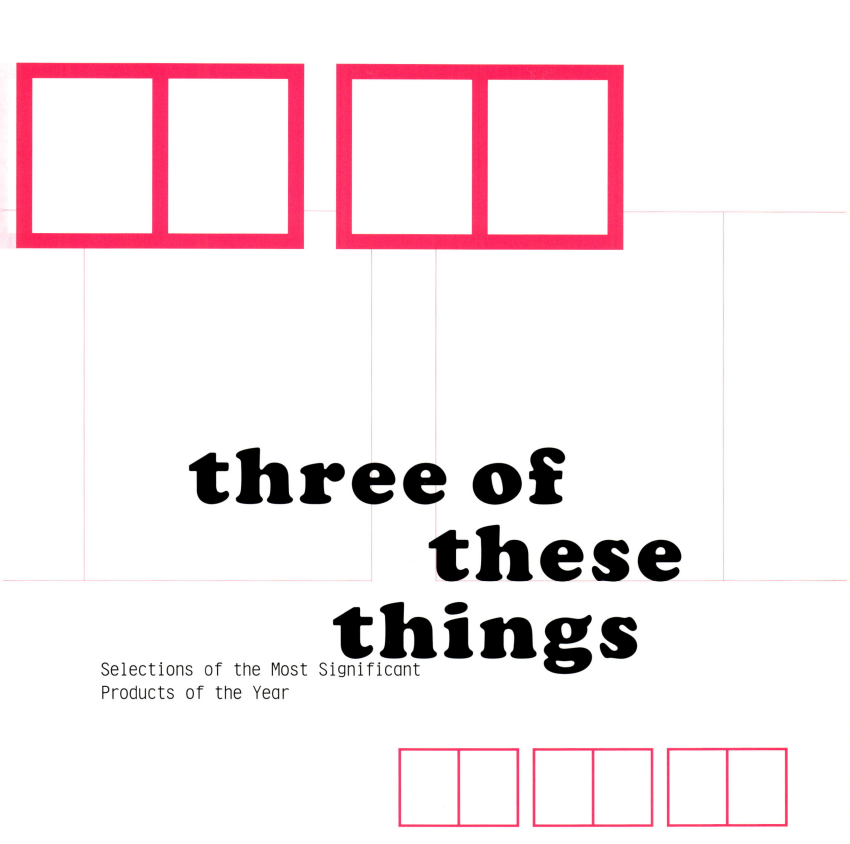

three of these things

Selections of the Most Significant
Products of the Year

Figure 1. Manhattan 96th Street subway station mosaic designed by Laura Bradley. *Courtesy, MTA Arts for Transit. Photo: Mike Kamber*

Forward Furniture

susan
yelavich

Figure 2. Manhattan subway station grillwork designed by Laura Bradley. *Courtesy, MTA Arts for Transit. Photo: Mike Kamber*

When I was first asked to think about the three most important artifacts of 1995, I realized that my own product epiphanies would be of little use. The fact that I am still reveling in the new freedoms acquired with my first cordless phone and dishwasher last year seemed only to illustrate the time lag between invention and consumption – say, a decade or two, for a family somewhere in the middle of the economic food chain.

Furthermore, the icons of excellence within the professional realm of industrial design had already been well established in the fall/winter issue of *Innovation*, conveniently routed to my desk in the waning weeks of 1995. However, as it was irrefutably the publication of record on the subject, I decided to conduct my own analysis of the winning entries to test a theory I'd been harboring for some time now. With only one gold medal awarded to a quasi-public space – the ESEO Federal Credit Union in Oklahoma, it seemed that product design was rarely associated with the civic realm. Or, if it were, no one was much interested in writing about it or in giving it prizes.

So I set my sights on the public sector. As it happened, I didn't have far to look for my first candidate. I found it in the East 96th Street subway station in Manhattan, pushing my way through what I now know is called a highwheel exit. This particular revolving web of interlocking bars was not the usual menacing black comb, but a glistening series of stainless steel arcs.

Here was an object vastly improved, if not totally reinvented, that I didn't have to buy, beyond the price of my token. This new exit turnstile – to be put in place throughout the entire New York subway system – turned out to be the brainchild of an artist named Laura Bradley. Without the benefit of a design team, Bradley employed all the now voguish anthropological tactics of the design trade – endless hours of observation, public interviews, meetings with police officers, station managers, engineers, fabricators, and agency administrators – to radically rethink an everyday artifact of the commuter's life.

Bradley was originally commissioned by the Metropolitan Transit Authority's Arts for Transit program to design the mosaic leitmotif of the 96th Street station (figure 1). Subsequently, Arts for Transit introduced her to the system-wide effort underway to "harden" the entries where fare beaters had cost the MTA millions of dollars annually.

Figures 4 and 4a.
JCDecaux accessible public toilet in San Francisco.
Courtesy, JCDecaux

Figure 5.
Interior of JCDecaux accessible public toilet.
Courtesy, JCDecaux

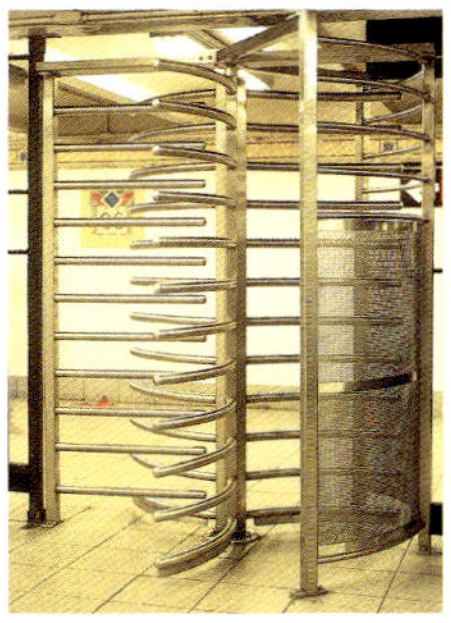

Bradley seized the opportunity to soften the prison aesthetic of the new floor-to-ceiling grillwork by successfully proposing two new railing designs that featured modular decorative motifs and fit the vagaries of the historic system (figure 2).

The idea to improve the exit highwheels was also entirely Bradley's. With the support of Arts for Transit, she succeeded in convincing a reluctant agency to halt its own plans and adopt hers because of the meticulousness of her specifications and the assurance that her design would cost no more than the highwheel in current usage.

Figure 3.
Manhattan subway highwheel designed by Laura Bradley.
Courtesy, MTA Arts for Transit.
Photo: Peter Hamblin

Figure 3a.
Highwheel detail.
Courtesy, MTA Arts for Transit.
Photo: Peter Hamblin

The results: the gently arced bars immediately signal which way to push (no more jamming in the wrong direction); the skirt, which envelops the user once inside, is lowered slightly to give more visibility and is patterned with delicate perforations (figures 3 and 3a.) The overhead canopy, which had heightened the sensation of entrapment, is eliminated. Bradley's training in anatomy and fascination with the economy of measure in mosaics made her designs for the MTA keenly responsive to the needs of both the body public and the body politic.

In contrast to the almost puritanical modesty of the origins of the highwheel, there is the unquestionably commercial saga of JCDecaux. A French street furniture company, JCDecaux has also made bodily functions the mainstay of its business by grafting advertising onto public toilets, kiosks, bus shelters, and newsstands.

For cities throughout Europe, JCDecaux had commissioned litter baskets by Phillipe Starck, park benches by Martin Szekely, and bus shelters by Norman Foster — all inspirationally hip and forward-looking. So I was heartened to learn that an American city had struck a deal with the French firm to upgrade its sidewalk amenities, particularly after New York City's controversial public toilet debate in 1992. San Francisco, in all its civility, had indeed signed on for a suite of twenty accessible public lavatories, twenty public information kiosks, and seventy newsstands. Described by the local press as "Parisian-style," they recall not so much the Paris of the Grand Projets as the Paris of the Beaux Arts (figures 4 and 4a).

Be that as it may, the inside of these latter-day *pissoirs* is quite another matter, which is why I am nominating their fully accessible interiors as my second selection. (It also neatly sidesteps the politics of profit associated with the advertising carried on the outside of each commode.)

For a mere quarter, the door slides open, offering city folks and tourists, in wheelchairs or on foot, a safe, clean, attractive restroom (figure 5). After use, the toilet neatly retracts into the wall where it is disinfected and blown dry before reemerging. Sensing the user's hands, the sink dispenses warm water and soap without a command. There are two red call buttons for emergencies, one on the floor and one on the wall, which can send off a call to the local 911 operator via a speaker and microphone located inside the unit. Users are accorded eighteen minutes before a recorded voice informs them that the doors will open in two minutes. A failure or inability to exit in twenty minutes sets off an alarm. The heady efficiency of it all is like a rare fulfillment of the prophesied future of World's Fairs past.

Figure 6. Armchair and Tripod from the Puzzle Series designed by David Kawecki.
Courtesy, 3-D: Interiors

Figure 7. Salon Table (left) with Tripod Table and Tansu Cabinet designed by David Kawecki.
Courtesy, 3-D: Interiors

If urban design is a conservative endeavor with little stomach and even fewer tax dollars for idiosyncratic taste in its street furnishings, one can always exercise one's first amendment rights of taste at home, bringing me to my last selection – a piece in the Puzzle Series designed by David Kawecki (figure 6).

A former computer graphics designer, Kawecki's studio consists of a mouse and monitor. The furniture is the product of his newest software programs and the economic constraints of a start-up enterprise. To be affordable to both producer and consumer, the line had to be made from one material in a single-run fabrication process, with no assembly. Each element is precisely notched by laser. His two-person San Francisco based firm, 3-D: Interiors, can then ship the flat, stacked components at the ludicrously low cost of twenty-five dollars a unit to customers who assemble their birch-ply, three-dimensional, jigsaw puzzle in about fifteen minutes.

Belying the ascetic nature of their structure and almost Luddite inversion of Kawecki's computer application is the playful character of the pieces themselves. Offered in a palette of slightly off-key pastel hues, the salon table, which I purchased in lime, is rife with associations (figure 7). Notches animate the surface with a Morse code of dashes that bring to mind stitched leather. The key holes on the side panels have a whiff of roboticized carpenter Gothic with their serialized stamped-out repeat. French literary concepts of absence may account for the designer's muse and discipline, but the aesthetic is decidedly American – casual, hybrid, bordering on frugal.

Clearly, this San Franciscan's leanings are more on the vanguard than his counterparts at City Hall who selected his home town's more traditionally styled kiosks. Perhaps more official tastemakers would do well to talk to Laura Bradley and David Kawecki, or, for that matter, any number of progressive American designers. They might be inspired to take modernity out of the water closet and back to the streets again.

Figure 1. *Martha Stewart Living*'s Araucana Colors. *Courtesy, Martha Stewart Living*

Big, Loud, and Smelly

tucker
viemeister

Can something as normal as a shoestore foot gauge or as simple as, as fashion designer Joan Vass says, "a glass of water" be significant? What is it that makes a product significant? Don't they have to be big or loud or really smelly? Shouldn't they be the result of complex scientific investigations like micromachines or artificial fat? If something is presented by a famous personality (i.e., Cindy Crawford plugging soda-pop) isn't it important? Significant things (such as the Reebok Step) can be really stupid, or (such as the A-Bomb) can be really mean. William Gibson and Steve Jobs have proved that things don't even have to exist to be significant in our lives.

Even though there are many ways to define a significant product, a year is lucky to have even one: 1850, Levi's; 1876, Bell telephone; 1903, Wright brothers' airplane; 1908, Ford Model T; 1939, World's Fair; 1949, Xerox copier; 1952, Salk's polio vaccine; 1964, Mustang; 1967, Sgt. Pepper's Lonely Hearts Club Band; 1969, moon landing; 1980, Sony Walkman; 1984, Apple Macintosh; 1985, Graves' teapot; 1987, The Simpson's; 1989, Good Grips kitchen tools; 1990, McDonald's cardboard boxes; 1991, Stealth bomber; and 1994, Chiat/Day's virtual office.

Looking for this year's significant products, I perused the one hundred fiftieth anniversary issue of *Scientific American* with its predictions of key new technologies for the twenty-first century: mag-lev trains, high-temperature superconductors, optical networks, self-assembling materials, artificial intelligence, and artificial organs. Then I scanned *Popular Science's* "Best of What's New" awards and found IBM's butterfly ThinkPad, Rollerball rollerskates, Nippondenso's Micro-car (the size of a grain of rice and it runs), Boeing's Sea Launch self-propelled rocket launchpad, and Engelhard's catalytic technology that cleans air while you drive. I surveyed my designer friends and asked some smart people. I rounded up the usual suspects from the Industrial Designers Society of America's IDEA awards in *Business Week*, and *I.D.* magazine's Annual Design Review.

Luckily for me, there have been many significant designs this year — IDEO's wall switches, Bill Gates' Windows '95, Nintendo's VirtualBoy, Myst, I.M. Pei's Rock and Roll Hall of Fame, Paola Antonelli's "Mutant Materials" show at MoMA, Boeing's 777, OJ's Isotoner gloves,

Newt's Contract With America, McVeigh's Oklahoma bomb, Farakan's Million Man March, and the Beatles' reunion album. But what could be more significant than the birth of my daughter Josephine, a product of millions of years of genetic development? As everyone who has a kid knows, a birth causes a paradigm shift in the perception of all things – not just sharp objects, but the air, the noise, the events!

A product is significant when the design is good, when the designer does a good job of integrating all the elements – the ergonomics, versatility, sustainability, efficiency, materials, power, ease of use, market success, social influence, innovative technology – and it looks beautiful. Though it may last longer than our taste, a beautiful thing is a wonder to behold and a lasting record of itself.

Unlike the bathing-suit competition of a beauty pageant, the reasons *why* I selected these three beautiful things are as important as *what* I picked. All of them are designed, are pretty, and are generally available. Like the three bears, one is big, one is medium-sized, and one is flat. One is high-tech, one medium-tech, and one is low-tech. All are American – one from the West Coast, one from the East Coast, and one from the Midwest.

Although I like the Buick Riviera and the new Mercedes E-Class, my first choice goes to the '96 Ford Taurus and Mercury Sable (figure 2) because "everything you touch is soft," as the TV ads say. They are a second generation that is actually better than the '86 original. The lines and forms are more resolved and expressive than the original "soap bar," which in '87 began to, as the Republicans say, "de-evolve" yearly. The edges of the box began to poke through the soap, until the '95 models looked really bad. The new Taurus is pretty radical.

Ford's vice president of design Jack Telnack says the curvaceous car is not evolutionary. "We followed the philosophy that, in product design, form contains function. We aimed for a tension and tautness in the surface to express the energy beneath . . . A one-piece overall silhouette, a seamless look of quality with everything integrated." (Porsche design axiom: "good design is the dominance of the whole over the parts.") The original exterior designer John Doughty and interior designer Briton Chris Clements were replaced in the final stages by Doug Graffka. The design is based on ellipses. They have more ellipses than an Infinity J30.

Figure 2. 1996 Ford Taurus.
Courtesy, Ford Motor Company

My next selection is Acer Aspire computers by frogdesign (figures 3, 3a, and 3b) although I also like Hewlett-Packard's Pavilion computers by Lunar Design. "The design language of the Aspire is part embraceable curves and part the apt expression of technology's new looser, cartoony mood," says frog's visionary steven skov holt *(sic)*. "The intent of the design was based on moving away from the typical hard-lined, putty-gray computers . . . giving it a dash of color and soft, smooth shapes," says designer Barbara Sauceda. "Our code name for the project was 'Jetsons,'" designer Matthew Barthelemy says, "and that pretty much sums up our conceptual approach, which was to take the technology and make it fun for the home environment." Chris Lenart pipes in, "the shapes are the result of many hours devoted to George, Jane, and Elroy." Although he says they were "pushing the goo," even cartoon computers don't come with a built-in telephone, fax, and answering machine. Dan Harden and Garry Goh completed the frog team that created an object with some really cool textures, colors, and curves that looks nice even when it's turned off. holt adds that, like all good design, "the Aspire will become the company's best advertisement."

Figures 3, 3a, and 3b.
Acer Aspire Computers.
Courtesy, Acer Computer Inc.

The Taurus and the Aspire are good examples of a new design style that is showing off at the Consumer Electronics Show, the Housewares Show, and auto shows. steven holt calls them "blobjects." The boys at Ford are moving toward what they call "biokinetic." More than an updated streamlining or slick biomorphic, both of these products exhibit distinctive forms of a new movement that needs a new name. Let's combine "aerodynamics" and "organic" to get "aerganic." These kinds of forms not only express a smooth, unified exterior skin, but the inner components, like an alien, seem to be alive under the membrane, the way rocks on the riverbed create waves on the surface, or the carburetor bulges the hood of the TR-3.

All hardware, from interactive kiosks to dial telephones and even baseballs, have software components. Aerganic designs have more psychonomic* power than simple, cold, platonic shapes. Plain geometric shapes are more intellectual; curvaceous blobjects are more emotional and unusual. Complex shapes have more personality, offer more opportunity for poetry, and allow meaning to evolve into a relationship with the users. People are attracted to aerganic forms because, simply put, they think they are more friendly.

Like all design styles, this one is made possible by contemporary design tools. Streamlining was not only an expression of the new technology and speed of the '30s, it was easy to draw with pastels and natural to model with plastiline. The trim, slick boxes of the '70s were not only a result of international-style modern design, but were easy to make out of Foamcore and Magic Markers. Now, designers are free to create complex forms using powerful personal computers and electronically controlled tooling machines.

My final selection is a two-dimensional product: paint. *Martha Stewart Living*'s Araucana Colors (figures 1 and 4). Based on the natural colors of Araucana and Ameraucan chicken eggs, it's a color palette created by Martha's chickens. Everyone in her office admired the beautiful bluish, greenish, and brownish eggs that she brought back from her country house, especially when they decided to create a new color story for the magazine *Living*. The series was the result of a collaboration between Martha Stewart, Gael Towey, Eric Pike, Eve Ashcroft, Steven Earle, and the chickens. When they made swatches and put the recipes together into a menu, they knew they had a "good thing." Then they sold the idea to the manufacturer Fine Paints of Europe.

Figure 4. *Martha Stewart Living*'s Araucana Colors. *Courtesy, Martha Stewart Living*

*Psychonomics is the non-physical twin of ergonomics. I coined the word to describe the exploration of the reasons why we like things that don't work right. It addresses the fact that if you like a chair, it will feel more comfortable, even if the ergonomics are wrong. Just as an ergonomic handle makes it easier to pick up a pan, a psychonomic handle gives people a reason to use it. It sounds crazy, but if we improve our understanding of understanding, we'll be able to design more enjoyable and better things.

There are two reasons these paints are a significant product design. First, from a paradigm-shifting point of view, when you see the colors, you think, "Oh, they're nice, but I'll just go in the back of Janivick Plaza and save fifteen bucks by finding some ordinary paint to match." But as you search through the chips, you realize that all the other colors don't have the clarity and freshness of these. It opens your eyes. Second, these colors have the power to make other things look better, not by simple factors but geometrically. "Using paint color as a basic design for a room can accomplish ends that other decoration can't . . . Color is an opportunity, in fact, for a unique kind of comfort," William L. Hamilton writes in *Living* (April 1995).

Color is a design element that everyone likes. Everyone has a favorite color, so it would seem that even if forty percent of Americans are illiterate, maybe they can read design and color better than designers think. Martha Stewart gives them the tools to make their home look nice. Anyone can use this fool-proof menu. Any two colors go together. Martha Stewart's paints sell okay, considering that they are horribly expensive. Meanwhile, Ralph Lauren came out with Polo house paint. Color seems destined to become a "designer" commodity.

What makes any product design significant is that it adds value by improving our lives. Normal people think that beautiful products are a significant part of their lives – maybe more important than scientific discoveries or even new TV shows. They love their furniture, cherish their souvenirs, and polish their cars. They fight wars over their property. My Zen conundrum is: if "beauty is only skin deep," why is making things look good so important? If it is not right to judge people by how they look, why did my Dad insist that I get a haircut so that I would "look nice"? Why is beauty so important to me if "you can't judge a book by its cover"? My teacher at Pratt, Rowena Reed, said, "pure unadulterated beauty should be the goal of civilization." The designers of the Taurus, the Acer computers, and Martha Stewart *Living*'s Araucana Colors have done more than their job, they have done their duty to our civilization!

Figure 1.
A busy dangling string
Courtesy, Xerox Palo Alto Research Center

Designing Calm Technology

mark weiser and john seely brown

Introduction

Bits flowing through the wires of a computer network are ordinarily invisible. But a radically new tool shows those bits through motion, sound, and even touch. It communicates both light and heavy network traffic. Its output is so beautifully integrated with human information processing that one does not even need to be looking at it or be near it to take advantage of its peripheral clues. It takes up no space on your existing computer screen. In fact, it does not use or contain a computer at all. It uses no software – only a few dollars worth of hardware – and it can be shared by many people at the same time. It is called the "Dangling String."

Created by artist Natalie Jeremijenko, the "Dangling String" is an eight-foot piece of plastic spaghetti that hangs from a small electric motor mounted in the ceiling (figures 1 and 3). The motor is electrically connected to a nearby Ethernet cable, so that each bit of information that travels by causes a tiny twitch of the motor. A very busy network causes the string to whirl madly, making a characteristic noise. A quiet network causes only a small twitch every few seconds. Placed in an unused corner of a hallway, the long string is visible and audible from many offices without being obtrusive. It is fun and useful. The dangling string meets a key challenge in technology design for the next decade: creating calm technology.

The Periphery

Designs that calm and inform meet two human needs not usually found together. Information technology is more often the enemy of calm. Pagers, cellular phones, news services, the World Wide Web, e-mail, television, and radio bombard us frenetically. Can we really look to technology itself for a solution?

Some technology truly does lead to calm and comfort. There is no less technology involved in a comfortable pair of shoes, in a fine writing pen, or in the delivery of the *New York Times* on a Sunday morning than there is in a home PC. Why is one so often enraging, while the others are frequently calming? The difference is in how they engage our attention. Calm technology engages both the center and the periphery of our attention. In fact, it moves back and forth between the two.

The word "periphery" describes what we are attuned to without attending to explicitly. Ordinarily, when we drive, our attention is centered on the road, the radio, our passenger, but not on the noise of the engine. But we will notice an unusual engine noise immediately, which shows that we were attuned to the noise in the periphery, and were able to quickly attend to it.

Periphery does not mean on the fringe or unimportant, however. What is in the periphery at one moment may in the next be at the center of our attention and therefore crucial. The same physical form may even have elements in both the center and the periphery. The ink that communicates the central words of a text – through choices of font and layout – also clues us peripherally into the genre of the text.

A calm technology moves easily from the periphery of our attention to the center and back again. This is fundamentally calming for two reasons. First, by placing objects in the periphery we are able to pay attention to much more than we could if everything were at the center. We are attuned to objects in the periphery by the large portion of our brains devoted to peripheral (sensory) processing. Therefore, the periphery informs us without overburdening us. Second, by centering on an object that was in the periphery, we take control of it. Peripherally, we may be aware that something is not quite right, such as an awkward sentence that leaves us tired and discomforted without knowing why. By moving the sentence construction from the periphery to the center, we are empowered to act. We may stop reading or we may accept the source of irritation and continue. Without centering, the periphery could easily be a source of unconscious frenzy; with centering, the periphery is a fundamental enabler of calm through increased awareness and personal power.

Not all technology needs to be calm. A calm video game, for example, would probably get little use, since its purpose is to excite. But too much design of technology focuses on the object and its surface features without regard for context. We must learn to design technology for the periphery. In this way, we will most fully command it, not be dominated by it.

Technology in the periphery is related to the notion of affordances, originated by James Gibson and popularized by Donald Norman. An affordance is a relationship between an object and the intentions, perceptions, and capabilities of a person. The side of a door that only pushes out *affords* this action by offering a flat pushplate. The idea of affordance, powerful as it is, tends to describe the surface of a design. It does not reach far enough into the periphery where a design must be attuned to but not attended to.

Figure 2.
An inner-office window
Courtesy, Xerox Palo Alto Research Center

Three Signs of Calm Technology

Technologies calm as they empower our periphery. This happens in two ways. First, as already mentioned, a calming technology may be one that easily moves from center to periphery, and back. Second, a technology may enhance our peripheral reach by bringing more details into the periphery. An example is a video conference, which, compared with a telephone conference, enables us to tune into nuances of body posture and facial expression. This is calming because our enhanced peripheral reach increases our knowledge and, therefore, our ability to act, without creating information overload.

The end result of calm technology is to put us in a familiar place. When our periphery is functioning well, we are tuned into what is happening around us, to what is about to happen, and to what has just happened. We are connected effortlessly to a myriad of familiar details. We call this connection to the world around us "locatedness." It is the fundamental gift that the periphery gives us.

To deepen the dialog, we now examine a few designs in terms of their movement from center to periphery, their peripheral reach, and their locatedness.

Inner-Office Windows

These glass windows that look out into hallways from inner offices are a beautifully simple design that enhance peripheral reach and locatedness (figure 2).

The inner-office window extends our periphery by creating a two-way channel for clues about the environment. Whether it is the motion of other people down the hall ("it's time for lunch," "the big meeting is starting"), or noticing the same person peeking in for the third time while we've been on the phone ("they really want to see me," "I forgot an appointment"), the window connects the person inside the office to the nearby outside world.

Inner-office windows also connect those who are outside the office to those inside. A light shining out into the hall means someone is working late. If we see someone tidying a desk, it may be a good time to interrupt for a casual chat. These small clues become part of the periphery of a calm and comfortable workplace.

Inner office windows illustrate a fundamental property of motion between center and periphery. Compare them with an open office in which desks are separated by low or no partitions. Open offices force too much to the center. For example, a person hanging out near an open cubicle demands attention by social conventions of privacy and politeness. There is less opportunity for the subtle clue of peeking through a window without eavesdropping on a conversation. With inner-office windows, however, the individual, rather than the environment, is in charge of moving objects from the center to the periphery, and back.

Internet Multicast

A technology called Internet Multicast may become the next World Wide Web phenomenon. Sometimes called the MBone (for Multicast Backbone), multicasting was invented by Steve Deering while he was a graduate student at Stanford University.

While the World Wide Web connects only two computers at a time, and only for a few moments during which information is being downloaded, the MBone continuously connects many computers at the same time. For any one person on the information highway, the Web lets only one car on the road at a time, and that car must travel directly to its destination with no stops or side trips. In contrast, the MBone allows streams of traffic – many people at a time – enabling the flow of activities that comprise a neighborhood. Whereas on the Web, one ventures timidly to one location at a time before scurrying back home again, on the MBone, ongoing relationships are sustained between machines, places, and people.

Multicast is fundamentally about increasing peripheral reach, derived from its ability to cheaply support multiple media connections of video, audio, photographs, interactive drawings, shared objects, etc., all day long. Take video, for example. Continuous video from another place is no longer television or videoconferencing. Rather, it is more like a window of awareness. A continuous video stream brings new details into the periphery ("the room is cleaned up; something important may be about to happen," "everyone arrived late today on the East Coast; there must be a big snowstorm or traffic jam").

Figure 3.
A calm dangling string
Courtesy, Xerox Palo Alto

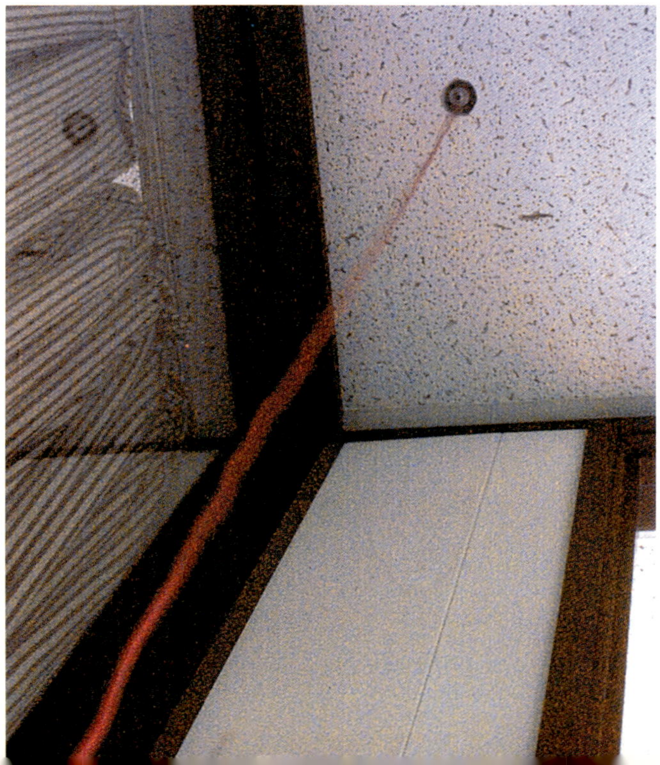

Similar to videoconferencing and television, Multicast allows an increased opportunity to tune into more details. Compared with a telephone or facsimile, however, the broader channel of full multimedia more fully projects the person through the wire. The responsiveness that full two-way interaction permits enhances this presence.

Similar to the inner-office windows, Multicast enables control of the periphery to remain with the individual, rather than with the environment. A properly designed real-time Multicast tool will offer but will not demand. The MBone provides the necessary partial separation for moving between the center and the periphery, which a high-bandwidth world alone does not do. Less is more when less bandwidth provides more calmness.

At the moment, Multicast is not so easy to use, and only a few applications have been developed. This was also true of the digital computer in 1945 and of the Internet in 1975. Multicast in our periphery will utterly change our world in twenty years.

Dangling String

Let's return to the dangling string. At first, it creates a new center of attention by just being unique. But this center soon becomes peripheral as the gently waving string moves easily into the background. Because the string can be both seen and heard, it increases the clues for peripheral attunement.

The dangling string increases our peripheral reach to the formerly inaccessible network traffic. While screen displays of traffic are common, their symbols require interpretation and attention. They do not move to the periphery well. By contrast, because the string is a physical object, our brains' peripheral nerve centers are organized so as to "take it all in." In engineering terms, the impedance of our senses and the physical world are matched.

Conclusion

In the face of frequent complaints about information overload, it seems contradictory to claim that more information is calming. It seems almost nonsensical to say that the way to become attuned to more information is to attend to it less. These apparently bizarre features may account for why so few designs properly take into account the center and the periphery to achieve an increased sense of locatedness. But such designs are crucial. Once we are located in a world, the door is open to social interactions among shared objects in that world. As we learn to design calm technology, we will enrich not only our space of artifacts, but our opportunities for being with other people as well. In this way, design of calm technology may come to play a central role in a more humanly empowered twenty-first century.

Bibliography

Brown, J. S. and Duguid, P. "Keeping It Simple: Investigating Resources in the Periphery." From *Solving the Software Puzzle*. Ed. T. Winograd, Stanford University, 1996.

Brown, J. S. http://www.startribune.com/digage/seelybro.htm

Gibson, J. *The Ecological Approach to Visual Perception*. New York: Houghton Mifflin, 1979.

MBone. http://www.best.com/prince/techinfo/mbone.html

Norman, D.A. *The Psychology of Everyday Things*. New York: Basic Books, 1988.

Weiser, M. http://www.ubiq.com/weiser

Design Offices

About the Contributors

Caryn Aono has been the art director of the California Institute of the Arts Public Affairs Office for eight years. The nontraditional elegance of her design work is evident in the material she has produced in her two-person office. Eschewing house style in favor of a diverse, content-driven approach, she has nurtured young talent through rotating one-year internships. Aono received her M.F.A. from Cranbrook and teaches in the graphic design program at the California Institute of the Arts.

Barbara Glauber runs her New York-based studio Heavy Meta, focusing on the design of publications, information graphics, and other materials for clients in the arts, education, and entertainment industries. She curated the 1993 exhibition *Lift and Separate: Graphic Design and the Quote Unquote Vernacular* at Cooper Union, as well as editing its accompanying publication. Glauber teaches at Yale University. She received her M.F.A. from the California Institute of the Arts and occasionally collaborates with Somi Kim of the Los Angeles design studio ReVerb.

Catherine Gudis is a Ph.D. candidate in American Studies at Yale University, writing a dissertation on highways and outdoor advertising in America. She works as a freelance exhibitions and publications coordinator and previously served as editor at The Museum of Contemporary Art in Los Angeles.

Marlene McCarty is a partner in the New York design firm Bureau with Donald Moffett, whom she met as part of the activist art collective Gran Fury. Her powerful graphics can be seen on the street or in the gallery. McCarty's widely ranging projects include posters for the American Civil Liberties Union, film titles for Geoffrey Beene and filmmaker Todd Haynes, graphics for the Women's Action Coalition, as well as large-scale typographic paintings. She has been on the graphic design faculty at Yale University and spent her formative years studying design at the Kunstgewerbeschule in Basel, Switzerland.

John Seely Brown is chief scientist at Xerox Corp. and the director of its Palo Alto Research Center (PARC). He is co-founder of the Institute for Research on Learning, a member of the National Academy of Education, and a fellow of the American Association for Artificial Intelligence. With a B.S. in mathematics and physics from Brown University and an M.S. and Ph.D. in computer and communication sciences from the University of Michigan, Brown has published over sixty papers in scientific journals.

Mark Weiser is principa scientist at the Xerox Palo Alto Research Center (PARC). After starting two businesses in the '70s, he talked his way into graduate school, with no bachelor's degree, after his businesses folded. He has a Ph.D. in computer and communications sciences from the University of Michigan. He was assistant and associate professor and associate chair in the computer science department at the University of Maryland, and has published numerous papers. The focus of his work since 1988 has been on "ubiquitous computing," a program which aims to replace PCs with invisible computers imbedded in everyday objects.

Jan van Toorn has been a freelance designer in the Netherlands since 1957. His socially conscious design work has centered around the design and editing of exhibitions and publications for governmental and cultural institutions. Van Toorn is currently the director of the Jan van Eyck Akademie, Centre for Fine Arts, Design and Theory in Maastricht, the Netherlands, and teaches in the graduate program at Rhode Island School of Design. He has previously taught at various academies and universities throughout the Netherlands, and has significantly influenced younger generations of Dutch designers.

Tucker Viemeister is vice president of Smart Design Inc. Called "Industrial Design's Elder Wonderkind" in America's hottest forty by *I.D.* magazine, Viemeister graduated from Pratt Institute in 1974, and is on the faculty of Yale University and Parsons School of Design. He has taught at Pratt, California Institute of the Arts, University of Cincinnati, and Ecole Nationale Supérieure de Creation Industrielle. His work was selected for the first Presidential Design Achievement Award (1984), and is in the permanent collections of the Cooper-Hewitt National Design Museum and the Museum of Modern Art. He was chair of the 1995 national conference of the Industrial Designers Society of America and is on the board of directors of the American Center for Design.

Susan Yelavich is the assistant director for public programs at the National Design Museum, where she is responsible for the development of the museum's exhibitions, education programs, and publications. Recently, Yelavich directed the development and implementation of the museum's new graphic identity program and the accompanying exhibition *National Design Museum: A New Identity for Cooper-Hewitt*. She has launched a major exhibition on the North American city to open in 2000. She has served as a juror for *I.D.* magazine's annual design awards, and has contributed to *Statements*, the American Center for Design's magazine. She is a graduate of Brown University and Cranbrook Academy of Art.

Production Notes

Page Composition
A template of the design was created on the master pages of a QuarkXPress 3.32 document. Text provided in a word processing format was imported into the document and low-resolution versions of the images were placed for position.

Images
Original images were provided as original pieces, line art, slides, or color transparencies.

Film Input
The images were scanned on Crosfields 656M and 636E. The QuarkXPress files were opened on a PowerMac 8100. Page makeup was done on the Mac by replacing the positional low-resolution images with color-corrected high-resolution images.

Film Output
High-resolution post-script files were then sent to the Scitex Dolev 450 for final film output at 175 line screen using Kodak films and Kodak processing chemistry.

Proofing
Machine-pressed proofs were created on Dainippon KF-124-GL on European matte art paper and using Japanese Morohoshi ink to evaluate colors.

Printing
The book text was printed inline on Heidelberg Speedmaster 102 using Fuji printing plates and solvent-based four-color process inks. The cover was printed with gloss lamination. The book text was printed on Nymolla Matt Paper 150 gsm. The cover was printed on Nymolla Artpaper 135 gsm from Stora Nymolla AB.

Binding
The book was thread-sewn in 16 pp, separate ends, square-backed, fully cased with head and tail bands and jacketed.

Book Design
Barbara Glauber
Heavy Meta
New York

Editor
Therese Rutkowski
American Center for Design
Chicago

Production
Todd Reece Douglas
Chicago

Design Assistance
Beverly Joel
Heavy Meta
New York

Portrait Photography
Amy Rothblatt Photography
Chicago

Student Intern
Susan Auer
Chicago